To Pat, with happy memories
of the time spent with your
brother Dick in Tripoli,
Best wishes from
Jean Sheldon

Letters from Libya
1966 – 1969

Jean Sheldon

CLOSE PUBLICATIONS

Letters from Libya 1966 - 1969
by Jean Sheldon

First published 2018
by Close Publications

ISBN 978-1-9996371-8-7

A catalogue copy of this book is available from the British Library.

Printed and bound by St Andrews Press of Wells.

Whilst every effort has been made to trace the owners of the copyright material reproduced herein, the author would like to apologise for any omissions and will be pleased to incorporate any missing acknowledgements in future editions.

Dedicated to my grandchildren
Melissa, Daniel and Charlotte

Preface

This is a warm and enthusiastic tale of a young provincial bride who travels to Tripoli in a BA VC10 'plane. She gauchely wears the same cream bouclé suit that she had first put on fifteen months previously when travelling to Guernsey for her honeymoon. But once landed she is quick to adapt to an expatriate life far removed from her previous suburban life, commuting from South Norwood, London. Packed in her suitcase are four homely cotton shift dresses that her sister had made for her in readiness for warmer climes. The length of these dresses, just on the knee, is determined by local custom and not the latest London fashion. She had been forewarned by her husband, who had taken up his appointment as manager of a sub-branch of The Commercial Bank SAL a month before, that it would be discourteous, and maybe even dangerous to flaunt her legs in such a strict North African Muslim country.

Everything is beyond past experience, she has nothing to relate to, but nevertheless finds herself happy to live in the suburbs of Tripoli in a roughly furnished apartment with tiled floors and fly netting at the windows. A day after her arrival she sits out on the first floor balcony of the apartment and bathed in October sunshine she writes her first letter home, telling her parents of the wonder of her surroundings; a palm tree that is so tall it blocks the light from a side-window; sheep and goats wandering in the sand road beneath grazing on weeds that sprout from boundary walls; donkeys braying in the distance; the call to prayer reverberating over nearby wasteland. These letters home form the basis of the book telling of a way of life long since gone.

Jean's story is made up with extracts from this correspondence, full of detail that lends an authentic flavour to the period being portrayed. For example, in 1966 it was not unusual for the wife of a businessman to be expected to be part of the team and to entertain people of a similar social standing in the interests of commerce. But amongst the younger hierarchy of the banking world fellow expatriates from overseas branches of Barclays Bank or the British Bank of the Middle East, the entertainment took on a much livelier tone. At one dinner party a couple gave a demonstration of how they liked to argue and the meal finished with blobs of food being flicked across the table and sliding down the opposite plain emulsion walls. It was not too long before the pretence had turned into real anger and the wife was left sobbing on the settee whilst her husband stormed out and drove himself home. On other occasions the young men would arm themselves with rolled newspapers, and after being blind-folded would lie flat on the floor whacking all around them and shouting 'Are you there, Moriarty?' It is amazing to think that the next day these same men would be in their offices at eight o'clock looking every bit the serious banker, carrying out their various tasks whilst in all probability nursing massive hangovers. The drink always flowed freely when bankers were gathered together.

During the day Jean would attend or give coffee parties that were far more sedate than the evening entertainments. The ladies would exchange and talk about books; swap recipes; recommend a hairdresser; and complain about the lengthy hours their husbands worked. Later, after the Six-Day Arab-Israeli War, Jean took a job at the British Embassy. There were official functions to attend and Jean remembers vividly, and pens an account of the experience to her parents, of the occasion when she was introduced to the Queen of Libya.

Jean loved to swim and Tripoli provided ample beaches with soft sand and clear water. Snorkelling was a favourite pastime with plenty of fish to be gazed at through her glass mask. When the waves frothed she could body-surf all day long and when the sea was smooth she had the choice of water-skiing around the bay. 'Legs bent, arms straight' was the command from the shore but she hardly ever got it the correct way round – to everyone's exasperation. A different lifestyle could be tasted when, by special permission, entrance onto the American Airbase at Wheelus was granted; where genuine hamburgers could be had as well as the opportunity to swim undisturbed by the stares of Libyan men and boys.

This carefree way of life continued for three years until the day of departure arrived on 1st September 1969 when Jean and her husband awoke to discover the borders closed and a curfew in progress.

Introduction

When clearing my mother's flat following her death in 2010 I found a box of airmail letters tucked away in the attic. I was amazed to discover that she had kept every single letter that I had written home during my time spent living abroad. In that instant I decided to do something with them, not only for my own satisfaction but to say a belated 'thank you' to her for keeping my writings.

As the following extracts from my letters will illustrate I was a naïve, self-centred and unworldly person in October 1966 when I went to join my husband John, in Tripoli. He was on secondment to the Commercial Bank of Libya. The bank was 51% Libyan owned, with the remaining 49% belonging to the Eastern Bank – an overseas bank where he was employed at its head-office in Bishopsgate, London.

Why did we break our ties with England after only fifteen months of married life? At the time we were renting upstairs rooms in a house in South Norwood, London and not seeming to be moving forward. We were trying to save towards a deposit for a house of our own (average cost £3,840 at the time) but it was proving difficult with a joint monthly income of only £55, out of which we paid our rent of £22; food £20; train season tickets; utility bills and incidentals that included running an old Morris Minor car. Petrol was 26p a gallon and we limited ourselves to two gallons every Saturday allowing us to visit our respective parents at weekends. This was well before the introduction of the MOT and our tyres were so poorly maintained that the journey to Stoke D'Abernon, Cobham, in Surrey to visit John's mother and stepfather had to be taken slowly and cautiously for fear of losing grip on the road.

We commuted daily to London from South Norwood railway station to our work places, John to the City and myself to the West End to National and Grindlays Bank in St. James's Square. Our flat was conveniently near the station but passing goods trains turned the white net curtains grey within a very short time and left a residue of greasy smuts on the inside of the sash-window ledges. It was a dull and mundane existence.

A weekly trip to the local laundrette was classed as a highlight if we included a visit to a nearby pub for a half pint of bitter whilst waiting for the clothes to dry. However, this treat meant that we forfeited an outing to the cinema later in the week. We could neither afford to buy or rent a television and so filled our evenings reading library books or playing cards.

One of my most hated chores was undertaken on a Friday evening when I did a weekly shop at the Sainsbury's Victoria store on my way home from work. Carrying full and heavy shopping bags on the commuter train and putting up with being squashed and pushed around, arms aching painfully, was not an enjoyable experience. Neither was there anything to look forward to once indoors, only preparing and cooking the evening meal and having to justify my purchases to an anxious husband who worried that I'd overspent the housekeeping allowance.

We were certainly not part of the 'swinging sixties' wearing colourful pants and flowered shirts nor did I wear my skirts extremely short (my flirting days were over). Pop music only held a momentary interest for us as we were mainly into jazz, both of the traditional and modern kind. Pirate Radio had emerged at this time and various boats were anchored offshore filling the airways with the latest hits so I was aware of groups such as The Monkees, Beatles, Rolling Stones, Mamas and Papas, Beach Boys, Supremes etc. plus others with a more serious message like Bob Dylan and Joan Baez, who made political protest through their music and lyrics.

One song particularly stuck in my mind and even today, over fifty years later, I can more-or-less remember the words extolling the sixties: 'England swings like a pendulum do, Bobbies on bicycles two by two, Westminster Abbey the tower of Big Ben and the rosy red cheeks of the little children.' It painted a picture of a country in love with its traditions, where everyone was wrapped in bucolic contentment. It forgot the Braybrook Street massacre where three policemen were shot dead in the August of that year, and failed to give reference to the Ian Brady and Myra Hindley trial in Chester where the couple were found guilty and sentenced to life imprisonment for the sadistic murders of three children.

The world was in an unsettled and sometimes frightening turmoil of change and protest during the sixties. In the UK anti apartheid marches and South African boycotts held the headlines whilst in the USA people were wondering what their 'boys' were doing fighting a war in Vietnam that hardly seemed relevant. American troops were eventually to number 500,000 in that part of the Far East. At the same time, in New York, Dr. Martin Luther King jnr. made his first public speech on the Vietnam War.

The so-called Cold War cast a cloud over the whole political scene and impinged on the lives of everyone. Russia and the US vied for political control of the world throughout the sixties and beyond, leaving populations in fear of one side or the other annihilating half the world by deploying an atomic bomb. A race was also on to land a man on the moon and on February 3rd an unmanned Soviet Luna 9 spacecraft made a controlled landing there. Eventually, however, in July 1969 the Americans won the race, safely landing Apollo 11 and putting two astronauts on the moon's surface.

Other antagonistic military manoeuvres were occurring at the time and at the beginning of the year a B-52 bomber collided with a KC-135 Stratotanker over Spain, dropping three 70-kiloton hydrogen bombs near the town of Palomares, and one in the sea. And in May six French fighters crashed above Spain.

Unfriendly acts continued unabated. In October 1966 Spain closed its border with Gibraltar to non-pedestrian traffic; in Malaysia it was decided that British troops were to stay until a peace could be settled; and on the last day of January 1967 the UK ceased all trade with Rhodesia. Nearer home Ireland made the headlines in March when the Republicans destroyed Nelson's column in Dublin.

John and I were staunch Conservatives at the time and were aghast when Harold Wilson's Labour Party won a 96-seat majority in the 1966 General Election. Perhaps that was the tipping point that set us looking outside the UK to further our life together.

The following extracts from my letters home have only undergone minimal changes for the sake of clarity and grammar.

Letters from Libya
1966 - 1969

Thursday 6th October 1966

A cream boucle suit, the jacket collarless and buttoned to the neck; a modest knee length skirt; fifteen-denier stockings; polished medium heeled brown shoes, with matching brown cotton gloves; two suitcases; and one piece of hand luggage. After five weeks of separation I was on my way to join my husband wondering if I was suitably equipped to spend the next three years in Tripoli, Libya, as a 'bank wife.'

On a high of enthusiasm and excitement the twenty-two year-old young wife that was me boarded the VC10 and with few regrets settled into a seat between two middle-aged women. Perhaps I should have thought a little more deeply about my parents and sister and considered the effect of my departure on them but at the time I could only look forward, imagining how I would love Libya and its people and that they, the Libyans, would love me in return.

JEAN SHELDON

Letter No. 1 (Handwritten airmail letter)

The Commercial Bank SAL
PO Box 2308
Tripoli
Libya

Friday 7th October 1966

Dear Mum, Dad and Diane,

Thank you all for the marvellous send off. It was very good being able to see you as I boarded the plane. I was fortunate once aboard, everyone had seats to go to (no mad rush) and I was placed in the middle of an English lady, Miss Baldock, also travelling to Tripoli, and a Scottish wife, heading for Accra. This Miss Baldock had £1.15/- worth of dog on her lap which was a six week old white miniature poodle. We all chatted quite generally and so passed a pleasant three-and-a-half hours. I didn't get much of a view but caught a glimpse of the French coast and Mt. Blanc. We had lunch, served on a plastic tray with containers that fitted into it. Hors d'oeuvres consisted of cold hard-boiled egg with white sauce, asparagus, mushrooms and smoked salmon. Main course was hot roast chicken, runner beans, mushrooms, tomatoes and rice. Pudding was half a peach, raspberries, sponge and cream. Then cheese and biscuits and coffee. Although the above sounds a lot it was only really a taster, the helpings weren't immense but it was all very nice.

Miss Baldock does not advise Diane to come here and Mrs Norman, the GM's wife, later said the same. Even twenty-two years of age is considered to be rather young here, especially if you are alone.

Well you can imagine my excitement when I saw Tripoli harbour from the air. Then we flew over quite a lot of reasonably cultivated desert to the airstrip. The customs took an age and it was so clammy and humid waiting to be passed and all the time John and I could see each other through a crowded doorway. We waved furiously at each other grinning all the time with excitement.

Eventually we were on the road home, having to collect some cutlery from Barbara Howarth (another bank wife) on the way. I suppose the first thing that struck me was the Arabic script number plates on Felicity Fiat (a white Fiat 600 that John had bought from someone who was leaving Libya). We drove for ages along a straight bumpy sand road, hooting loud and clear before over-taking.

Some male Arabs stand at the roadside and stare and stare. Others just squat, or sprawl and kip down, again on the roadside. The day was extremely close and rather dull (weather wise).

The flat is in a sandy road with palm trees along the edge and there are lots more roads leading off, all looking the same and like a maze. On the roof of the flat opposite we saw some turkeys. Inside our flat it is spacious and the ceilings high. Furniture so far consists of two carpets; which will have to be beaten. (Mrs Norman, the General Manager's wife, is arranging for some Arabs to do it); two rugs either side of the bed (which has a form of chicken wire for springs); a bedroom suite (but the wardrobe is a different, darker wood); and a dining suite (comprising a kitchen table and chairs, and a cabinet where the shelves are rough and unfinished). In the lounge we have a green 3-piece suite stuffed, I think, with straw and wood shavings. The coffee table wobbles but is okay. On the whole the furnishings are like bad utility but I suppose serviceable. We have a huge fridge, which is a must; even the bread goes in it. For milk we buy powder and mix it up ourselves. The second bedroom is a junk room at the moment but it has a chest of drawers and a wardrobe. The shower in the bathroom is only a short rubber hand–held tube fixed to the bath taps, so one has to shower sitting in the bath!

The windows and French doors have shutters, then mesh mosquito screens and glass. The flat has a fine covering of sand over the floors and they need scrubbing. It is tiled throughout so once the worst is cleared it shouldn't be too bad to keep clean. The place has been freshly decorated (emulsion walls and cream woodwork) but the emulsion is all over the light switches and splashed over the stone skirting boards.

We went shopping about 7pm (6pm your time) at a supermarket (Italian) and bought some sauces, pickles, drink etc. and Birdseye beef burgers, which had defrosted by the time we reached the cash desk! Also Walls sausages and some vegetables that were not very fresh but just about edible. Then we called at a group of three other Italian shops, that had a great variety of goods between them considering their small size.

The gas for cooking is in cylinders and not terribly efficient. This morning I tried to light the oven but eventually John had to help me. I left him doing it by himself for a moment and suddenly there was a terrific bang and a flash of flames which leapt out of the kitchen doorway. Fortunately only the hairs on the back of his hand were missing and, except for a red mark where they had been, he seems okay. It could have been nasty and there was no difficulty in extracting a promise from him never to play around with the oven again.

There is such a lot to tell you and my writing has become almost unreadable trying to cram it all in but I hope you will understand and get a good idea of conditions. Everything is very strange and I've not quite made up my mind how I'll feel about it all once the novelty has worn off.

Poor John, he really has lost weight but is eating like a glutton now, filling up with frozen bread and peach jam between meals.

The GM, Mr Norman, and his wife, asked us to their villa in Giorgimpopoli for midday on Friday and after drinks we were taken to the Underwater Club for lunch. (Fried shrimps and chips, surprisingly very tasty). We walked down to the water afterwards but there is no sand only rocks. It is very expensive to belong so I don't expect we will be able to join. After we left the Normans (4pm) we drove through Tripoli itself stopping at the Elizabethan Club for a look round. It was very pleasant; not posh but friendly.

So far we haven't found the beaches most used by the Europeans. Other beaches would be foolish to use as the Arabs cluster round staring, which can be most disconcerting. Fortunately if they so much as touch a woman they get six months hard labour but believe me, they are most unnerving. John assures me it is perfectly safe to shop alone in the day as long as you ignore them and just keep walking. The Arab women wear barracans (which cover the whole of their body leaving only one eye exposed so that they can see where they are going).

On the other side of Tripoli is an American air base called Wheelus* and we can pick up their radio trash. Tonight we heard the songs 'Big Bad John' and 'Norman' just to give you an example.

Tomorrow is a public holiday so we will probably explore and hunt for a suitable beach to swim from. Incidentally, the weather was bright and sunny today, in fact gorgeous.

I've seen one camel to date, lots of donkey carts, plus ants in the bathroom, and we killed two cockroaches in the kitchen. By 'we' I mean I spotted them and John fired the pest killer!

The flat and furnishings are bad by the standards achieved in the other Eastern Bank postings but the Commercial Bank has to pay for these things out of its profits and as it is a comparatively new business they haven't been very good so far. As you know 51% shareholders are Arabs so the bank cannot borrow money from London.

Still, although there are difficulties we are managing and I feel very optimistic and happy about the venture with the knowledge that it can't get worse only better. Please explain to anyone who asks that I can't write much at the moment but I'll do so when the floors are scrubbed and the curtains etc. fixed.

Give my love to Grandad and everyone else. John sends his love to you all. Don't forget to write.

Lots of love,

Jean XXXXXX (2 each).

NOTES:

*ref. Wheelus. '...The United States was entitled to retain the air base at Wheelus Field ... up to the end of 1970. ... Wheelus was, in fact, the country's largest single source of regular income and the largest single employer of Libyan labour – apart from farming – before the oil boom.' [Wright, John, Libya: A Modern History. pp.84-85, ISBN 0-7099-2733-9]

Letter No. 2 (Typed airmail letter)

Thursday 20th October 1966

Dear Mum, Dad and Diane,

Thought I would make use of this opportunity, and type you a legible letter for a change*.

We have discovered one rather nice shop in Tripoli. It is an Indian shop and although the goods are pricey they seem to be excellent quality. They had some jade pieces and Mrs Norman said there is also a jade shop in Tripoli, but before you decide I would make very sure of prices in England as things seem quite expensive here.

I have your letters here and will answer your questions. Don't talk about fresh fish or fresh anything here, the vegetables walk home with you they are so crawling with insects, as for fresh fish I wouldn't dare try any. But we can buy frozen fish and the other day I bought some Ross kippers. John is looking a little fatter now, mostly due to his customary bread and jam in bed of a night. Jam is pricey about 4/- a jar.

Thank you for sending all the bits from National and Grindlays Bank. I have now posted them back. Also thanks for sending John's income tax rebate to the Eastern Bank. If you could have a close look at my final statement I would like to know what debits the Insurance and Travel Department put through. It isn't important but would be interesting to see. The Insurance was for luggage and my life for the duration of the flight and the Travel was for air freight.

Incidentally we still haven't been able to collect the freight as, firstly the bank car was due to go into the garage and secondly we have quite a few formalities to complete.

We had a nice time at Jim Graham's party and met a young couple called Nancy and Alan Stewart*. We actually called on them last night but couldn't get an answer, so we popped into the 'Lizzie' Club and met Jim and Florence* and some other new people. They were having a Scottish Dancing session so John and I felt the odd ones out as most of the people were Scottish. I write the last sentence jokingly as really they are very nice people.

On Monday Mrs Norman called for me and we drove into Tripoli looking for china and cutlery and other odds and ends for the flat. I liked her better this time as she didn't keep staring hard at me when talking, as she did the first time I met her. We had a chauffer-driven Rover which is the bank's car and were hopping in and out all morning going to different shops. We bought the china, which is white with a gold square-type of design round the edges. It is Czechoslovakian and of poor quality. When the stuff is stacked it looks like a pile of bent records. We (or rather I) couldn't see any cutlery that I liked, except the more expensive type, so she is going to get us some like the manager's (Jim Deasey). The same thing happened with wine and sherry glasses, so her husband told John we could have theirs and I expect they will get new ones for themselves. Still it should be better stuff than I saw in the shops. She is going to send the car round for me on Monday to have coffee with her. I expect she has asked some other people as well so it will be best party manners for me. John seems well in with Mr Norman so I must keep my side up.

The weather is lovely still. This morning it was 64 degrees and this afternoon it has risen to 80 degrees (with 50% humidity), so it is rather warm. We only have one sheet on at night and that seems plenty. Mrs Norman has given me three blankets ready for the winter. I asked her about beds for the spare room and she will try to get two singles in there. She can't get a double as Mr Norman thinks they are a waste for people who might come out later and need singles if they have children.

Mrs Norman knows you are coming out and didn't raise any objections, so that is good.

This evening we called on Nancy and Alan again and they were waiting for a Dr Biome and his girl friend to call and take them to the American base called 'Wheelus'. When the doctor arrived we all had a beer and then went our separate ways after arranging to see them again at the girl friend's house on Saturday for a curry

I am at home now and can smell the chicken cooking ready for tomorrow's picnic at Sabratha. Sabratha has some beautiful Roman ruins by all accounts and also a beach. We are looking forward to it. It is John's only day off work*.

I am trying to think of other things to tell you without repeating myself. Did I mention we have two types of police here? The ones in white uniforms are traffic police and the first thing you know of an offence is a stinking great fine when you go to buy your next licence. The khaki dressed ones are ordinary 'bobbies'. All the police look very young and on the whole handsome. John said they never stay in the force long as they end up as big business men.

All business is conducted by bribery and corruption apparently. We heard that one ex-pat girl who works at the hospital got her electricity bill knocked down by £60 because one of the utility bosses' wives' needed some treatment. Mind you, the hospital can't be up to much as Florence is coming home to have her baby and she should know as she is a nurse.

John and I have been weighing up the odds about transferring to Eastern staff. He definitely likes Tripoli better now and everyone who has been abroad reckons it is a bad posting, so at the moment his mind is running towards staying abroad. One of the main delights is the extra money and being able to have a beer when you feel like it. Unfortunately entertainment is sadly lacking but the social life is good.

I am beginning to get the hang of things and can do all my housework in the morning and then please myself after 3.30pm when John goes back to work. Or I can trot off and visit in the morning providing I'm back about 1.30pm to prepare lunch. All in all it is a good life.

Well I have no scandals to tell you about as yet, but have acquainted you with a few of our new-found friends in readiness. Please send love to Grandad and look after yourselves.

Lots of love from us both,
    Jean and John XXX XXX XXX

NOTES:

In the afternoons I sometimes returned with John to his Giorgimpopili branch and made use of a typewriter there. The bank was only open to customers in the mornings but John usually had to go back after lunch to write up and balance the ledgers.

Friday was the one day in the week that the bank closed and that John had off.

Jim and Florence Graham. They were a Scottish couple of about our own age and Jim worked for Barclays Bank in Tripoli.

Alan and Nancy Stewart were another Scottish couple and they were employed by the Libyan Government at Inas Hospital, in Tripoli.

Ref. INAS '...through the expansion of the National Social Insurance Institute (INAS – Istituto Nazionale Assicurazione Sociale), first set up on a limited scale in 1957, Libya by 1969 was well on the way to becoming a model welfare state providing lifelong social security.' [Wright, John, Libya: A Modern History. *p.114, ISBN 0-7099-2733-9]*

Letter No. 3 (Handwritten airmail letter)

Thursday 27th October 1966

Dear Mum, Dad and Diane,

This week seems to have flashed by, mainly because I have been getting about more.

Last Friday whilst you were banqueting and dancing, John and I were in bed exhausted after a day in the open, we had gone to Sabratha* – you pronounce it with a hard 'T'. The ruins were extensive and we walked to the top of the ancient theatre and had a good view of the pillars and general layout of what was once a thriving Roman town. It is difficult to imagine how it once was, as most of the outer walls are missing from the shops and public buildings, with only pillars and pavements left. We had hoped to spend the rest of the day there on the beach but it smelt awful and didn't look very appealing so we lunched sitting on a wall overlooking the beach (a Roman wall needless to say) and had an hour's drive back to *13 kilometre beach where we had a little swim. We tried to sunbathe but by this time the sun was low in the sky so we didn't get tanned.

After a hair washing session and a meal we fell into bed and must have been asleep by 10pm.

Saturday evening saw us at Jetta's villa (Dr Biome's girl friend) where she had prepared a delicious curry. We called for Nancy and Alan (Alan can't drive yet so they haven't a car) and met the hospital secretary Janet, who comes from Canterbury. Everything was going fine and we were sitting and nattering comfortably whilst waiting for Dr Biome to arrive. When he eventually turned up the conversation went a bit flat, I think he sensed that John and I instinctively disliked him. He is a big-headed Sudanese chap and I think he could turn nasty if you said something that he didn't agree with. After the curry and more drinks we prepared to leave (about midnight) and this Biome said 'When shall we all meet again? Monday at Nancy and Alan's flat, alright?' Well we all said 'alright' but when driving Nancy and Alan home John and I backed out of the invitation. It was rather a cheek on his part anyway as it isn't even his flat. He is a pushy character and I feel that once you had accepted a couple of invitations all your free time would be spent with him.

I had my just deserts on Sunday, violent pains just above my waist. Well I thought I'd contracted a rare desert disease but John said that it was only indigestion. Anyway I felt fed up so in the afternoon I went back to Giogimpopoli and typed a letter to Kathy Jones. So as you can see Sunday wasn't very exciting.

On Monday I was still suffering but had to buck my ideas up as the bank car called for me and took me to *Giogimpopoli, where Mrs Norman lives, for a coffee morning. The one person she particularly wanted me to meet didn't turn up. But there was an American lady present who held us all enraptured as she described how she had spent last night. Apparently an English woman went mad and rushed to this lady's house clutching a bottle of poison, which she said her husband was using on her. Anyway the story went on but I can't tell you the outcome as the mad lady was still at Mrs Craig's house (the American lady) and no one knew what to do with her. She has aged parents in England, so couldn't go to them and there is nowhere suitable here. Anyway if I ever discover the ending I'll let you know.

Mrs Norman has got our cutlery, stainless steel from the super-market, not very thrilling. I was packed off home in the bank car full of stuff for the flat. Then in the afternoon she called for me again and we went round Tripoli. She is quite a nice lady but you have to be careful what you say as it all gets back to her husband.

This is rather a day to day account but I keep a scant diary which helps when I write.

Tuesday the pains had shifted down but they only lasted a day this time.

One afternoon John's cashier at work said to him 'I'll just say my prayers'. So he placed some blotting paper on the floor and knelt facing the wall and bowed up and down praying, then he got up and lit a cigarette but still kept muttering. John wasn't sure if he'd finished or not.

Tuesday night I was awakened by the sound of running water only to find the toilet broken again. John had woken up by this time and he mended it with a hairgrip but yesterday I went to flush and nothing happened, another part had broken, so we have to lift the plunger thing manually now. To cap it all John went to raise the blinds in the lounge when the pulley snapped and has now disappeared completely. So I'll have to call Mohamed, the caretaker. He is a nice Arab and has the sweetest little boy. They live just below our bedroom in a spare carport and Mohamed makes his boy say his tables and alphabet (at least that is how it sounds) every evening.

Wednesday I visited Florence and we spent most of the time discussing cameras. I wonder if you could ask *Albert Mascal the advantages of a 'Super 8'. Apparently you get a 50% larger picture. But if I sent Super 8 films home for you to see, would he be able to show them on his projector? There are some lovely scenes to take and I'd love you to have a *preview before your visit but don't be too disappointed when you see things in real life as they look much cleaner and romantic on film, that is according to Florence, who has seen some recent films of Tripoli.

The weather is still fabulous, they promised a high of 90 degrees today. The sun is shining and it isn't humid at all. I hope you have good weather when you come.

I am waiting for the bank 'truck' to call at the moment and take me to the airport, as we haven't collected our luggage yet. John was talking to Alan last night and he also has golf equipment here. So one of them may join the club and split the cost (£70 odd). Jim Graham overheard and said he would like to go as well, but he hasn't any clubs, so between the three of them it should be a laugh – one member and a small assortment of clubs. Nancy, Florence and I will sit and watch when they finally pluck up courage.

There is still a lot to tell you, all the funny bits and minor frustrations but I'm running out of space. As you can tell though, we are both enjoying ourselves and have made four good friends and have loads of acquaintances. I'm longing for you to see it all yourselves.

Take care and lots of love from both of us,
Jean XXXXXXXXX

P.S. Have now collected luggage from airport. It is all O.K. and no customs trouble.

NOTES:

*Sabratha, located about 40 km east of Zuwarah city, is one of the best preserved Roman sites outside Italy, and one of the world's best archaeological sites to visit. Its strategic location by the sea and the magical groves and trees surrounding its impressive collection of buildings, busts and temples ... makes the city one of the best Roman destinations in Libya. ... When the Phoenicians arrived in the first millennium BC,

Sabratha became a trading post, and then was transformed into a majestic city when the Romans invaded the area'. [Extract from www.temehu.com © 2006-2012]

*13 Kilometre Beach was the name given to a beach that was thirteen kilometres outside of Tripoli.

*Giorgimpopoli was a suburb of Tripoli, housing mainly American oil workers and their wives. It was where John ran a small sub-branch of the Commercial Bank. He had a staff of four to help him.

*Albert Mascal was a work colleague of my mother's at I.C.L. in Beckenham

*We were hoping that my parents would be able to visit us in June 1967.

Letter No. 4 (Typewritten airmail letter)

Thursday 3rd November 1966

Dear Mum, Dad and Diane,

Thank you for your last letter and the information about my account.

You mention the soup at the Grosvenor, well I've tasted that stuff twice before and the last time it even had bits of scrambled egg in it. Ugh. Next subject … You mention Christmas gifts I can't think of anything really but if you do send try and remove the wrappings so it does not look new. The customs are funny about new stuff coming into the country.

It doesn't seem like November one little bit here. The weather is rather blustery after a heavy storm on Monday night but the sun still shines. This storm woke John and I up at about one o'clock. The wind was howling and lightning was continuously flashing. We couldn't see the sky for the rain, which was the heaviest I'd ever experienced. We made our way round the flat and pulled down all the shutters then groped our way back to bed.

The next morning the electricity was off, the roads were just huge millponds and palm trees were down. John drove to work and found the electricity was cut in Giorgimpopoli as well. At ten o'clock that evening he had just finished posting his accounts by hand at home. Fortunately he balanced. Our own electric came on in the afternoon, just as I'd finished wiping out the fridge, which had defrosted. I then went shopping and discovered that we had lost the palm tree in the front garden. On the main road I saw the cause of the electric cut - namely a palm tree had crashed through the overhead cables tearing them down. On the radio Wheelus said the wind had reached 83 m.p.h. and stayed at that speed for half an hour. (A hurricane is 60 m.p.h. so it was pretty fierce).

We went to Wheelus last Friday in the evening (after spending the morning at 13 kilometre beach). Some of the boys from the Lizzie Club and some from Idris Airport made up two rugby teams and gave a fifteen minute display on the base. Not that we were interested in the rugby but you need a pretty good excuse for getting into Wheelus so we took advantage. It is just as you would imagine an American town to be. It has everything any American could possibly want and therefore did not appeal to me at all with its complete lack of North African character. We also discovered that the lost atomic bombs over Spain had originated from Wheelus.

One of John's Italian bank customers invited us to his new supermarket opening at Gurji (near Giorgimpopoli). We drank celebratory champagne out of plastic cups as flies galore flew in through the open doors. My legs and arms are still in a horrible state where they kept biting me. Anyway we decided to buy a few things just to help with his overdraft and when we came to pay he knocked quite a bit off.

Mrs Norman came on Sunday morning and stayed for over an hour drinking coffee and discussing curtains. I've got to unpick three pairs at the hem and the ones for the lounge have got to be joined half way down. Talk about economy drive I'm getting fed up with all this scrimping. She even begrudged £Ll for two vegetable dishes.

Anyway we have a list of necessities and when John finishes work this afternoon we are going into Tripoli to buy those which she has ticked (all the cheap things) and then put in a claim for a refund.

I visited Florence on Wednesday only to find her as pleased as punch because she has now got her camera. It isn't as nice as the one she really wanted but it was only £30 as compared to £72. I feel sure I shall be getting mine pretty soon after Christmas. Don't forget it will probably be a Super 8, which seem to be the newest idea. The chap in the shop didn't think many more of the other ones would be made from now on. I have since found out that Albert will not be able to show them on his projector (unless it is specially adapable) but perhaps he will get the craze and change to Super 8 equipment.

I hope Diane likes her new pin-up boy (a post card is coming showing King Idris in full splendour). At least he is pro British which is more than can be said for the Crown Prince who apparently favours Nasser. By the way Idris Orange Squash seems to be the most popular brand here.

While on fruity subjects the situation is improving and the new crop of fruit is appearing in the shops consisting of green tangerines and oranges and half green grapefruits. So now, Mum, we are getting our quota of vitamin C. For lunch today I did stuffed green peppers. I didn't find them too bad but John liked his a lot. They are not hot but have a distinctive flavour. By the way he has gone off jam sandwiches at night, it is now cheese sandwiches, and then we get complaints about sleepless nights . . .

It is evening now. We went into Tripoli and got a few odds and ends but spent a lot of time looking at paintings. Some were originals and very good. They didn't have prices on them so we didn't ask, but I expect we will get one soon. I looked at a few jade pieces and those with prices on were pretty expensive (£14 for a ring, remember it is a £ for a £L here) but I haven't yet found 'The Jade Shop' that I've heard mentioned. Whilst out we decided it would be best to skip Christmas gifts as we can't see anything suitable at all.

We had a look at the Norman's villa this evening as they have gone to Malta for a few days. They wanted John to check against burglars. Well in the front garden we saw an ant's nest being made. The ants were burrowing down and bringing out little balls of sand which were placed round the edge making a wall.

Another insect tale – John had to get Mohamed up to the flat this evening to change the kitchen gas cylinder and he saw a praying mantis on the garden gate when he went to fetch him. He then took me down to have a look but luckily it had gone by then! I was actually frying pork chops (frozen ones) at the time and had to hide them away in the empty oven in case they upset Mohamed because his religion does not allow the consumption of pork (unclean).

Before I forget, I'm glad *Jean, Derek, and John made it. He is a lovely little boy. I expect you, Mum, made a great fuss of him.

Well until next week I'd better close,

Love from both of us, Jean xxxxx

NOTES:

*Jean and Derek mentioned at the end of this letter, were good friends of mine. I had worked alongside Jean Andrews at National and Grindlays Bank, St. James' Square, for five years.

Letter No. 5 (Handwritten airmail letter)

Friday 11th November 1966

Dear Mum, Dad and Diane,

I hope you are all feeling fit once more, I think it must be the cold weather. This clime is just about perfect and quite frankly I've never felt better. Mind you it plays the old hay fever up which is now more a 'dust fever' but only when I'm sweeping the floors.

You asked about exotic fruits. The answer is NO and even melons have gone out of season. It is grapefruit all round at the moment.

You say you went to the travel agents, have you decided when exactly you will be coming? Sometimes May can be chilly if the summer is late so I should think June would be the safest. Don't forget that Malta is meant to be nice so if you do manage a long holiday I would definitely suggest a few extra days there. (Not that we don't want you but we feel rather guilty about you spending so much in fares just to visit Tripoli, which has nothing very much to offer the holiday-maker). Fortunately Florence can drive and although she will have her baby by the time you come (should be three months old by then) I daresay she will run us about a bit so that you can see the 'sights'.

We had a small dinner party last night and it went off very well. Nancy was telling us that she visits an old Arab three times a week to give him injections and the old man's son pays her £50 a month and also offered to buy her a car! We also made a tentative arrangement to spend Christmas day at Florence and Jim's with the six of us 'chipping in' but John thinks he is working Christmas day. The only consolation is that Dec. 24th is *Independence Day and a national holiday so we may celebrate a day early.

We slept in very late this morning so we had a huge breakfast and then went to 13 kilometre beach. It was cloudy and the water was very chilly, but nevertheless we managed a good swim. We then tried to sunbathe but without success so we came home, bathed and sat around reading. John is now in bed exhausted (8.45pm!). He is getting quite a fatty now, and quite lazy also. On Wednesday evening he was very late home, 8.30pm, and I was sitting feeling sorry for him having to work so late when he came in grinning from ear to ear 'Just dropped into the Lizzie on the way home'. I was so relieved I forgot to tell him off.

We have now got a new Ascot and it works very well. The plumber also unbunged the sink and fitted a new lead on the hand shower. Our only problem is when you run a bath the hot has to go in first as when you turn the cold tap on simultaneously the gas goes out.

Mohammed's little boy is getting quite friendly, he smiles and waves and looks so cute. He is quite chubby, not like some of the poor kiddies here with matchstick legs and straggly unkempt hair.

Nancy had us in stitches describing how the Libyans come up to her in the hospital, kissing her and full of gratitude. And how one chap in the ward had two of his relations in bed with him as they thought he was feeling lonely. When one of them falls ill the whole family arrive in attendance but the sad thing is that when it is a sick child they won't leave without it, so they take the child away. In one case it was pointed out that the baby would die unless left at the hospital 'So what, we will have more.' And with that they were gone, the baby as well. Everything is 'will of Allah' which I suppose is a good thing as it would be heartbreaking if their attitude towards life and death was the same as ours.

I don't think anything very exciting has happened this week. I am finding it increasingly difficult to write to people as what was new and thrilling at first is now just part of ordinary life. It is still very enjoyable but nevertheless the novelty has gone. However, I expect you will both re-live it for us when you come.

Oh, dear my cooking! Just one failure after another. I was told that a 'Mary Crocker' cake mix would be the answer, as apparently you just can't go wrong, but out it came, burnt at the bottom and flat on the top. I'm afraid I blame the oven but I suppose I'll get used to it. I did manage my first shoulder of lamb this evening and found that by using tin foil and putting the shelf up high in the oven it cooked well, but the roast potatoes got rather stuck to the tin. It was very tender (for a change) and tasted of kidney. We have found this kidney flavour prominent in the lamb chops also. Apparently they don't hang the lamb for long after the killing so they are probably 'super fresh.'

Mrs Norman loves to bargain and when buying our bath mat she got 200 mls off. (4/-). I still get in a muddle with the currency though. It is easy to convert back to English equivalents but 200mls can also be 20 piastres so when shopping you have to decide whether the pricing is in piastres or milliems. (Piastres are the old coins and dying out).

By the way I found out about the lady who said her husband was poisoning her. They sent her up to Wheelus for a week and when she got back home she gave Mrs Craig (the American lady who had her at her house overnight) a box of chocolates for looking after her, but she made no reference to it and seems to have forgotten. Mrs Norman thought it sounded like DTs.

I had a letter from Barbara Bass (National and Grindlays Bank) and she tells me that two of the boys from *Pay In have handed in their notices and another got the sack. Also Jeanette has moved upstairs to Securities so that only leaves Willy, Jack Warmsley, and a new chap, Geof. I told John it was because they couldn't stand it any longer without me there.

Pass on love to Grandad also tell Dorothy and Bob and Len and Joyce I haven't forgotten my promise to write. I will do so soon.

Love from both of us, Jean XXXXXXX

NOTES:

*Libyan independence was proclaimed on 24th December 1951... Early in the morning, the last powers held by the British and French Residents were transferred to the provisional government'. [Wright, John. Libya: A Modern History. p.73 ISBN 0-7099-2733-9]

*Pay In' is the department where I used to work at the bank in London. It was a desk job entailing opening mail and making sure that any enclosed cheques were written up and sent to the correct account for crediting.

Letter No. 6 (Handwritten airmail letter)

Friday 18th November 1966

Dear Mum, Dad and Diane,

Thank you for your letters Mum and Diane, it was lovely getting them. I suppose by now 'Hello Dolly' will seem distant (a week ago as I am writing). Anyway I hope you all enjoyed it.

About Christmas presents, I think it would be better not to send anything out as I understand they sometimes charge duty. But when you and Dad come in June I will probably ask you to pack some extra stockings and cosmetics.

I'm still answering questions; yes I'm still in dresses but need to wear a cardigan up till about 10am. In the afternoon it is much warmer out than in.

So far the washing does not present a great problem. I do it every two or three days, soaking it overnight in the bath and then just scrubbing John's collars and cuffs before dunking them about in the kitchen sink. I discovered today that the Ascot in the bathroom works in the kitchen also. I never dreamt the plumbing stretched so far.

On Tuesday evening we were wined and dined along with Peter and Barbara (Howarth) by the Normans. They took us out for the meal and it went off okay. I had had about an inch chopped off my hair and the hairdresser had put it up. The Normans said how much they liked it. In fact I found it rather awkward, as I wanted them to think I'd done it myself but Mrs Norman asked where I went.

Barbara and Peter came back to the flat for a coffee afterwards and to my utter shame I found the kitchen full of cockroaches. They took it in good part and between us we got a good dozen. Three cheers for 'Pif-Paf'. We think they got in through a ventilation opening high up in a corner of the room. The thing that makes me shudder is the thought that they probably come out every night but get back in before morning and we only discovered them because it was late.

Before I forget, the Normans spent about four days in Malta a couple of weeks back and didn't like it much. It is very English and the food isn't very good – still it's not much to rave about here.

I went shopping one afternoon and got stranded in one of the shops by a terrific rainstorm. I only had a dress and sandals on and no umbrella so I had to ring John's bank and ask him to leave early to collect me. The embarrassing part was that as soon as I'd rung the rain stopped.

Monday was quite a day. I had three Arabs from Tripoli branch call to beat the carpets and lay them. Then Mrs Norman called with an Italian curtain maker, so I was rushing around sorting out pelmets and laying out curtains. When she had gone Florence, and a new dog of hers, arrived unexpectedly. So I made coffee for us and gave the Arabs some squash and tied Whisky, the dog, to a chair. Eventually they all left by which time I had quite a headache so poor John had a horrid lunch of a failed pizza mix and had to fill up on cheese and biscuits. I retired to bed and when I finally awoke in the late afternoon I quickly washed up and had only just finished when Mrs Norman popped in and whisked me into Tripoli to buy a candlewick bed cover. It cost £4.10/- and she thought it expensive but I certainly didn't think it dear.

I've been feeling rather tired as Monday entailed getting up at 6.30am. Tuesday was very late, about 2am by the time Peter and Barbara left, and Wednesday we went to the British Council to see Pickwick Papers, which didn't end until 11pm. It was a jolly good film with James Hayter as Pickwick. We all sat in a classroom and the projector was outside on a balcony being shown through a window. The poor fellow doing the projection looked frozen when it was finished.

Thursday I went shopping early (about 9am) and had to wear my thick brown roll-neck sweater over my green skirt and black jumper but it was getting warmer as I came home. Mohamed (the caretaker) came up later in the morning with a chap from the gas people. He is going to fix a pipe between two gas cylinders so that when one runs out I only have to turn a knob and the other one comes into use. It saves calling Mohamed up at, perhaps, an inconvenient time to replace individual cylinders.

I had a doze in the afternoon and then John took me into Tripoli and we purchased two whips. John's is plaited leather with an inlaid handle and inside the handle is a dagger thing, which looks like a meat skewer and just about as lethal. My one is a short, firm, leather one, more of a horsewhip. Actually I bought mine for a purpose as we may be getting a dog. It is just in case any other dogs cause trouble when I am out walking ours, I shall be able to bang them on the nose. The dog will be useful to me as a) it will frighten the Arabs and b) it will make sure I go out for walks as my figure is deteriorating.

Today we did the same as last week, a late breakfast (frozen Ross kippers) and onto the beach around midday. Besides John and myself we had one family of four and another of three using the beach, so we weren't crowded. We went in for a swim and found it warmer in than out for although the sun was shining brilliantly there was a strong chilly breeze.

John bought two lots of meat on Thursday. He had asked for veal chops and two pieces of steak but we haven't decided which lot is which as both were red and both tasted the same. They were tough as well.

We are hoping the weather remains good for at least another week as Monday is a public holiday and next Friday we want to visit Leptis Magna with Jim and Florence. (More ancient ruins but apparently a lovely beach).

I had a postcard from *Carol and she and Alan have taken a late holiday and been to Hollywood and Las Vegas, amongst other places, on a 5,000 mile trip. Sounds rather exciting but I should think tiring as well.

On reading your letter through again I've missed two questions. Sometimes my hair goes up, depending on how it feels, and if I've got time. For drying clothes I have a balcony off the kitchen and a line going across the carports to a tall post. It works on a pulley system, the same as the one we had at Wheathill Road. Things only take a short while to dry if it is sunny and not humid. I now also have a newish iron which goes cool when on 'cotton' and is at its hottest when on 'rayon' and 'nylon'. Typical.

Well must leave you now. Glad to hear Grandad is keeping well. I hope you are all free of colds once more.

Love from both of us, love Jean XXXXXX

NOTES:
*Carol, who is mentioned towards the end of the letter, had been my friend since we were both five years old. We had started Infant School together in 1949. Carol and my sister and Dorothy and Bob Ashby's 3-year-old daughter, Rosalind, had been my bridesmaids on 5th June 1965, at St John's Church, Penge, London. Carol emigrated to Canada with her boy-friend Alan Colton in July 1965. They later married.

Letter No. 7 (Handwritten airmail letter)

Saturday 26th November 1966

Dear Mum, Dad and Diane,

Sorry Diane that I haven't answered your letter yet, but will do so soon.

This letter should be headed 'Ode to Rupert' as we have now got him. He is brown and white and rather plump. He is nearly three months old and to my absolute horror completely unhouse trained. I collected him from some private kennels on Wednesday afternoon. Florence kindly drove me to them and he cost £1 plus £1.5/- for his distemper jab. He loves cars and yesterday we drove to *Leptis Magna, about seventy miles, and he snoozed under my feet all the way. We let him off the lead on the beach and he played with Jim and Florence's dog completely tiring himself. We then went and looked at the ruins (Roman) and Rupert kept falling over with exhaustion so we had to carry him most of the way. The ruins were far better than Sabratha but the trip out was not so interesting, it was along the coast road towards Benghazi. We took some photos, or rather Jim did, and we will send you some after they are developed. Would you prefer prints or slides?

Now it is time again to answer your questions. The little boy is called *Ali and he seems to like Rupert but is too frightened to pat him.

John's people still plan to visit next October but only for two weeks otherwise Kay will loose her wages but she may have two extra days if she can afford it.

I am hoping to hear that Diane passed her driving test. I expect I will hear the result before this letter reaches you though.

Last Monday (21st) was a public holiday. The weather was quite bright and sunny but as we were half expecting Peter, Barbara and the two boys to turn up we stayed in and changed our spare room and dining room around. It has made the dining room more cosy and the spare room will now take two single beds instead of one, so Mrs Norman will have to spend out. *Anyway Peter and

Barbara never came so we went round to them in the evening and discovered that poor Peter had been working in Tripoli and didn't get home until 8pm. Disgusting hours. Apparently the GM went in for a short while and inquired where John was. John's job should really only involve Giorgimpopoli so I don't see why he should have to go into Head Office on a holiday.

Christmas is very doubtful now as 24th December falls in the middle of Ramadan which is a time of fasting for the Arabs and may be brought forward to the beginning of December, so I suppose John will have to join us in the evening when his work is finished.

The Libyans have banned imports of Coca-Cola and Ford cars as these companies are exporting to Israel. Ford spares will be allowed in for a couple of years though. Peter Howarth has an Anglia and it might make it difficult to sell here before he returns to England.

Rupert needs milk in the morning, a meal at midday and another about 7pm. Florence lent me an old collar and lead and in the afternoon I walked to her flat but he kept yelping and sitting down as he doesn't like the lead so I ended up putting him in my shopping bag and carrying him, which he seemed to like. On Thursday I took him shopping. I had to carry him some of the way and on the return he fell asleep whilst I was waiting to cross the road. He really is cute though.

It gets very chilly in the flat in the evenings. We have an old-fashioned oil heater but we are promised another. The only thing lacking is a container to fetch the paraffin in but I've mentioned it to Mrs Norman. Also I'm hoping to get a Squeezy mop soon when the shop gets some delivered.

We have received Dad's letter and John will be writing separately.

Love to you all, Jean XXXXXXX

NOTES:

ref. Leptis Magna. 'Leptis Magna … was a prominent city of the Roman Empire. Its ruins are located in Khoms, Libya, 130 Km (81 miles) east of Tripoli, on the coast.... The site is one of the most spectacular and unspoilt Roman ruins in the Mediterranean'. [Wikipedia]

Ali, the little boy mentioned was Mohamed's young son.

We didn't have telephones in our homes so there was no way for Peter to communicate with us to let us know that he had to work late.

Letter No. 8 (Handwritten on airmail paper)
A letter to my father from John

Monday 28th November 1966

Dear *John,

We now have our 'pooch' and I am regretting it bitterly already, although Jean is as enthusiastic as ever. I don't know quite what breed, or variations of, it belongs to, but I do know that if they ever hold a peeing contest, this dog would take the prize. Still, I expect you will get a very glamorous description of the animal when Jean writes next.

As regards your comments about the newspapers, there is no need to worry as we get the Daily Telegraph the day after issue, so we are not badly served. In actual fact I was only wondering today why we bother with papers here at all, as we don't really seem to ever read them. It is surprising somehow, but what is happening in England politically etc. just doesn't seem to matter any more.

Work is just as strenuous as ever out here, but we have now lost the consolation of good weather as it has turned quite chilly and we also get a lot of rain, some of it quite torrential stuff. Still, I suppose one advantage is that winter doesn't last long over here.

Well must close now, thanks again,

Yours, John

P.S. I nearly forgot, I enclose a cheque for you to please get something for *Grandad's Christmas and Margaret's birthday. You'd better keep this letter away from wandering eyes, or there'll be no surprise on the day.

NOTES:
*My father was also called John as was my husband's step-father. Quite confusing!
*Grandad refers to my grandfather, surname Tuesday and Margaret refers to my mother.

Letter No. 9 (Handwritten on airmail paper)

Friday 2nd December 1966

Dear Mum, Dad and Diane,

Apologies for my last letter which was rather late.

This morning we planned to sleep in but at 8.30am Rupert began banging a broom around on the spare room floor, so up I got, gave him his milk and then out for 'walkies' round the block. Yesterday I took him with me into Tripoli to the Post Office and then along the harbour road to Florence's and then all the way home. Today I am paying for it, I must have pulled a leg muscle because I can hardly walk and even sitting up in bed is agony.

John's Italian customer, Ortis Benimeto, took us with his wife and elder son (2 yrs 2 mths) to a mountain village called Garian. We had a long drive to it along a bumpy tarmac road and we suffered a puncture. Ortis jumped out and changed the wheel and then got the punctured one mended in Garian calling back for it after a stop for ham rolls and a drink. Once the straight tarmac road ended we were surrounded in front and to the sides by huge flat topped mountains. They were covered in scrubby grass and mouldy looking heather. Then we began the ascent; hairpin bends, with low white walls on the sheer sides. The actual village was scruffy in parts but at the end of the 'high street' were a couple of hotels with lovely green gardens.

We had a surprise when we got home. We had asked Ortis and family in for drinks only to discover that Rupert had somehow got indoors from the front balcony, where we had left him, leaving a trail of bones and a tooth-marked purse, which he had opened, scattering coins and notes all over the lounge. Also the bedroom was a mess of strewn shoes and socks. When we had left him that morning we had pulled the fly screens together but we think that possibly next door's cat had opened them for him.

Last Tuesday Mrs Norman took Barbara Howarth and myself round the suk. One part was a building with fish, meat and vegetables for sale. Some Arabs held chickens, with their legs tied together, and were selling eggs. Another part consisted of stalls with cheap brass, mats, and sheepskins. That part was rather trashy but some of the little shops had lovely ornaments and jewellery and one narrow street sells only gold. (Usually 22 carat).

We have made friends with the couple downstairs. He is American and she is English. They seem older than us at about forty years and thirty-five years but it is comforting to know we have English-speaking people on hand. Jack and

Audrey live together 'in sin' but what surprised me was when I saw her pink knitted bed-socks hanging out to dry on their washing line. So very unsexy. I think I had been expecting black negligée.

I'm fed up with the penny-pinching bank. The first thing was that Mrs Norman promised me a vacuum cleaner when it came back from the menders. Well she now informs me that Mr Norman wants it kept in the office to clean the two carpets there. I am allowed to borrow it for three whole days (lucky, lucky, me). The other thing was a strip of green carpet that Mrs Norman said we could have and cut up as we pleased. Well, just as we'd decided how to use it to its best advantage she came along and took it away, planning to cut it in half, one half for herself and the other for Barbara, leaving us with a smaller different piece raked out from somewhere.

Oh yes, the hardest cut of all, we have got to have a lodger for a week. It is Mr Norman's new secretary, and until her flat is ready she will stay with us. The trouble is the spare room will have to be furnished for her and poor Rupert will have to be put in the kitchen to sleep. No mention of payment has been made and also I can see it lasting longer than a week. Usually people are put in hotels but, of course, our bank would never think of doing such a thing. One good thing though, the two single beds have arrived along with green sheets and pillowcases, so they will stay put for your arrival. They were a great expense; £6 each for the chicken wire frame and £8 each for the 'top quality' mattresses. Honestly I think they were a bargain.

Well I'm rambling on but it is now Saturday and I'm doing the minimum of work as my leg is still painful. Florence has my Algipan as her back has been aching but I'm hoping to get it back soon for my leg.

I think John will have to take me into Giorgimpopoli to the vets this afternoon as Rupert's eye is swollen and red. I think a cat scratched it. I tried bathing it but he kept chewing my hand. Also John's bank is near a supermarket which I can use as I can't walk to the local shops because of my leg.

I'm really looking forward to your visit as I have so much to show you, also we will join the Underwater Club so you will be able to have use of a beach. Actually you swim from some rocks but they have a swimming pool there as well.

Hope Diane's test went off O.K. *Don't forget the anti-freeze as I expect it is pretty cold now. Our weather is chilly except for between 11am and 4pm when it is sunny and warm.

Better close now, love to everyone,
from both of us, Jean XXXX

NOTES:

The reminder about anti-freeze is due to the fact that my family had never owned a car before. Diane was in the process of learning to drive the old Morris Minor that we had given her in return for her making me four cotton dresses to take to Libya; hence also the enquiries about her passing her test. My father had yet to learn to drive and my mother never took up the challenge.

Letter No. 10 (Handwritten airmail letter)

Sunday 11th December 1966

Dear Mum, Dad and Diane,

Please don't mention your long Christmas break, you make us jealous. We still don't know for sure if 24th December is going to be a public holiday. The Normans have asked us for pre-lunch drinks on that day and quite frankly it is the last place I want to go. Completely messing up our day. (John thinks that staying half-an-hour should be sufficient).

I've gone completely off Mrs Norman, she mentioned to Jim Deasy (the manager) about my keeping Rupert in the spare room and how it wasn't 'furnished' for a dog. My goodness the furnishings consist of a wardrobe, tallboy, and a cardboard box, which she thought could be covered in plastic to look 'nice'. Honestly, my blood boiled. I got a form of revenge though, as when she called to deliver the bedding for the spare room Rupert 'accidentally' escaped from the kitchen and snapped round her ankles. 'He won't bite will he?' My reply, 'He might.' So I may have found a way to keep her from nosing around. Saturday 3rd was miserable. We were meant to go to a dinner and dance with John's customer, Ortis Benimeto, but I could hardly walk for my leg, so John had to cancel it, as dancing would have been impossible. Then Rupert's eye went funny, blood shot and a skin forming over it, so John drove me to Giorgimpopoli to the vet's. £L1 for a couple of eye drops and having his ears cleaned. Still he is okay now and can see very well. We spent the afternoon in the bank and although customers are not permitted, there was a great rattling at the door and a lumbering Arab came in, saliva on his lips. I thought he was drunk and was petrified. Rupert growled at him but John fortunately recognised him as the chairman's mental son and just served him as if all was okay. I felt sorry for him afterwards but at the time was very frightened.

On Sunday I limped round to the local shop, which is more expensive than the three Italian shops that I usually use, and met Margaret (an East German, whose husband is in the desert). I had a coffee at her flat and felt a little more cheerful. This was the first time I'd felt depressed and in need of some sympathy ever since I've been here. In fact I'd have gladly come home just to be tucked up in bed and have the pain go away. Anyway after working myself up into a hypochondriatic state Florence diagnosed a form of rheumatism and not the original pulled muscle I thought it to be. So I have been making every effort to keep warm and it seems a lot better. Anyway enough of my health you know how I get carried away with the thought of dire illnesses.

Before I forget, question time: the bedspread is pale green which goes very well with the dark blue carpet! As I mentioned we belong to the British Council Library, which has a fair selection of books. I can usually manage one and a half in a week; usually historical novels or just plain novels. The lounge curtains – Regency stripe – are awful, creased and hardly level and all the joins show. The other three pairs are quite good.

Florence is going home in the middle of January. The baby is due 1st March. Nancy and Alan will be looking after their dog, Whisky, if Jim can't manage it alone. The local 'desert dogs' here are like small Alsatians but are a white or creamy colour. Surprisingly even the stray cats look well fed and have shiny coats, the dogs likewise.

On Tuesday our 'lodger' arrives. John has got to drive out to the airport to meet her. (Mr Norman's orders). I'm not looking forward to it one bit.

Last Tuesday was awful. The weather turned wet and in the evening we were to have dinner at Nancy and Alan's with Jim and Florence. We just about managed the drive over there, through mud and water but when we left at about 1.30am the car wouldn't start. We tried pushing it through the mud and the boys were soaked about the feet, fortunately I had my old boots on. In the end *'Felicity Fiat' was dumped and Jim drove us home. He also kindly picked John up in the morning and took him into Tripoli office. I gave John sandwiches so he only had to be called for once to come home. Luckily the Bank driver took John back to 'Felicity' in Tripoli and she went first go. Peter Howarth had also had trouble as the rain had washed the sand from under his car and he couldn't use it. So all in all the storm caused havoc for the Commercial Bank.

Thursday also had its excitements as it was Jim's birthday and Florence had secretly arranged for us, along with Nancy and Alan, to eat there. Well we called for Nancy and Alan after doing some shopping in Tripoli and I discovered my handbag was missing with about £L11 in it. We shot back to 'Jollys' where we'd bought some cakes and there it was, waiting to be claimed. Relief swept over me as we proceeded to Jim's. We had a pleasant evening and the surprise worked very well. We gave him cuff links and Nancy and Alan gave him a cigarette lighter. He was very pleased.

Well that brings me to today. We lunched at the Lizzie and spent a quiet afternoon reading and writing. I wrote to Dorothy and Bob and Len and Joyce. (Practically the same letters so don't be surprised if they mention identical happenings). Anyway now I have written to everyone I promised and just wait to see if they answer. Carol, Jane and Barbara are my 'regulars'. Grandad and Mrs. Richens I don't really expect answers from but I still write now and then. I was sorry to hear of Kath Jones's holiday being so miserable. She hasn't answered our letter yet so we didn't know about it.

You mentioned my fur bonnet. Well I wore it the other day, but only early in the morning on Rupert's walk. He hates the rain and tries to go back home. Also he is scared of cats.

Well must get some shut-eye. Don't forget to tell us Diane's test result.

Love from us both, Jean XXXXXX

NOTES:

'Felicity' was our pet name for our Fiat car.

Letter No. 11 (Handwritten airmail letter)

Saturday 17th December 1966

Dear Mum, Dad and Diane,

Well I didn't write yesterday as I was too tired, and today I am still tired so I have a feeling this letter will not be a good one. Poor John, yesterday, as you know, is his day off but we both went into the bank for the morning and today I went back in the afternoon and have been typing and calling back figures etc. for him. His neurotic *Italian machinist developed 'nervous' trouble the week before Christmas and has taken sick-leave making John short staffed. My leg is okay now and I feel fine, except for being tired.

We have our lodger now. *She is very pleasant and only has coffee and about four cigarettes for breakfast. She loves Rupert and he goes to her for a fussing whenever we tell him off for misdemeanours. You will be pleased to know Mrs Norman told Joanne (the lodger) how mature and 'with it' she thought I was. Naturally I was pleased to hear I had 'gone down' well, but found her idea of me rather surprising. (I haven't altered a bit, except got fatter).

Ramadan began with a bang. A twenty-one-gun salute was fired at about 10pm on Monday when the new moon was sighted. All the Arabs then flew from the streets for feasting and orgies. The next day they looked miserable as nothing must pass their lips until sunset. About 6pm a gun fires once allowing them to eat until morning.

Fortunately the *24th is a declared holiday so our Christmas is settled. Florence has ordered a sixteen-pound turkey so we shall eat well.

Don't be taken in by the pamphlets on Tripoli as I got some here only to find them grossly exaggerated. For example a 'typical beach' was a photo of the Underwater Club and only available to members, a fact which they omitted to mention.

One good buy here is knitwear. I bought a lambs wool Lyle and Scott twin set for £6 and Nancy bought a cashmere twin set for £12.10/-. Also they have very attractive jumpers, with fancy collars and pretty designs. (Not flashy but very smart looking).

I haven't done anything exciting this past week. I did a little Christmas shopping and bought five toys: two for the Howarth's boys; two for Ortis's boys; and one for our little Ali. It was amusing the other afternoon, I was walking Rupert down our road when Ali came along and Rupert jumped up at him and caught the seat of his pants in his mouth and poor Ali got in such a state he started running around in small circles with Rupert following. I separated them as quickly as possible but there were a few tears in Ali's eyes from fright, however I managed to get back in his good books the next minute when about five little Arab boys started shouting 'Ali, Ali' and waving big tree branches towards him. Ali took one look, pointed to them and burst into quiet tears. By a mixture of my pointing to them and pretending to hit him he nodded that they were ready to gang up on him so, quite childlike he clung to my hand and I escorted him back to the flats. He is a dear and even John talks fondly about him and how he waves whenever he sees him. I sometimes give him sweets but he never takes them for granted and is rather shy.

We have received quite a few Christmas cards but I can't get used to the fact that Christmas is so near. *I hope you will forgive our not sending you a birthday card, Mum, but the shops are full of Christmas things at the moment. We sent some money for Dad to get you a little gift and hope you had a happy day.

Diane must forgive me for still not answering her letter and could you please tell Grandad I'll write to him soon. Rupert is to blame for my lack of free time and also, because John works so late now, the short evening is taken up with eating, washing up, 'walkies' for Rupert, and then bed.

Before I forget, could you look up in the Telephone Directory the address of 'Prestige', only I have been trying to get a 'Squeezy' mop ever since my arrival and the shop is still waiting, so I thought I'd drop them a line and try to hurry them up.

In answer to your question about my feet, yes I do still use the powder when they get itchy. The sand from the road seems to get into my shoes and irritate.

Well I'd better rush off, John and Joanne are going to bed (separately, of course) and I must take Rupert out for his last minute toilet.

If you don't hear for more than a week don't worry, as it will be due to the festivities. Also don't worry if you don't get time to write over the holiday, as we will understand.

Incidentally, I take it Diane didn't pass the test as you said Rodney went as a 'co-driver'. Please tell us how *Bertha is going. Felicity seems to be having trouble starting at the moment.

Love from us both, Jean and John.

NOTES:

It was later discovered that many of the machinist's errors were caused by her rather well endowed figure unintentionally touching the keys as she leant across the machine.

24th December Independence Day. The anniversary of Libyan independence in 1951. During World War II Idris, as leader of the strong Senussi Muslim tribe, sided with the U.K. in the fight to rid Libya of the colonial Italian authorities. He remained friendly towards his British and American liberators right up until his overthrow in September 1969 by an army coup led by Col. Gaddafi. King Idris was Libya's one and only king. One of the two main streets in Tripoli was named '24th December Street', the other was called Sc. Istaklal.

My mother's birthday fell a week before Christmas on 18th December.

Joanne came to Tripoli as secretary to Mr Norman. She was a single woman who had also worked in Iran. She was extremely intelligent and excellent company.

Bertha. Our name for the old Morris Minor that we gave to my sister when we left England.

Letter No. 12 (Handwritten airmail letter)

Tuesday 27th December 1966

Dear Mum, Dad and Diane,

Well I'll zoom into details of our first Christmas away from home. Thursday 22nd John and I went shopping in the evening and bought a leather pouffe for Nancy and Alan and a small alarm clock for Jim and Florence (which was rather funny as they had bought each other gold wristwatches for gifts).

On Friday we went into Tripoli again and bought another pouffe, for ourselves this time, and then lunched at the Lizzie. I made mince pies in the afternoon and in the evening we went to the pictures and saw an English film with French and Arabic sub-titles.

Saturday was our Christmas Day and we started off with pre-lunch drinks at the Norman's, which was a nuisance as when we finally got to Jim and Florence's they were all quite 'high' whilst we were pretty sober.

We had turkey, peas, sprouts, Xmas pudding, cream etc. but it was not a very jolly time. We sang a few carols and Scottish songs but I think the six of us had our minds either on England or Scotland. Nancy looked quite tearful, so we all danced and twisted to records. Alan had a dance with Florence but she is quite big now so they couldn't hold and we all laughed at them. John and I left before midnight and Nancy and Alan were following. We should have had a more cheerful time as everything was laid on but I guess we were missing home.

The gun just went off at my last full stop so the Arabs will be stuffing again. It's about 6.15pm. Apparently they are awful to work with at Ramadan as they sit up all night feasting and talking instead of eating now, going to bed and then having an early breakfast, consequently they are tired out at work.

Christmas Day - John at work and myself flat cleaning. In the evening Ortis took us back to his house for a drink. He has two boys. Fabio is about three years old and the younger one is about eighteen months. Fabio is dark eyed and has dark hair but the baby is fair with blue eyes. Fabio is like Ortis in colouring and the other takes after his wife, Irene. The living room was heaped with toys but for all his money the furnishings were not very nice. His mother and her father were there and also another middle aged lady. They looked poor and scruffy but took us for a meal and onto a nightclub which had a very good floor show. The dancing girls were smart and slim and they had a Spanish troupe as well, which was good. This was followed by a fire-eating act and as we were sitting in the front you could feel the heat, and smell the fumes strongly. I was scared but after that there was a knife throwing act, which was worse. At one point the man was blindfolded, and the lady lined his arm up before taking up her position against the board. He threw three knives down one side of her body but when he moved to attack the other side the first knife bounced out having hit a knot in the wood. I let out a gasp, as at first I thought it had landed in her. Some friends of Nancy and Alan said they had seen the act on a previous evening and had remembered seeing the same couple in America in 1946. This friend apparently spoke to them later and discovered they were the same people. Fantastic coincidence!

Well that was our Christmas and poor John has been working his heart out at the bank trying to get things ready for the end of the year balance. His machinist is still away ill and he has had to do a lot of posting by hand, as well as all the extra work. I thought he would be weighed down by gifts but only Ortis and another shopkeeper remembered. Ortis gave us a little cupboard shaped like a beer barrel with whisky, vodka, cherry brandy and Italian vermouth in it and the other shopkeeper let John have a whisky, sherry and six bottles of beer free.

I had a nice letter from Jean and Derek, they were coming down for Christmas and hoping to see a few shows in London, leaving Jean's mum to do the babysitting. The baby, John, is doing very well and eats proper meals now. Unfortunately Jean's father has recently gone blind but she thinks something may be able to be done for him in the near future.

Rupert is also doing well but everyday he gets into mischief. He even managed to get the lid off the waste bin and ate all the bits we'd thrown out, uncooked pastry included, then he pulled the bread off the table and demolished that too. We discovered all this when we came back from the Norman's to collect him to go to Jim and Florence's. Needless to say he was sick in the car going there but fortunately on some old newspaper we had in the back. His last growth spurt seems to have finished and John and I are holding our breath hoping it was the final one. His eyes are smallish and when he pulls on the lead go blood-shot. His ears either stand up giving him a foxy look or fall forward into his eyes. We can get scrap meat from the butchers, 2/- for a kilo, or lights for free, also Spratts' 'Top-Dog' and other makes of tinned food, plus 'Gains' miniature biscuits, so feeding is no problem.

I'll remember to look for 'Hawaii' in the library tomorrow and I offer Alister Maclean's 'The Last Frontier' as a reciprocal suggestion for you to read.

By the way the photos taken at Leptis weren't much good except for one of John, myself and Rupert on the beach but we had another taken at Christmas round the table so I hope that turns out okay.

You mention Arab customs. Well I learnt a new one the other day. A lot of the men here wear baggy trousers and this is because they believe Mohammed will be born again by a man and the baggy trousers are to catch him in.

Love to you all, love from both of us, Jean XXXXXXXX

Letter No. 13 (Handwritten airmail paper)

Friday 6th January 1967

Dear Mum, Dad and Diane,

Our New Year started terribly. Myself and Rupert sat up until 4am before John came home, white and exhausted. He still hadn't balanced his current accounts and the manager, Jim Deasy, had been helping until 3am. After three hours sleep John went back to work and I joined him in the afternoon. Mr Norman came in and checked through all the entries for the day where Jim and John had ascertained the difference stemmed from, eventually it was discovered as being a machine error. Something very difficult to find as you take it for granted as being correct and only by checking the entry and the total thrown out can it be found. We stayed on until 9.30pm tidying up and getting balances written up. John now has until the 10th to get his final sheets ready. Still he is looking better again and as today is Friday he is going golfing with Jim and Alan. I expect Florence, Nancy and myself will watch.

Peter Howarth has handed in his notice. His original term was for a year but it had been hoped he would stay on. Still, by the time a replacement has been found he shouldn't be seeing England until May when his twelve months would be up anyway. I think Barbara is the most fed up of the two. She is living out at Colina Verdi and can't get into Tripoli at all. As with a lot of people here she is tied with the children and hasn't found any friends. I am a little better off as I have a nearby friend Margaret round the corner (she has two young boys) and Florence in Tripoli. Also when Florence leaves Nancy might be on night duty so I should be able to see her some days.

At the moment I have borrowed Florence's movie camera and am itching to use it. It is loaded and ready and all it needs is for John to finish doing some work that he has brought home so that he can stand on the front balcony and be filmed. One half will be of our surroundings and the other half will be Rupert as I want him on film before he gets too big. (Otherwise I'll need a wide-angle Cinerama type of camera to get him all in)

Last night we watched Jim and Florence's first movie. It wasn't bad at all. The first part was taken at Leptis Magna and the dogs have come out marvellously well. The second part was taken on the beach with Nancy and Alan. That was much better photographically.

7.1.67

Dear Rupert. He was car sick five times on the way to the golf course yesterday, but seems perkier today and has even obeyed the 'sit' command. This morning he woke me up at six by thumping and yowling at the balcony door; still he had good cause as it was just beginning to rain. In fact he is quite intelligent where his own comfort is concerned.

John has been getting home about 8.30pm lately. We have dinner and then we are so exhausted we go to bed. I think we are still tired from the end of the year stint. My going back to the bank for a few afternoons put me behind with housework and another tie is that shopping needs to be done nearly every day as it gives Rupert a longish walk. But I can only manage one bag at a time as I need a free hand to control him. By the way it is still a great joke that he can't cock his leg yet.

I don't know how quickly time has passed for you but it has gone really fast for us. It hardly seems possible a third has gone until you come out. I'm really looking forward to showing you around. *The New Mosque on the main road near us is nearly completed and John filmed the top, which we can see from the front balcony.

While the boys were playing golf yesterday we three 'golf widows' walked along the beach (scruffy) on the edge of the course and on the way back found lots of balls. They were really smart ones with a bright red stripe round them. But apparently they are specially marked as they belong to a practice driving range, so we are going to try to bleach it off. John was the worse player of the three and today he is still stiff and sore so it shows how out of condition he is.

The course isn't bad, a bit sandy with a thin grass covering. John at one point thought he'd lost a ball up a palm tree but it had actually dropped down okay.

We bought a rather nice vase the other day made of platted palm leaves and highly varnished. I haven't got anything to put in it though but they do have several florists' shops in Tripoli so perhaps tomorrow I'll get something. The lounge looks barren again as the Christmas cards have been taken down and our 'bar' table with bottles and glasses on it has been put back in the dining room.

We received three more cards today and also Barbara Bass sent a stainless steel tea strainer.

I'd better go now, dinner is nearly ready and John is home.
Love from us both, Jean XXXXXXX

NOTES:
The New Mosque, known by that name, was on the Ben Ascuir Road.

Letter No. 14 (Hand written airmail letter)

Friday 13th January 1967

Dear Mum, Dad and Diane,

First things first, do tell us more about *Uncle Terry's misdemeanours! Has he come back from Josie's yet?

I have had my hair cropped, literally. I keep thinking I'd do well as Joan of Arc. In fact there aren't two pieces the same length so I shall just have to keep having it trimmed round the bottom until it levels off again. John was rather annoyed at the time but now I think he alternates from pity to laughter. The chap who chopped it was nattering away in Italian most of the time and only glanced at what he was cutting occasionally.

At last …. we are getting a movie camera. John can get a 20% discount so we intend splashing out £50 on the projector, which will show both ordinary films and Super 8, and then buying a cheaper camera to last for perhaps three years. The idea being that after that length of time we will know exactly what we want the movie to do. i.e. zoom; Super 8; fully automatic. By the way I have taken a film using Florence's camera. If it is any good we will send it on to you and perhaps *Albert will show it (doubtless). Most of it is of Rupert.

Ramadan ended on Tuesday evening. John and I went out about 10pm looking for the new moon but all we saw was a 'moving star' (probably a satellite). But at nearly 11pm the guns went off and a three-day holiday began. John caught up on his work on the Wednesday and the temperature reached 75°F so we were longing to go to the beach on Thursday, but it rained and rained and turned very chilly (55°F) so we couldn't go. In the evening Nancy and Alan came over for cards and we all enjoyed it. We wondered if you could purchase a book on the various rules of card games and send it out. We would like to play canasta and cribbage but we are uncertain exactly how.

John stayed in bed until midday today and I teased him about perhaps staying there for lunch. In the afternoon we went to the beach with Jim and Whisky. You will be able to see on the film how rough the sea was. I got some good shots of the dogs playing and you will find it hard to believe that two months before the film was shot Rupert was smaller than Whisky (about half the size). He is now tired out and at the moment sound asleep on the settee. He has improved a lot in the last few days and is getting quite obedient.

Our caretaker Mohamed has gone to Homs for the holiday and we gave him £L1 for himself and a popgun for Ali and a tiny sort of jewellery casket for his wife. (We didn't realise he had a wife until Tuesday morning when he said he was going to see her, so I took the opportunity of getting rid of the casket which Nancy and Alan gave me for Christmas; sounds ungrateful but I couldn't take to it at all). Anyway although they were all wrapped up and he didn't know what was in them he seemed very pleased and little Ali's eyes lit up.

Yet another shutter has broken, making it the fourth. The canvas tapes that you pull on, to pull them up or let them down, seem rotten. It's only 6/- for new tape but it means Mohamed has to come up and take down the top piece and side pieces of wood to replace them, leaving a load of dust plus greasy fingerprints on the paintwork.

We met a pleasant man at Jim and Florence's named Philip. He was telling us of some of the Christmas gifts he has received from customers – crates of liquor, tape-recorders, full sets of golf clubs in kangaroo skin bags. etc.

Florence flies home next Friday (20th). She is rather worried as her exit visa has not yet been sorted out. If they don't hurry she will be in the soup, as the airlines won't take her after the 25th anyway. Jim says she will have to go by boat to Malta to have the baby there, as a last resort. Barclays are paying the £75 fare home, which is jolly good. She could have it here okay but she thinks she will need a caesarean, which would cost £200. It costs £14 for a pint of blood even if you bring your own donors. One woman who Nancy knows had a hysterectomy and that cost £300.

The Arabs are like a football crowd in Tripoli. They are full of celebration and keep going up to each other with shouts of 'kerfalik' (hello) and much hand shaking.

All the little huts selling soft drinks are open again (they cater for the Arabs) and the people all look cheerful once more.

John is still working hard but the pressure of the year-end is now off and he is pretty well up to date. Naturally he is dreading tomorrow, as after 3 days of no business the Yanks will be swarming into his branch. Some of them come in three or four times a week to draw cash.

Did I tell you that Peter Howarth is leaving? It seems likely *Terry Dowrick and his wife will now have their villa. They are welcome. I'd hate to be stuck out there.

Our latest film here is Genghis Khan! I wonder what next week will bring.
Love to you all from both of us,
Jean XXX

NOTES:

*Uncle Terry was my father's elder brother. He was married to Eileen and they had two daughters, Valerie and Janis, both slightly younger than me. He was conducting an affair with Josie at the time.

*Albert was a friend of the family and a work colleague of my mother. He was a good amateur photographer and made an excellent movie film of our wedding in 1965. In 1970 his nephew, Richard Clark, married my sister, Diane.

*Terry Dowrick had been away on 'home leave' from Tripoli and John had been his replacement at Giorgimpopoli for the duration.

Letter No. 15 (Handwritten on airmail paper)

Saturday 21st January 1967

Dear Mum, Dad and Diane,

I have two letters to answer, Mum's and Dad's. Dad's arrived today so I think I will discuss your visit first as it is most exciting. John and I decided this lunchtime that Mum and Dad have our 'guest room' and we will loan a mattress from Jim and Florence and Diane can sleep in the lounge. It won't be cold and I doubt if you will need more than a sheet in the way of bedding, so Diane will probably be the most comfortable of everyone. (Also Rupert might be sleeping on the balcony that leads from the lounge and Diane will be well placed for his 7am 'walkies'). I hope you all agree that this is the best way. It will mean a little more work but if we all 'muck in' I should have plenty of time to spend with you. I only hope the Fiat manages six (Rupert included!) for trips around, perhaps you would all go on a diet. Anyway it sounds as if it should be quite a jolly time and it is good to think of seeing Diane as well. Incidentally it is an interesting drive from the airport, you pass through a few villages with little rows of shops, see mosques and Arab huts, some signs of cultivation and maybe a camel or two. As Dad put it 'Roll on June'.

Do take care about your visas, they are not understanding here and will turn you out sooner than phone the embassy. Also try and hurry them up. Nancy and Alan had to collect theirs in-between the flight down from Scotland and the flight to Tripoli, which was most worrying for them when they first came here.

You know I feel so excited that the rest of this letter will be a huge muddle. Actually I think one of Mum's letters went missing as we were surprised when we read 'what do you think of Diane's change of job?' Please tell us all about it as it is the first we have heard. It is hardly surprising that a letter has gone missing as Barclays Bank haven't had any London mail for eight days, all because of the end of Ramadan festivities which left the post office knee deep in mail. But, amazingly, Dad's letter only took four days.

Is 'Hawaii' (film) the same story as the book you recommended by Michener? I haven't found it yet but I keep looking. Do try 'South by Java Head' by Alistair MacLean, even better than 'The Last Frontier'. Also have you read Daphne Du Maurier's 'Flight of the Falcon'? I expect you have, I found it absolutely gripping.

Don't be insulting mum about Florence. She doesn't come from England but Scotland, and very proud of it. We saw her off yesterday (Friday) and she only has about half an hour to wait at London for the connecting flight to Glasgow. Nancy is now on night duty so I shall be able to see her some days as a 'replacement' for Florence. Nancy and Alan are also Scottish.

You ask two more questions; no we didn't have to pay duty on the tea strainer, but it took a month to arrive. Secondly we get quite exotic flowers in the florist shops but I haven't actually seen any growing in the ground here. The things in the garden of the flat are very thick and shiny and I haven't seen a flower on them yet. I do have a couple of geraniums in the window box and the grapefruit seeds I planted have come through, surprisingly.

Joanne only stayed five days and then she went to the 'Hotel Grand'. She is paying £L1 a day and the bank is paying the rest, until they find her a flat.

Did I mention John can get a 20% discount on the camera if we buy from the Kodak shop? We have chosen the projector, a £50 Canon which shows 8 mm and Super 8 mm. The cameras here are all good makes and therefore expensive. Meantime we will borrow Jim's and he can use our projector in return.

We are now into the coldest part of the year with temperatures below freezing some nights, which is not very pleasant with our high ceilings and stone floors. Apparently it warms up after the middle of February.

I forgot to mention one cruel thing they do here; slaughter sheep in their garages. I was taking Rupert for a walk around the block when I saw a couple of Arabs pushing a sheep along. It was baaing away and then it dawned on me, as they drove it up a driveway towards a prepared garage at the side of the house. This was the end of Ramadan, so I guessed it was for a feast. I just hurried past feeling slightly sick. Fortunately I never heard anything, but Mrs Norman hears them actually killing the sheep in a villa near to her.

I went to my usual Italian butcher shop the other day and two halves of a pig were hanging up. I asked for two pork chops so the chappie went over and hacked two off the side. Then I asked for kidney so he enquired 'two?' 'Yes' I said, and back he went and took both the kidneys out. Nancy and Alan asked for two pieces of frying steak, which he cut off a slab of meat on the counter. Then mince, so he cut off some more and minced it, then roasting beef, so off came another chunk, which he tied up for them. By the way new potatoes are in again (the second time since I arrived). I hope you don't get tired of the food here. We rely a lot on frozen and tinned stuff but I hope salad things will be available in June as I don't expect you will fancy much else in the heat.

Well better go now, I hope all the bookings go through okay. Longing to hear a definite date.

Love from both of us, Jean XXXXXX

P.S. Please tell Grandad I'm rather behind with my correspondence and will write to him shortly, also send our love.

Letter No. 16 (Handwritten in pencil on an airmail letter)

Saturday 28th January 1967

Dear Mum, Dad and Diane,

I feel awful having to use pencil but Rupert has just destroyed my last Biro pen.

I hope my previous letter regarding the holiday has arrived okay, only the post is funny at the moment. Just in case it hasn't arrived, you are all to stay at the flat and we are looking forward to it very much.

Last Saturday I was taking Rupert down the road when a man made encouraging 'doggy noises' and Rupert dragged me over to him with his tail wagging like mad. He jumped up and covered the man in muddy sand (it had been raining) but he didn't seem to mind. He introduced himself as David Pugh, British Consul. He then invited John and I to his villa, diagonally across the road from us, for drinks later in the evening. He has a nice wife named Susan and two children, Sally, 9 and Martin, 6. Guess what – they have a house in Bromley where they have been living for four years. Anyway, Susan has made lots of friends already so things should brighten up regards coffee mornings. Not that

I ever feel lonely but it sounds agreeable to meet more English people living locally.

Yesterday, being Friday, we went golfing. But we took Sally and Martin along with us as their parents were lunching at the ambassador's residency and they didn't know what to do with them. We called for Jim and Whisky and then onto Nancy and Alan's and a friend of theirs called Vic. Nancy, Alan and Vic took Rupert in their car, which was good as he was sick.

Nancy, the children, dogs and myself settled on the beach and after half an hour the dogs had disappeared. I went hunting for them with Sally and found Whisky but no sign of Rupert. I was frightened in case he had slipped off the piled up seaweed and was trapped between it and the sea. In some places the seaweed is a couple of yards higher than the small piece of shore, forming lots of hiding places. Eventually though, I spotted him at the huts where you pay to use the course, chasing golf balls around. I had to carry him back as Whisky wanted to play again and go even further from the beach. Then we saw Nancy and Martin coming towards us. Nancy had had to leave the part of the beach we were using as an Arab had appeared and had started urinating. Anyway the children played on another piece of sand and we tied the dogs up. Then we went to the café and had hamburgers and Pepsis. By the time the menfolk arrived off the course the children were restless and fighting a bit, so John wasn't very happy. Once the children were home John said 'Never again' but I argued that they had been good most of the day. Then he confessed he hadn't known what to say to them. In fact he hadn't even said 'hello' because he said he didn't know how to address children. Funny man.

The other day John nearly gave in his notice as Mr Norman has been up to his tricks of never saying anything critical to John's face but telling Jim Deasy and then getting him to mention it. That way John has no chance of defending himself. Anyway with both the 'accusations' John was perfectly in the clear, so after much ranting and raving about it privately he finally told Mr Norman and since then he has been as nice as pie to John. Mr Norman is the most two-faced person I have ever met. He never says anything directly but just gossips behind one's back. Another thing is that the GMs from the Chartered and Eastern banks are coming out to see the accommodation, as word has reached London that the furnishings etc. aren't up to much, so here's hoping. Not that I expect anything really, but I'd like better carpets as the two I've got are badly marked, plus a vacuum cleaner

John has bought a nice short sword for £L3.10/-. It is quite pointed and the blade is pretty sharp.

I went into Tripoli to collect the slides but they still haven't arrived. I had taken the film in to be processed on 31st December.

You won't forget the book on card games will you? We are playing every week now.

Many thanks for the letter, please pass on last week's regrets once more to Grandad. I really will try this week, but I am engrossed in reading 'The African Queen' at the moment.

Looking forward to hearing from you and your comments on my last letter.
Love from us both, Jean

P.S. Finally secured a Squeezy mop. A new lot have just arrived in town.

Letter No. 17 (Handwritten airmail letter)

Tuesday 31st January 1967

Dear Mum, Dad and Diane,

Only four and a half months to go. It was lovely getting your date of arrival. What a smashing birthday present. All three of you in your best 'wrappers'. I'm glad you're flying direct, it will mean less complications. I've been here four months now so I hope the next few pass as quickly. Mind you, you chose a good time to come with the bank half year. Still with a bit of luck perhaps Nancy and Alan will take us around if John is working hard. The first two Fridays should be okay though. I daresay we will have to get Jim or Alan to drive out to the airport with us to meet you because the Fiat won't be able to cope with you plus the baggage. It's all very exciting.

I have an address for you: Villa Agosta, Sc. Di Rossi (off Sc. Ben Ascuir), Tripoli. (In other words just past the New Mosque).

At long last I've written to Grandad. Does Diane still see him?

Rupert can now 'shake paws' but he expects a reward each time. Everyone remarks on his size but I don't think he will get much larger. He can now reach the kitchen table-top and take things from it, which costs me a fortune.

Thanks for the card game book it is 'just the thing' (as Nancy would say).

Don't worry about towels, we have five large ones, two smaller ones and odd hand towels. Once washed they will only take a minute to dry.

You ask if my hair is growing. Well sprouting would be a better choice of words. It's an awful mess, so tomorrow I'm going to my usual shop and see if he can tidy it up a bit without taking much off. I want it to look nice for 6th and 7th February. (Cocktail party in honour of GMs from London and a masked dance with Ortis and his wife).

We've racked our brains for ideas on birthday presents, as you know we are well stocked up with clothing and anything that wears out can easily be replaced here (e.g. vest and pants for John in cotton at 7/- each; stockings at 3/- a pair) so we decided that a plain linen table cloth would be a good idea as our dining table hasn't a nice surface. It measures five and a half feet long and two and three-quarters feet wide. A light fawn colour should look very good. Also if Dad could get a tube of plastic wood to repair Rupert's teeth strengthening efforts on the fly screen we would be grateful.

Our new friendship with the consul and family is budding. They are very pleasant people and very chatty. I don't know if I mentioned before how everyone here discusses salaries and outgoings quite openly and even the Pughs mentioned that they are a bit hard up at the moment.

Our wretched toilet has just broken again and John has had to join the ball cock stem onto the water flow control with a hairpin to stop the water flowing continuously. It often overflows down the over flow pipe but when you wriggle the ball cock it stops and the Ascot lights up. All this is very frustrating. When John is washing in the morning I can only get a trickle of water in the kitchen and whenever I turn the cold tap off in the kitchen the Ascot in the bathroom leaps into life.

Our caretaker Mohamed actually has a second son, a little boy named Salim. We bumped into him yesterday evening when we were out with Rupert. He was carrying Salim (about 2 years old) and was accompanied by his barracaned wife and little Ali. Salim is very like Ali, chubby and with huge soft eyes. I don't know how Mohamed managed such lovely children as he only has one eye and could never be described as handsome. He is a cheerful person and seemed very pleased to have his wife with him. They must have been very cramped last night in his little converted carport.

Well nothing much has happened, my daily social life is brighter with Susan for company and John has had 'trouble at mill' with all the messengers on a day's strike because of poor pay rises.

Will write later in the week, love from both of us, Jean xxxxxx

NOTES:

My parents and sister had booked their flight to Tripoli for my 23rd birthday on 15th June.

Letter No. 18 (Handwritten on airmail paper)

Saturday 4th February 1967

Dear Mum, Dad and Diane,

My writing may be a little shaky as I'm trembling like mad. I am writing this whilst baby-sitting at the Pugh's. (They have gone to a cocktail party at the embassy). As John was late home I had to leave him his meal before seeing him. About half-an-hour ago he called in whilst taking Rupert for his late night walk. We left Rupert in the garden as the Pughs have just acquired a nine year old cat-killing boxer and we didn't want the dogs to meet, just in case. Well John only stayed for a short while before we both went into the garden to catch Rupert, but he hared past and pushed open the front door (left ajar). The boxer, Peaches, growled and Rupert got too close, wagging his tail, until she leapt onto him snarling and biting. Rupert's squeals of agony were horrible but he managed to get away into the children's bedroom where we had a repeat performance. I threw myself onto Peaches and managed to haul her off allowing Rupert to wriggle away, yowling like mad. John grabbed him and went. Unfortunately I'm still stuck here and very worried about Rupert. I don't think Peaches' teeth are very sharp but she has a lot of weight and was on top of him at least twice. One good thing, the children slept through the din and I've just peeped in to find them both rosy cheeked and sucking their thumbs. Anyway I'll write a P.S. when I've returned home and checked that Rupert is okay. (I hope).

On Thursday I had my first ride in a gharry. Susan and I have decided to buy our meat weekly and then treat ourselves to a morning in Tripoli with coffee and pastries, followed by a gharry ride home. A bit expensive all round but definitely enjoyable. In the evening John took me to the Italian shop I use and we bought a supply of groceries so my shopping problem is solved.

Wednesday evening we went to Nancy and Alan's along with Jim (and Whisky) and another couple of chaps. We had a meal and then played cards. Whisky disgraced himself by cheekily cocking his leg against Nancy's ankle and then looking round quite unperturbed as we all burst out laughing (except for Jim who was too ashamed).

On Friday – golfing with John and Jim. I played this time and actually won on one hole (a fluke). My drives were feeble but fairly accurate and I think I could get to like the game. I don't feel at all stiff, as John did after his first game here, so I must be in reasonable condition through shopping and having Rupert tugging away on his lead.

Will write again next week but can't concentrate at the moment.
Lots of love, XXXXXX

P.S. Sunday 5th February 1967. Have just received your letter so will answer it before I seal up. Firstly Rupert is okay but his stomach is a bit out of order, probably fright.

We have just noticed the 'Blue Max' is showing this week so we will make an effort to see it. It is only on Monday to Thursday but we are cocktailing on Monday night, clubbing on Tuesday and I daresay going to bed early on Wednesday so Thursday it will have to be.

At long last I have got the slides. Leptis Magna; John; Rupert; myself on the beach at Leptis; a gharry; and a view of the harbour from Jim and Florence's roof. Look at them with the plain side towards you.

Question time: – The Pughs are attached to the British Embassy so usually when they go out it is at the ambassador's invitation, either at the embassy or his residence. So the Ambassador's is not a hotel.

Jim Deasy is the manager of Tripoli, Commercial Bank, with Mr Norman as GM of Tripoli, Giorgimpopoli and Benghazi. Actually Mr Norman has been very pleasant to John just lately. I don't think he can have any valid complaints as the amount of money deposited in John's branch has nearly doubled since September.

If possible could you bring out half a dozen Marks and Sparks Trubenised collars for John, size fourteen and a half, and I would like a couple of suspender belts, please.

I've just been listening to the top twenty and the Archers on Radio Malta. I wonder how much longer they will be allowed to broadcast?

The Pughs have lent me their vacuum cleaner so I am cleaning everywhere ready for the inspection. Then they can't say the flat is dirty and that we don't deserve better furniture.

Well must close now, love from us both,
Jean XXXXX

Letter No. 19 (Handwritten airmail letter)

Friday 10th February 1967

Dear Mum, Dad and Diane,

I think I'll just plunge into recent happenings. Sunday morning I received a shock by discovering a baby lizard in the washing-up bowl. It was still alive and John threw it into the garden for me. I expect it had fallen down from the ventilator hole in the kitchen ceiling. The rest of the day was spent in the flat tidying and I borrowed Susan's vacuum cleaner.

Monday was the bank's cocktail party in honour of the two visiting GMs from London. John and I had planned a drinking session at our flat afterwards, but before we could ask anyone Mr Norman had invited us to dinner in the restaurant of the hotel. We had to accept and it quite spoilt the evening. After the cocktails we trooped down and Mrs Norman absolutely fawned over the chairman's Italian mistress so I felt cheesed off. Anyhow we were all 'placed' for the meal and I sat between one of the GMs and an Arab director of the bank. John was miles away so we couldn't say a word to each other. The chairman gave Mrs Norman a carnation from the table centrepiece, then Mr Norman gave one to the Italian mistress and so the GM on my left felt obliged to pass one to me.

I was glad when it was over. It was sickening watching the Normans crawl. By the way, getting back to the actual cocktail party I was introduced to the ambassador. I saw him come in and was immediately attracted to his blue eyes and greying hair. He looked a typical ambassador. Later in the evening David (Pugh) asked if I wanted to meet anyone in particular so you can guess my answer. Anyway he chatted very pleasantly and even although he didn't remember my name when he took his leave I still felt 'bucked'.

On Tuesday we had the flat inspection. I don't think anything will be done but I can write another list of things, so I shall try again for a vacuum cleaner. Rupert was bribed with an early meal and several biscuits and behaved reasonably well. He was on the back balcony but started whining and scratching when the GMs got to the bedroom near to him.

In the evening John left him alone in the lounge for about fifteen minutes whilst he bathed and I got ready for Ortis to take us out. During those fifteen minutes he completely destroyed the library book John was reading. We left him in disgrace and didn't get home from the night club until about 2am.

Wednesday passed tiredly away – we were asleep by 9.30pm.

Thursday morning I went shopping with Susan. We got lots of meat but have to go back on Monday for lamb and liver. I had to pay 21/- for the destroyed library book but the librarian wasn't annoyed, she just felt sorry for me and said she wished it had been a cheaper one. I also managed to buy some shoes to replace my 'Granny' boots, which Rupert had eaten. We came home by gharry.

John then came home so we went shopping again and after dinner saw the 'Blue Max'. We didn't like the story very much but enjoyed the filming of the planes. We came home and John took Rupert out whilst I got the hot water bottle ready.

Jim's dog, Whisky has just caused £75 worth of damage. He has ruined a G-plan settee and Jim will have to replace it.

The weather is wet and windy at the moment and rather miserable. Fortunately John backed out of golf today so we are both peacefully sitting in the lounge. Jim, Alan and Vic are coming later for cards.

Love from both of us, Jean XXXXXX

Letter No. 20 (Handwritten airmail letter)

Friday 17th February 1967

Dear Mum, Dad and Diane,

I hope I'm not being too optimistic but after a light shower this morning it looks as if summer is beginning. The sun is brilliant and the sky a bright blue with a few streaky clouds.

Only a couple of answers required for question time. Yes, I have got fatter. A lot of the trouble started during my five-week stay with you in August/ September last year and I haven't lost any since. John calls me 'hippy' but I can still get into most of my dresses, so I think a 25" – 26" suspender belt will do fine. Make-up is okay here; I can get anything I need. If I think of any more things I'll let you know and don't worry about money as I'll pay you back in June. I would like some more 'Dipitydo' for hair sets, perhaps you could manage two jars. And also, if you each bring hair lacquer you could, perhaps, be persuaded to leave it behind as it costs about 18/- a can here.

The toilet has finally given out. John fortunately woke up at 3 am and discovered it. He had stepped out of bed and I heard a squelch and an exclamation (unrepeatable). We both mopped up the flood but the bedroom carpet was saturated. The overflow hadn't been able to cope with the amount of water coming in and the water was all over the bathroom floor and down as far as the dining room as well as in the bedroom. It's been temporarily patched up by Mohamed.

18.2.67 (Saturday)

We spent an hour on the beach yesterday. It would have been warm enough for swimming only we didn't have our things with us.

This morning I had a quick cup of tea at Susan's and their dog Peaches caught and killed a cat whilst we were indoors. Susan was very upset about it, yet at the same time she wants to get rid of all the stray cats that come into her garden.

Also this morning Rupert got round to the back of the flat (I'd left him playing in the front) and I looked out only to see him getting the worse in a 'friendly' with the Alsatian owned by the *Spaniards. Fortunately the Alsatian was chained (a long chain) and is not vicious so I managed to rescue Rupert with only a cut gum injury. I was worried at first as his mouth seemed full of blood but he ate some food so it can't be too bad.

Actually yesterday's weather changed into a ghibli in the late afternoon. If you can imagine a drizzly day in England where everything is turned to grey just substitute light brown for grey and you get the effect. Of course this morning I had lots of sand to sweep up but the back balcony was more affected than the front one so not too much came into the flat.

I have loads more free time now as John takes me shopping Thursday evenings. We get a week's groceries and on Saturday I get a week's meat with Susan. Just for a rough idea on prices, this week I spent £7.12/- on groceries which was over stepping the mark a bit. (I usually spend between £5 and £6). Anyway this cuts my shopping time down a great deal and I have been able to keep my housework up to date and have time for visits to Susan and Margaret.

Sally Pugh was nine on Thursday. She is a tiny little girl with a thin face and large eyes. Apparently she was two months premature and only weighed 3lbs at birth. Martin, who is six, is bigger than Sally already. Anyway you will be able to see them both soon.

We spent yesterday evening there playing canasta. It was the first time I'd played so I partnered David and John and Susan (both rusty) were partners. Out of the two games David and I won them both so I was very happy. Also I drank three watered down whiskies and felt very merry once outside and walking home. John made me drink an Enos before going to bed and so I returned to normal and had a lovely night's sleep.

I had lunch with Joanne (our guest before Christmas) and she was telling me how Mr Norman is perfectly horrible to his wife and she also gets the impression he doesn't care overly much for me (how sad). He doesn't like Rupert and says he chews the furniture, which is a lie and he hadn't even seen our flat when he made the accusation.

Must close, love from us both, Jean XX

NOTES:

*The Spaniards lived in the ground floor apartment next to Audrey and her American partner, Jack. Mr and Mrs Agosta (the Italian owners of the block) lived upstairs opposite ourselves.

Letter No. 21 (Handwritten airmail paper)

Friday 24th February 1967

Dear Mum, Dad and Diane,

Many thanks for your letter. I certainly had a chortle when you said you were starting on your fourth pen. I imagined you scrabbling about from drawer to drawer and muttering away as you looked for a fresh one.

I have heard from Florence, the baby is due in about two weeks. She spends all day in bed and finds it an effort to go to the 'loo' (her phrasing). She has to get up on Wednesdays though, for her hospital check up. (All this is written with my tongue in cheek). Nancy was only saying this evening how silly Florence is about it. Jim did everything about the house so she never had any exercise. Mind you she was always ready to go out in the evenings. (Catty).

As today is Friday we went to the beach. Firstly we collected, at long last, a Canon projector. We then had our first dip of the year. The water was very cold but the sun was lovely and hot. Rupert came in up to his tummy and then got chased around by two dogs a quarter of his size. We stayed for a couple of hours and have caught the sun.

Saturday 25th

I wrote the last page in bed so decided to carry on today. John managed to work the projector yesterday afternoon and I must admit our first film is rather a failure, but I'll forward it and edit it later. In lots of the shots we had both thought we had the subject central but on the film they have come out either to the side or too low e.g. mosque top (too low!) and Rupert's hind parts (to the side). I'll send the film next week as we plan to have a 'showing' with Jim's first film, plus his wedding film, and our one. When you have seen it could you then please post it to the *Morrison-Scott's: 13 Vincent Road, Stoke D'Abernon, Cobham.

The projector is full of bright ideas. We cut a special notch at the end of the film and once this part has gone through the projector clicks and it is rewound before you even have time to turn the lights on.

We played cards last night with Nancy, Alan and Vic. Nancy's parents are coming on June 29th so you should be able to see them once or twice before you leave.

Joanne (who stayed with us before Christmas) came for a meal last week and I made a cherry pie. I left it on the dresser and Rupert managed to get it down, lick all the sugar off the top and make three nibble holes in it. So we were minus our pudding. In spite of his lapses he is pretty good and as long as he isn't excited he will obey commands ('In your basket'; 'on your throne'; 'sit'; 'shake hands'; and if you are lucky 'stay'). I took him for his rabies injection the other day and he now has a little tag to wear.

This morning I went into town and bought some dry skin cream as my face is a bit flaky and I have a couple of really dry spots on my chin (not too unsightly but annoying). I then paid nearly £L1 to replace broken china. After that I got the week's supply of meat and treated myself to a gharry ride home. Rupert was frightened at first and kept fidgeting around but he soon settled down and sat quietly on the floor. The gharry drivers are all smiles to start with and I got today's man down to 25pts (5/–) but when you get out and hand them the exact amount they are very grim faced. To my mind they charge quite enough and don't warrant a tip.

This afternoon I went to Wheelus Air Base with the Pughs and had a swim. In two days my back has turned quite brown and my face is covered in freckles.

We've managed a few games of *canasta with the Pughs so we shall be all set, come June. (Rupert nearly had the book of games for an extra course the other day but I rescued it just in time).

Better close now, love from both of us,

Jean XXXXXX

P.S. Sorry to hear about Mr Lawson. Let me know if there is any more news on his illness.

NOTES:

*The Morrison-Scotts' at Cobham. They were John's mother (Kay) and step-father (John).

*Canasta. My parents used to play with friends in England. John and I intended playing with them during their stay in Tripoli.

*Mr Lawson was our next door neighbour at Pelham Road and father to Dorothy who Diane and I used to play with when children. Dorothy was about four years younger than me.

Letter No. 22 (Handwritten airmail paper)

Friday 3rd March 1967

Dear Mum, Dad and Diane,

Firstly my congratulations to Diane. Well done. With no disrespect to your driving ability but did you wear a 'mini' skirt?

You asked about the Pughs and where they lived. Well you know Bromley College, the old house that is falling down? You continue down the hill and you come to some shops on one side of the road and a park on the other. They lived in a road behind the shops. John keeps well clear of their children and doesn't go over unless they are in bed (8.30pm). Still I daresay one day he will get over his awkwardness (me-thinks he'll have to). I hope that when we have children he will play with them, but I daresay there are many men who feel as he does but get over it when they have their own.

John at the moment is exhausted. He has had six months of really hard work and in my opinion needs a holiday. He is off his food and when he gets home he is only fit for bed and his hair gets greyer every day. My friend Margaret's two children have chicken pox and I thought it a good idea if John went and played with them, but apparently he has had it. I feel sure John would enjoy the life here if he had more free time. Jim Graham, who works for Barclays, has it easy compared with John and he likes the life. John is thinking of changing to Barclays when his time is up. The only thing stopping him at the moment is the age factor (he is too young) and that he is married.

Jenny and Terry Dowrick came back last week. They were married in January. If you remember, Terry was the one who jilted Brenda and then got jilted by Jenny. It appears she changed her mind. I hope his arrival will relieve John's burden a little, but I doubt it as Terry is said to be a great one for skiving.

He told us himself that he plans to do as little as possible. He will probably get away with it as he crawls to the GM and is his 'favourite' boy. (In fact we don't like him much). Jenny is very pleasant, she's Scottish.

One afternoon I glanced out from the back of our flat. We have a row of flats facing us at the back with a road and a patch of green shrubbery in between where sheep graze. A dustcart was collecting rubbish and one of the Arabs crept away from the cart and headed towards the green patch. He was hastily pulling down his trousers and the last thing I saw before withdrawing my gaze was a bare bottom preparing to squat. When I dared look again he was making his way back to the cart pulling up his trousers.

On Wednesday I met Margaret whilst out with Rupert. I mentioned I was on my way to Tripoli and she asked me to cash a cheque at Barclays for her. In the bank one side had been labelled 'Pilgrims' and there were hoards of Arabs buying travellers cheques etc. ready for a pilgrimage to Mecca. Rupert was in his element nipping and chasing the tassels on the Arabs' blankets. In fact he made my arms ache so much I decided to spend 10/- (50pts.) and try my luck with a choke chain. He was much improved on the walk home.

Saturday 4th.

Yesterday John went golfing. I didn't go as Nancy wasn't going and I didn't feel very energetic. Jim came back for a meal and we learned that he is now a 'Daddy'. He doesn't know any details except that it is a boy and that they are both okay. (He is going to be called Stuart Alexander Graham). He didn't seem overly excited although he wore a smug look on his face. Funnily enough I wrote to Florence on Wednesday, which was the day he was born.

We had a short film show when Nancy, Alan and Vic arrived. We showed our film, and Jim's one taken here, and also Jim's wedding film. Jim's wedding film was done by a professional using a Super 8 film, the difference in size certainly makes it worthwhile investing in the Super 8. Please tell Albert from us both that we consider our wedding film to be far the best of the two. All the professional had done was aim the camera at the groups when the stills were being taken. Also he was shaky on the few panning shots he had bothered to take. We hope to get John's mum to send our wedding film out so we can see it again. John is far more enthusiastic now we have the projector and wants to buy a ready made film.

The weather is lovely now and I'm beginning to wear summer dresses (with a cardigan though).

Hoping you are all okay. Love from both of us,
Jean XXXXXX

Letter No. 23 (Handwritten airmail paper)

Saturday 11th March 1967

Dear Mum, Dad and Diane,

Thank you for the letter, Mum, and all the trouble you took to sell my wedding dress I am glad the nurse looked lovely in it. John's mother wrote and said she'd seen some Russian radios advertised giving world coverage for only £9.19.6d so we are letting her get one to bring out for us, so the £10 covers the cost nicely. It is unfortunate that our present radio will only pick up local stations, and Malta if the weather is fine. With the new one we should get London World Service giving us news and plays.

I'm glad Mr Lawson is getting on okay. You must tell me how you enjoyed yourself at Lyn's. I presume it was from her you found out about Mrs Wade; Mrs Meekins and Mr Huggins. All very interesting.

Today must be your Ladies Festival, are you wearing the red dress that you made? And don't forget to mention what gift you get.

On both Saturday and Tuesday I had to go back with John in the afternoon. On both occasions we were working until 9pm. It seems I have to help out when John's staff take sick leave.

This morning I went and got the meat only to discover they had no lamb and only two pork chops, so we are eating beef this week: casseroled; fried; pie; mince and roast. Apparently the lamb is usually 8/- per pound when imports are allowed but imports are stopped when the local lamb is available and that costs 12/- per pound so the butcher won't buy it. (Neither would I at that price). Pork is usually a bit difficult to buy anyway as only a few Italians are allowed to keep pigs (religious restrictions).

On Thursday a new acquaintance named Julia gave a coffee morning. Susan and I went together and there were four other ladies, two Canadians and two others whose husbands work for an oil company. The two Canadians live at Giorgimpopoli and whilst we were talking Julia mentioned that 'Jean's husband manages the Commercial Bank at Giorgimpopoli.' Well you should have heard the screams of delight and praises sung by the Canadians for John, so it seems he keeps his customers satisfied. As David says he probably checks their 'figures' when they come in.

As Julia's husband is in the desert she gets rather lonely and enjoys company so I offered to stay behind and help wash-up (John doesn't come home for lunch on Thursdays). But before we started washing-up she ran the two oil company ladies home and took me along. We firstly went into Josie's flat and saw her three-week-old baby Michael. He is a lovely baby and I held him for a short while. Then we went into the other lady's flat, Olga. She is a dress designer and showed us two of the dresses she had made up for her youngest daughter (14 years). They were gorgeous but she doesn't want to set up as a dressmaker here, which seems a shame, as all six of us at the coffee morning would have been willing customers.

Actually, Susan has a Freeman's catalogue so I have ordered two cotton dresses: 55/- and 39/6d respectively. They will come through the diplomatic bag with her own order so we won't pay duty. I also want a new swimsuit but didn't see one I really liked so we are going to send for some more catalogues.

Yesterday we went to the beach. I had a little swim but the water is still chilly. Rupert had a good run round for an hour with the two little dogs that had frightened him last time we were there. He kept disappearing with them, then we'd hear yelps and he'd come back to us. Once the beach started filling up I caught Rupert and picked him up, but one of the little dogs followed and Rupert kept yelping. As Rupert is so big I couldn't see what was going on but John said the little dog was swinging on Rupert's tail. Anyway we found a convenient lump of rock with a hole in it and tied Rupert up for the rest of the time. The water is exceptionally salty giving me a crust on my eyebrows and leaving my hair feeling tacky.

Our suntan is beginning to come along quite nicely. My legs are still pale but my arms and back are healthy looking already.

This afternoon I went to an ice-cream party at *Jean Cate's villa. She and her husband Addie (or something) are Americans and they have a two-year old boy. Susan came along with Sally and Martin and Julia brought her daughter, Catherine. There were lots of other children but they all sat separately in the garden whilst the adults sat under a covered patio. We ate ice cream and drank pink fizz.

I'm glad we don't live in a villa because the Cate's have been burgled twice and lots of people in villas have had robberies.

Love from us both, Jean xxxxxx

NOTES:
The Cate's were American and lived in our road on the opposite side. Addie taught

at the University. Their son, David was adopted from Germany and was a blond, light skinned little boy. Parentage probably an American forces father and a German girl.

*Ref: Lyn; Mr Lawson; Mrs Wade; Mrs Meekins and Mr Huggins. They were all neighbours in Pelham Road. Although, by now, my parents had moved to Orchard Court in Beckenham.

Letter No. 24 (Handwritten airmail paper)

Friday 17th March 1967

Dear Mum, Dad and Diane,

Last Sunday was a public holiday for the King's birthday. John went into Tripoli office for the morning but I stayed at home and Julia Parker left her eight-year old daughter, Catherine, with me whilst she went shopping. She is a quiet little girl and very clever. Julia drives a huge Plymouth which is twenty years old, and when she came back from shopping she drove straight here. I made her coffee and we chatted and then they both went home. It wasn't much later, when I took Rupert out, that I noticed she'd left her car behind.

In the afternoon John and I drove into Giorgimpopoli to get our car battery filled and on the way home we explored some back streets. You'd never guess who I bumped into? Miss Baldock (the lady on the plane) and her little poodle. I jumped out of the car and she said I could call on her any time. She is a bit odd but at least it's someone else to see occasionally.

The evening was spent chatting at Peter and Barbara's. It is a shame they will be gone by the time you arrive as they are very friendly.

On Monday Julia (her husband, Norman, is in the desert) took me to meet an old New Zealand friend of hers. He was having a few drinks before going home for a holiday. A Maltese couple were also there, with two children who sat as quiet as mice. Anyway after two whiskies I was well away and have practically disposed of Rupert. You see, Julia has a tiny stray female dog and is frantically trying to find a home for her. She also knows some people who live way past Giorgimpopoli (six kilometres) and they want a large male dog. So I said to send them round and if they want him I'll take her stray. Actually I blame the whiskies, but to be honest I have often thought that if anybody really wanted him and had a garden for him to run in I'd let him go. I feel rather sad and in some ways hope these people don't come, but Rupert is really too big both for me and the flat. The reason why Julia can't keep her stray is that she visits

England for three months every summer. Anyway, I'll let you know if anything more happens.

Susan Pugh was taking me to a Women's Guild meeting on Tuesday but as her New Zealand home help was ill she couldn't come. I went with Mrs Drysdale instead, whose husband works at the embassy. She is also an acquaintance of Mrs Norman, so I had to watch it. We saw some flower arranging but I didn't learn much as it looked too complicated. Then the meeting discussed a forthcoming bazaar. Susan has been landed with 'Beach Wear' so I had to listen to what was said. We intend making some towelling robes and some children's shifts etc. I didn't care for the vicar's wife and my impression of her wasn't improved when she was talking about the church flowers for Easter. 'I want all gold and white, we don't want any reds and purples and things'. Which is rather cheeky as flowers are very expensive here and one usually chooses by the price rather than the colour of the flower. (5/- for a dozen anemones).

The weather has taken a turn for the worse, winter clothes and top-coats, which seems daft as we were out sunbathing a few weeks ago. It is very blustery (20–30 mph gusts) and showery with temperatures in the fifties.

We called on Jim Graham in the early evening on Thursday and were surprised that Whisky was not bounding to the door with him. The poor dog was lying in his basket covered in 'gents in violet' nursing a bitten leg and stomach. It appears he escaped from the flat one evening when Jim came home from a shopping expedition. Jim had dumped the shopping in the kitchen and when he went to retrieve Whisky he just kept running. In the end Jim gave up and two days later a very chewed-up Whisky appeared at Nancy and Alan's at 2am. Anyway he has been to the vet and should recover.

Nancy is a Sister and Alan a Lab Technician at Inas Hospital in Tripoli. One day Alan was given some urine to test for pregnancy and when the test proved positive he was told it was Nancy's. What a way to find out one's wife is pregnant. We haven't seen them ourselves but Jim says they are thrilled at the news. In England they had been told it was doubtful if they'd ever have children as Nancy is nearly infertile and Alan's 'count' is low. They have been wanting a baby for some time. Anyway Mum, get knitting. If you do get a spare moment it would be nice if you could make something but don't worry if you can't as it is understandable with all your decorating.

I have ordered a pram blanket from a Freemans catalogue for Florence and two cheap dresses for myself. It seems a good way to get things here.

You asked about the postage stamps showing an Exhibition. It is called TIF, Tripoli International Fair. Lots of countries have stands showing their produce e.g. Rolls Royce from England; glassware from Czechoslovakia etc. It is meant to be quite good but we haven't been able to go because of John's working hours. The TIF building is permanent and impressive. The street has flags and lights strewn across it at the moment but the flags are twisted up now because of the ghibli. Anyway you will be seeing the building in June.

In the Freemans catalogue the undies were pricey so I'd like four new bras (two white and two black if poss.) 34 medium should do. Perhaps Marks and Sparks or D. Perkins in the 5/- range. I'll square up with you later in either Libyan or English money as I'm sure my requests go far beyond a birthday gift.

Well I'd better close. Last night we went to a St. Patrick's Day drinks party and were rather late home.

Love from us both, Jean XXXXXX

Letter No. 25 (Handwritten on airmail paper in pencil)

Saturday 25th March 1967

Dear Mum, Dad and Diane,

As you can see I had my Biro on 23rd and I only got as far as the address. Today I used it to write a shopping list and just before I left for the shops both the Biro and list were missing. I am now home again; feet aching and a parched mouth, so whilst I drink my squash and rest my corns I'll write my weekly epistle.

Sorry to hear that you, mum and Diane have been sick. Any ideas about the cause? Do you both feel okay now?

Dad was lucky going to Truro, I'd like to visit Cornwall again. When I think of England I always think first of seeing you and then I think of Devon and Cornwall. I'm not homesick but I do indulge in wishful thinking from time to time. When Florence left for Scotland I had an urge to sneak on the 'plane with her and drop in for tea.

I hope our first effort at filming has reached you okay. We could have done with a camera yesterday as we drove to Garian, onto Jefran and home through partial desert. We saw huge flocks of sheep, Bedouin tent settlements and hobbled camels. The rock structure of the mountains was very well defined and would have shown up beautifully. Also we saw a sort of oasis. It was a large area of lush grass and palm trees in a valley between these barren mountains of rock. We must have covered 300 kilometres (divide by eight and multiply by

5 for miles). Anyway we will make every effort to take you there in June. We went with Nancy and Alan in the two cars as it is better to go in pairs in case of breakdowns. Rupert was left on the balcony from 9am to 6pm and Susan Pugh kindly took him out once for me.

We have had a four-day holiday, Tuesday to Friday. Tuesday John worked until 3pm. Wednesday Jim Graham, his father and a friend came and spent the afternoon and evening here and taught us how to play bridge (very complicated). Jim's father's friend is 72 years old and has been courting a lady in Scotland for 50 years. Jim's father has seen Florence and the baby and they are both fine. Poor Jim has only had one letter from Florence since Stuart was born, which I think is mean of her, as he's longing to see them both.

On Thursday morning we had a look round the suk (market) but a lot of the shops were closed. Then we had lunch at the *Lizzie where we bumped into Nancy and Alan and arranged our outing for Friday. In the afternoon we drove out to Giorgimpopoli and had a look at some more shops. Then we went on to Seven Kilometre beach and let Rupert run around, he was exhausted after half-an-hour.

This holiday was in celebration of Abraham's message from God not to sacrifice his son but to kill a sheep instead.

Susan's neighbours have had a sheep tethered in their garden for weeks now and after the guns went off on Monday afternoon Susan said, 'I wonder what's happened to the sheep.' She went to look out of the window, screamed and said 'it's hanging by its back legs from a tree.' Just as we all crammed at the window for a look the Arab couple appeared and began taking it's skin off. Poor thing. This must have been going on all over the place as many Arabs have been seen lately walking around leading sheep on lengths of rope, obviously in preparation for the feast.

Last Sunday we had a huge thunder storm, which at the time pleased me because I thought it would help clear the air, as it had been dull and cheerless. But instead of just lasting a night we had odd claps of thunder and frequent downpours right up until Wednesday.

Anyway today is pleasant enough at 63 degrees Fahrenheit and it is helping to dry out the puddles.

Poor John was very dismal this morning at the thought of going to work; he said it felt like going back to school after the holidays.

When you visit the library try a Gavin Lyall novel. We've read 'Wrong Side of the Sky' and another which slips my memory, but they were both excellent adventures.

I expect you are knee deep in decorating. John's mum has had her hall done and the paintwork is now white which should make it brighter.

How are your holiday arrangements coming along? Jim's father had to come a week later than planned because his visa wasn't ready, so hurry them up.

Better go now, hope you have a pleasant Easter.

Love from both of us, Jean XXXXXX

NOTES:

The 'Lizzie' – an abbreviation for the 'Elizabethan Club' where expatriates tended to meet.

Letter No. 26 (Handwritten airmail letter)

Friday 31st March 1967

Dear Mum, Dad and Diane,

Many thanks for your letter, very pleased to hear you have chosen a camera. Do try to take a film to bring out for us to see, it would be lovely. Perhaps a few shots of the garden with Grandad on his birthday.

You ask about TV here. Well you can get sets but they only pick up Wheelus, so you only get cowboys, Batman and old films. But with all our reading we certainly don't miss it. (Anyway we never had one at South Norwood).

John's mother has bought the radio and says it looks very smart and works well.

Julia's little stray dog has been found a new home and no one came for Rupert so I'm keeping my fingers crossed they don't. I happened to mention to Pat (a neighbour) that I'd like a canary as I've seen some around here in cages and they look pretty and sing well. She said, 'Wait just a month and you may get one, cage as well.'

Don't worry too much about the tablecloth, we understand the size difficulties, but if you do see one we'd still like it.

Florence comes back on 27th April and at long last Jim has had some letters and photos of the baby. Whisky seems okay now. Jim's father goes back today.

We've had a quiet week, but I was worried about John yesterday. He only ate half a slice of bread and marmalade for breakfast and he brought back his lunch sandwiches untouched. Still he ate a fairly large evening meal and this morning he slept until 10am and seems okay. I expect the work has been exceptionally hard as it is the end of the month. We've often discussed whether to stay abroad and whether to change banks, but we'll talk about it all, with its various 'fors' and 'againsts' when you come out.

Rupert has been in some funny moods lately. He has taken to jumping on our bed, but worse still he loves combs. So one morning I was sitting on the bed combing my hair when he bounded in, jumped on the bed and made a grab for the comb, but he accidentally bit my head instead. I was furious and chased him onto the balcony. He didn't actually draw blood but it felt bruised for a while.

He is still puppyish in some ways but looks fairly full-grown now. He has desert dog in his blood as we saw many desert dogs last week and he is fairly similar. I was hoping the hot weather would calm him down but it just makes him ratty so I ignore him until he has cooled off.

The weather was brilliant for a few days (84 degrees Fahrenheit) but the last two have been overcast and airless, so I've had a permanent headache. I think November and December were the best months. Summer with its heat is coming slowly but surely.

I'm reading the 'Pillow Fight' by N. Monsarrat and enjoying it immensely. We also managed to get out Gavin Lyall's 'The Most Dangerous Game', which will mean we have read all four of his books.

We are very concerned about the *oil tanker off Lands End and only hope something can be done to clean the beaches. It was only last week I was singing Cornwall's praises, so in future I'll keep my mouth shut.

Next Thursday I hope to go bowling with Bertha (Dutch). For weeks now it has been arranged that we go but every time something happened and it had to be cancelled.

John begins 'summer time' tomorrow so we'll be up half-an-hour earlier (6.30am for me and 7am for John). I hope he'll get home half-an-hour earlier too.

Love from us both, Jean XXXXXX

NOTES:

The oil tanker off Lands End refers to the Torrey Canyon that struck rocks and spilled 31 million tons of oil into the sea.

Letter No. 27 (Handwritten airmail letter)

Saturday 8th April 1967

Dear Mum, Dad and Diane,

Thanks for your letter. I'm pleased to hear that the film received a showing. The reason why we took such a lot of Rupert was because he was still a puppy and I wanted to catch him like that.

We aren't too out of date here so the answer to 'Have I heard Englebert Humperdink's No. 1' is Yes. Personally I prefer 'Georgy Girl' and 'This is my Song.'

Jim Graham has received some photos of baby Stuart. He has a very fat face and unfortunately has a large birthmark on his forehead. It should go in a couple of years though. His father and old friend went back last week after a good holiday.

We went golfing with Jim yesterday morning and I completed nine holes and then gave up as it was so hot and exhausting. John and Jim did another five after a break. John's game has suddenly improved which pleases him a great deal. Can't say mine was any better. We left Rupert at home for over six hours and I was so pleased with him as he hadn't even puddled. He now cocks his leg on occasion and looks like a wobbly flying trapeze artist.

Jim spent the rest of the day with us and told us how one of his Libyan clerks came in one morning with his hair cropped. Apparently the police had pulled him in and cut it as it was considered too long. (It was only a fraction longer than Jim's, so you can tell it wasn't long really). Another, more important thing where Diane is concerned, is that the police are pulling in mini-skirt wearers and forcibly taking down hems. This applies to English, American and Italian girls. (The Libyans wear barracans). I think one or two inches above the crack on the back of the leg should just about pass muster, but no more. It is an absolute cheek on their part, as it is only because the Arabs are so over-sexed (or randy) that it has to be done. I can't see that the Libyan male can be sex starved as he can have up to four wives. Dad will probably be looked on in awe if we go into town together when John is working, they will think he has three wives.

Last Saturday we were taken to Wheelus along with Terry and Jenny Dowrick by one of John's customers. We had prawn cocktail, chicken, ice cream and drank champagne all evening. Although the place was cheapened by its Formica topped tables and fruit machines the food was good and the dance band were also good. We didn't get to bed until 3.30am. And it was work the next day, so I was up at 6.30am. John is on summer hours now and although he starts half-an-hour earlier he doesn't get home any quicker. Another eighteen months at this pace is enough for anyone. Jim Graham gets local leave and Barclays are paying their staff the return fare to Malta. Also he has just got a £450 p.a. rise, and it was backdated, so he had an extra £100 this month.

Sunday evening we planned an early night but John discovered a huge black insect swimming in the toilet. So he put it in a jam-jar and we took it across to the Pugh's for identification. David said it was a black cockroach, which put my mind at rest as it looked lethal. On coming home we dumped it in the dustbin and then I found a good ten or twelve ordinary cockroaches and black ants in the kitchen so that took up more time, getting rid of them all. I'm fed up with them and was seriously thinking of coming home. Rupert is pretty good though as he stubs them with his nose and eats them. Ugg.

I've heard from *Jane and she tells me that Carol is coming back for a month in May and then goes back to get married to Alan in June. They have purchased some land in Vancouver so I presume they will have a house built. I also heard from Jean and Derek and they sent some photos of the baby. He looks rather like Jean and is very big. They had him christened in Croydon and the vicar, according to Jean, really took to him.

On Tuesday I plan to have a coffee morning, so keep your fingers crossed for me. I think about seven should turn up so I have bought a couple of cups and saucers extra. In the afternoon I have been asked to Mrs Cate's. She was the American lady who gave the 'ice-cream' party. I expect this to be on much the same lines as she said most of the people coming have children but that they are all young wives she'd like me to meet.

The weather has been lovely and clear and hot lately but today it was close and sticky and now a ghibli is blowing sand around. Both balconies are gritty again and all the window sills are dirty. I only hope it doesn't rain and get chilly, as Monday is a public holiday and we have planned a picnic lunch on the beach.

Can't think of anything else. I am now wearing summer dresses without cardigans. Sorry this letter is a little late, but think yourselves lucky you're not Kay, as John hasn't written to her for ages.

Hoping all is well. Only nine weeks now,
   Love from us both, Jean XXXX

P.S. could you please get me two nylon waist slips, fairly plain. The cotton ones seem to make my dresses look funny and rucked up.

NOTES:

Jane was an old school chum. Along with Carol we used to hang out as a threesome at Balgowan School, Beckenham. Carol was one of my bridesmaids in June 1965 who left for Canada with her boyfriend Alan, shortly afterwards.

Letter No. 28 (Handwritten airmail letter)

Friday 14th April 1967

Dear Mum, Dad and Diane,

I'd better plunge into answering some of your questions. Terry Dowrick is in Tripoli office, unfortunately. If both he and John were in Giorgimpopoli all would be okay. His wife has a secretarial job now and is earning more than John so as you can imagine they are stashing the cash away and have a car each.

I still haven't been bowling. The Thursday before last Bertha's car was out of commission and this Thursday I couldn't go because John thought he may need me at the bank in the afternoon. You must be joking when you ask if it is on grass or an alley. I'm not that old, and anyway we don't have grass here.

The weather is most odd, it has been blowing gusts of 25mph and yet it has been in the 70's. Some days it is cloudless with brilliant blue skies and other days everywhere looks brown and dull. Today I went out for 'walkies' wearing a sleeveless dress, sandals (no stockings), headscarf and sunglasses. So you can guess how queer the weather is (and me too I suppose).

I gave my coffee morning on Tuesday. I was rather worried in case some of them didn't come because there was a mix up over the holiday. Monday should have been a holiday but as no one saw the moon reflected in water it didn't take place. John fortunately went to work at the usual time because he had some catching up to do for the quarter end.

Anyway Tuesday was the holiday and all my 'ladies' came. I invited a new lady along so I've helped her a little (also I wanted to have a look at her). The morning ended a little chaotically as the new lady's girls came up (ages 2 and 4) and then Susan Pugh's daughter, Sally, came in with a tear stained face, so I got out some Pepsi's and the children finished the cakes. Then Jim Graham came, so I introduced him to the 'ladies' and he sat down with us for about fifteen minutes until they left.

The plan had been for Jim to pick me up, collect John from the bank and go for a swim, but this was meant for Monday so as the holiday was a day late we decided to stick to our original plan and hope for the best. Anyway I quickly put on my swimming costume and off we set only to see John driving towards us (we were five minutes late and he hadn't waited). We turned and chased after him but we got right back to the flat before we caught him up and then he said he was tired, so he went to bed and Jim and I went back (a good 30 miles wasted). At long last I had my swim. It was okay once in the sea but pretty nippy on the beach because of the wind. We then had to rush back because I'd been invited to a 'tea-party' at Mrs Cate's. I met two 'young wives' at the 'tea' who live in the Bank of North Africa's building and who said I was to pop in when next in Tripoli. I felt pretty tired at the end of the day but had enjoyed all the 'social frivolities.'

I am listening to the American top-twenty at the moment and the Monkees have a newish record called 'A little bit you and a little bit me' and the announcer added 'A little bit free.' You will get a huge laugh out of the American way of making radio announcements. I thought it appalling at first but now I'm not sure if either they have improved or I have become immune.

Dear Rupert has nipped a hole in the fly screen on the front balcony so Mohamed is going to repair it for us. He is very useful for odd jobs and quick about getting them done. He charges for the materials only, as his labour comes in the £4 per month.

His little son, Ali, still has the popgun we gave him at the end of Ramadan, which pleases us. Yet Sally Pugh had either broken or lost the gift we gave her for her ninth birthday within a week of getting it. Actually Ali is an exception as most of the Arab children are destructive. Mrs Cate had to call the police as so many of her two-year-old's toys had been stolen or broken by local children, but she doesn't mind David playing with Ali as he is good.

John wonders if you can get him two Marks and Sparks collar attached cream shirts. If they have started doing double cuffs in cream he would prefer it but he doesn't think they have them. The size is 14½ for collar attached. Do say if you would like an English cheque or whether to wait and have Libyan money.

I hope your cold is better now, Mum. I've got hay fever pretty bad owing to the dust storms and feel wretched sometimes. On that cheerful note I'll close.

Love from us both, Jean XXXXXX

Letter No. 29 (Handwritten airmail paper)

Friday 21st April 1967

Dear Mum, Dad and Diane,

I'll plunge into daily events. Last Saturday I really lost my temper with a gharry driver. I asked for the New Mosque and when he understood that, I said 'just a few metres on for 25pts.' (5/-) so he said 'No. 30pts.' so I argued and got really annoyed as it is only just past the mosque to our turning. So I turned on my heel and said 'stick it mate' (which was the worst I could think of at the time). Then the driver behind said he'd take me for 25pts. I felt really pleased and on arrival I paid him and watched him drive off and up another side turning so obviously he wasn't doing me a favour at all but had got a passenger for his lunch trip home.

John has been 'off' for a few days, suffering from overwork and depression. I was quite worried as the problem seemed psychological but as he wasn't eating or sleeping well either I mentioned it to Susan Pugh. She pinpointed the trouble to drinking gin (which he has recently taken to in preference to whisky). She said gin was a depressing drink. I told John what she had said and he is now drinking beer and seems okay again. I still don't know if there is any truth in it but it worked.

John has got 'trouble at mill'. His cashier Lemin has been late for work recently and John told him off one morning so Lemin shouted back and the pressure built up. It ended the next day when a letter arrived for Mr Norman from Lemin saying how hard he works and that John had called him 'bad names'. Both these things are untrue. Fortunately Lemin is not well liked and may have to go.

David Pugh took myself and Susan to the suk and I saw some lovely sheep skins. I managed to get the man down to £L1-25pts. for a gorgeous thick white one. As you know I'm not keen on skins but as these animals would have died anyway I didn't feel too bad. The market is full of them now because of the recent New Year celebrations. If you would like one do say and I'll get it for you. When I got this one home I laid it down and Rupert cautiously sniffed at it. Then I teasingly twitched one end and watched as he hurled himself at the door in an effort to escape. He sat suspiciously eyeing it for ages and when I called him for his food he wouldn't walk past it to the kitchen so I had to move a chair for him to skirt round. Since then he has been wary and this afternoon he spent a long time barking at it.

I went to a coffee morning on Thursday and met yet more people who live round here. Life is really full at the moment with new friends and all this bazaar sewing. The bazaar is on Friday so I expect my next letter will be a little late.

We visited one of John's customers yesterday and watched some Italian television and talked a lot. He made us very welcome and although a shrewd businessman he seems very likeable.

Only Mohamed and Ali are living in the carport now. The wife and baby Salim only stayed for a short while and then went back to Homs. Mohamed and Ali went to visit them at the New Year and brought me back a gift of three dozen eggs. (I presume from their own chickens). He really is a 'gaffer' (caretaker) in a million.

A whole load of Arab men arrived in a truck at the flat opposite the other day and hoards of children turned up. They were back from the Pilgrimage to Mecca and to celebrate had brought four sheep with them in the truck. The noise was deafening. They have been there for four days now and they have killed two sheep to my knowledge. I saw the first one slaughtered from our balcony and I saw the remains of the second one when I got home from the shops. The children amused themselves by throwing stones at Rupert and myself. I shouted at them and warned them on two occasions and the third time it happened I decided to get a policeman, I was so annoyed. But as none of the stones had actually hit us I thought I'd see David Pugh first. He thought it best to give them one more warning and came up the road with me bringing a fierce looking Peaches. They seemed to take more notice of him (women being inferior) and so far I've not had a repeat performance.

I expect you are wondering about the cheque, well we thought it would be nice if you could buy something for Grandad's birthday for us, or if you can't think of anything just give him a £1 to treat himself with. Tell him it's not laziness that stops us choosing a present but lack of suitable goods.

Hoping you are well, I am getting very excited and all the English speaking neighbours know you are coming.

Take care,

Love from us both, Jean XXXXXX

Letter No. 30 (Handwritten airmail letter)

Tuesday May 2nd 1967

Dear Mum, Dad and Diane,

Many thanks for your last two letters, which I am about to answer at long last. As I warned you in my last letter that this one would probably be late, I trust you have not been worried.

I will now answer your questions before diving into my own news (for what it's worth). Yes, you will be arriving at Idris Airport, the reason being that it is the only one available before Benghazi . . .

You mention my taking a job, well John is rather 'agin' the idea as he likes his meals to be ready when he gets home as well as my general services e.g. he has only touched a tea towel on about five occasions since we have been here. Also with your coming to visit it would be foolish to tie myself down. Maybe after October I will look for a part time job just to last through the winter. I don't know yet.

The canary hasn't materialised and I don't like to ask Pat if it is likely to. Yes I think Rupert is still growing, but outwards now. He possesses a huge stomach. I was sorry to hear about poor Grandad. I have posted him a card so if perchance it hasn't arrived before this letter do tell him it is on its way. I think the post is rather up the creek because of the Maltese strike. Your letters have been arriving a day or two later than usual.

3rd May

Today has been a stinker, one hundred degrees. I have done very little work and spent the afternoon in bed hoping it will cool down enough to permit housework this evening. Every little task is a real drag and even Rupert has been good, he just flops down on the coldest tiles he can find and sleeps.

We had Ortis and his wife for a meal on 25th April and Terry and Jenny Dowrick as well, because Terry speaks some Italian. I did hors d'oeuvres (small salad), chicken casserole and trifle. They all reckoned the nosh but conversation was difficult. If Dad can remember his Italian it will be very useful here as the older Libyans speak it whilst the younger ones speak English. We were planning to entertain another customer, Nenis Nahaum and his wife Angela, along with Jim and Florence this Thursday (tomorrow) but Nenis can't come now so we will just have Jim and Florence and jnr.

I feel ashamed of my writing but my hand is so sweaty the pen keeps slipping and also it is hardly the right temperature for concentrating on grammar and spelling.

We played golf on Wednesday 26th as it was a public holiday. It started off well, weather wise, sunny and breezy but later turned hot and cloudy and the wind was so fierce it felt as if we were being rubbed down with sandpaper; the sand blew relentlessly into our faces, legs and arms. In fact the sand storm made it almost impossible to locate the golf balls as they bounced away into the murk.

Our new neighbours, *Gwen and Eric Neale came in for drinks one evening and Eric is going to make me some shift dresses. He makes all his own children's clothes and alters Gwen's things. If you see any pretty material either green or red predominating perhaps you could bring out 2½ yds. But there is no urgency in this request as you can get material here okay but a wee bit pricey. Also I'd be grateful for the patterns that Diane made up for me. don't know where I'd be without those dresses.

The bazaar was a flop from mine and Susan's point of view as very few people bought the new stuff we'd made but instead snapped up second-hand swimming costumes that had been given us. I got a costume for 5/- which was originally a £3.10/- Marks one. It fits perfectly and is in top condition. After the bazaar John and I visited baby Stuart. He was nearly asleep so I couldn't hold him. He has huge cheeks.

The rest of the week has been work, work and more work for John. I went back with him on two afternoons to call back figures but that cuts the morning short socially as I have to get all the chores done before lunch and then the evening is gone by the time we have eaten. I only managed to squeeze in one coffee morning but it wasn't a very exciting one.

Things have quietened down in the street regarding the pilgrims. I think they have all gone now.

John says not to bother with duty free drink excepting sherry. Whisky, gin etc. is only £1.7/- and £1.6/- approx. and he gets it cheaper from Nenis Nahaum anyway. Sherry is rather more expensive though £1.9/- (Dry Fly). The duty free allowances into Libya are pretty much the same as into England, and I would suggest that you make your purchases at the airport.

Everything is speeding up now. Only six weeks before you arrive. I intend taking up the lounge carpet soon and putting down rugs as it makes it look cooler and is easier to clean.

The area around here is looking lovely with huge flowers on the trees and in the gardens. My window box has had it though, thanks to Rupert. He managed to jump up and devour all four geraniums before they'd even had time to flower.

I will try to get the sheep skin for Diane. She will be lucky as it will have had time to de-nit itself. I found two tics and several other insects in ours, but thanks to Pif-Paf it is okay now.

Hope you are all well.

Love from both of us, Jean XXXXXX

NOTES:

*Eric worked for the United Nations and had also had postings in Africa. He and Gwen had two daughters, Tracy (about four years old) and Adrienne (about two years old). Adrienne's nick name was 'Winkle'.

Letter No. 31 (Handwritten airmail letter)

Friday 12th May 1967

Dear Mum, Dad and Diane,

My excuse for being late is that I haven't yet received your letter to answer. I have put off writing every day as I think 'tomorrow I will get a letter'. I am not 'getting' at you, as I know the post is to blame because John's Mum's letter was late this week.

I have been swimming today and at the moment I feel rather burnt. The wind was vicious and we couldn't stay on the sand as it was blowing onto our bodies and stinging but we later found some sheltered rocks to sit on. Flo's baby was crying a lot, as he is already cutting teeth. John didn't come but instead he got his car's timing sorted out with the aid of our new friend Eric.

I met a pleasant Italian girl, *Anna, at a tea party a long time ago and at long last I managed to call on her at her flat. She has a sweet little daughter, Gianna, who understands English (Anna's husband is English). When you speak to Gianna she answers 'si'.

Guess what I found? A tiny kitten. I named him Tiny Tim and we kept him for two days before I found a home for him. I gave him a bath in the sink and his fleas all jumped up onto his head. I had a grand time getting rid of them with spray and soapy water and they left me feeling itchy for days afterwards. Mrs Agosta took a great interest in him and when I tried to tell her he had gone away to a new home she looked very sad as she must have thought I'd meant he'd died. So I got some Italian girls in our local shop to write her a note explaining what had happened and when I gave it to her her dear old face lit up with pleasure. I hope Dad can remember some Italian as she seems so nice but I can't communicate.

We had a meal at the Dowrick's along with Joanne and a pilot named Jeff who was not only Australian but knew Burwood where *Dave Laurie went.

The Underwater Club is a bit of a let down regarding visitors as you have to get special permission. I expect it is to stop several people sharing one membership fee, but as you will be visitors (tourists) I daresay we can arrange something.

Now I have something lined up which involves the cost of £9 to you if you wish to partake. On Friday June 30th there is going to be a 'Poppy Dance' at the ambassador's residence. There will be a meal and wine thrown in with the £3 ticket and dancing until the early hours. So if you would like to us to get tickets please say and we will square up later. You should see quite a few of Tripoli's top nobs. Dress is either formal or dark suits for the men and Florence and I will be wearing long dresses. The whole thing will take place outside and the reason behind having the dance in June instead of November is to catch people before the summer holidays and so that it can be held in the open.

Florence has offered to take you out in their car once or twice, whilst I stay here and mind Stuart, and the Neales have offered to accompany us to Garian and Jefran as two cars are a better bet for comfort (and in case of break downs). I am getting very excited and trying to think of interesting things to do. Jim said his father was quite happy just looking at the shops and the suk and you will be able to use the Waddan swimming pool in town to cool off.

The Neales have found a large villa at the back of Giorgimpopoli and I have offered to help them clean the floors and woodwork. They are pleasant people and have traveled a lot with the UN.

We have received an invitation to the Queen's Birthday celebrations on 10th June at the embassy. We feel very honoured about it as this year they are cutting down on numbers. But as David Pugh was in charge of the guest list and I had told him how much I wanted to go I think he arranged it. It is for two hours in the evening.

I am giving a small coffee morning on Monday for Gwen, Margaret, Florence and maybe Susan, so wish me luck.

This evening we had roast duck. It was lovely and cost £1.8/- which I didn't think too expensive.

Well I must wash up now, take Rupert out and go to bed as I feel tired after the beach and swim.

Take care and believe me I can't wait for the 15th June.

Love from us both, Jean XXXXXX

NOTES:

*Anna (Whitchelow) married to John Whitchelow. John worked for the Bank of North Africa. They lived in an apartment above their bank on one of the main streets in Tripoli. Another BNA couple, Polly and Garry John also lived in an apartment in the bank building.

*David Laurie: An Australian boy-friend during my Bromley College days.

Letter No. 32 (Handwritten airmail paper)

Friday 19th May 1967

Dear Mum, Dad and Diane,

Many thanks for your letter. I'm longing to see your film of Coombe Woods. I expect it is very lush and green instead of our parched and yellow scenery. I was also pleased to hear that Grandad enjoyed it and also about his hand getting better.

You mention *'The Children of Allah'. Well a friend, Pat, has read it and is always saying how good it is, so most of the neighbours are longing to get their hands on it when back in England. Don't bring it here as it is banned but do try to read it as it is quite a conversation piece.

Poor *Johnny and Olive it must be pretty worrying for them but I daresay that with Olive's capacity for organising all will work out well for them. As for Johnny's description of Tripoli being a city of a million trees I think he would be disappointed nowadays. Mind you, the harbour is beautiful with the old city stretching beyond but things have been allowed to slide e.g. where the harbour wall has been broken due to car accidents along the *Adrian Pelt they have either left the gaps or filled them in with breeze blocks instead of replacing the balustrade. Tell Olive that we would love to stay in her boarding house, if not this leave, as it will be a winter one, but some time anyway.

Just think three weeks and six days to go. I have made a list of nine things of interest that you can do but I think you will also enjoy just looking around and sleeping most afternoons. John hopes he won't appear unsociable but he will probably have to miss out on some things as he is working harder than ever thanks to Mr Norman securing a large new account for him.

I must get the spare room tidied, as it is dusty and full of cardboard boxes that we keep getting when buying groceries. The Pughs are loaning us a mattress for Diane but Florence still says she can sleep at their flat, so Diane can always change her mind if the floor gets too uncomfortable. Actually I think she will be the coolest of us all. John and I are only using one sheet and a candlewick now and even that gets too hot some nights.

I gave a coffee morning on Monday and Gwen brought her girls and Margaret her boys and Florence her baby so with Susan and myself as well it was quite rowdy. Still all things considered I thought it best to have all the children together and have a quieter morning another day. I have three 'circles' now, 1) The Oldies, 2) The Younger Ones (I'm the baby though), 3) The Mums and Kids.

We had Joanne round for a meal on Tuesday and she told us some 'charming' things about Mr Norman e.g. he asked a friend of hers if he'd slept with her yet. I'll tell you the details when I see you, but it shows how odd he is.

I bought a summer skirt yesterday for £2.15/- which wasn't bad but the real object had been to get a cocktail dress but we didn't see anything under £11.11/- that would do. Even the £11.11/- ones would be half that price in England. Still, as the Normans haven't given any bank staff parties for ages I doubt it matters too much. I got 2½ metres of cotton for a shift dress for £1 and Eric Neale is going to make it up for me. (I'm a bit shy about having fittings though).

Little Ali showed us a photograph of himself with his maroon hat on. He looked very serious and his eyes were turned up, as if in fear but he was very proud of it.

Rupert has torn the fly screen again and has also eaten two of the photos Diane sent. At the moment he is lying on the sheepskin dreaming – his feet are twitching and his breathing has quickened and he is almost snoring. Poor thing, I wish he could get more exercise as his muscles seem flabby.

You mentioned that I didn't say much about baby Stuart. Well he looks like Florence and is teething already. He isn't very pretty and has, to my mind, funny clothes. He isn't a patch on Jean and Derek's John and in fact neither of us are impressed. I think our being biased is that since Florence has been back with the baby poor Jim has had an awful time. He has to shop after work and do everything that the houseboy doesn't do around the flat. Florence has the car all day but doesn't put herself out at all. She knows she can leave Stuart here anytime if she wants to shop but she'd rather let Jim do it all. I'm being very catty but whenever we see them Jim is always at her beck and call and she uses the baby to excuse her laziness. I'll quote you a typical example: on two occasions she was meant to be here at 10.30am (Stuart's fed at 10am). Well one instance was to take me to the beach and she didn't arrive until midday but the second occasion was for my coffee morning and she was here on the dot of 10.30am.

On Wednesday night we were leaving the Pugh's villa after cards and way in the distance could see almost continuous flashes of lightening. At first I thought it was a searchlight but I saw a couple of jagged flashes in distant clouds which disposed the searchlight theory and now, today, the sky has turned grey with thick clouds and the wind is getting up. So I think the hot weather is on the way out for a while. Apparently it has been too hot for the time of year – 80's and 90's.

The time passes quickly here, so the 3 weeks 6 days will soon pass for us and I daresay for you too with packing and purchasing. Did I mention not to bother bringing cardigans? I haven't worn one for ages and if we do need them I have got three.

Love from us both, Jean XXXXXX

P.S. Dad needn't bring a razor as John has his electric one and an ordinary one so you can choose. Also John has asked if you can get some plastic golf tees. He can get wooden ones but prefers the others. Thanks.

NOTES:
*The book 'Children of Allah' was written by the American Agnes Newton Keith. It recounts her time spent in Libya with her husband in the 1950's. He worked for the United Nations.
*Johnny and Olive were friends of my parents.
* Dr Adrian Pelt of the Netherlands was the UN Assistant Secretary-General and appointed as UN Commissioner in Libya. [Wright, John. Libya. A Modern History. p.59. ISBN 0-7099-2733-9]

Letter No. 33 (Handwritten airmail paper)

Friday 26th May 1967

Dear Mum, Dad and Diane,
I think I will answer questions to begin with. You ask about Mrs Agosta, well I presume it is her husband who owns our block and apparently he owns half the next block as well, so what with his day time job he must be rather wealthy.

You ask about luggage – well if you could pack your own toothpastes and soaps (very expensive here), as many dresses as possible, clothes hangers, sandals and flip–flops (I live in my flip–flops because the sand slides out of them quickly). If you have a suitable bag for the beach it would be useful. Sunglasses are essential, even a sun hat would be a good idea, but you can get them here. Bring a couple of dressy dresses in case we are invited out for cocktails. No need to bring towels or books, we have quite few paperbacks here in the flat.

Don't bring shorts, not even for the beach. As you know you can't change on the beach. Most women wear dresses over their costumes and take off their dresses on the beach and even then the Libyans can't take their eyes off you. Some women do wear slacks but I think they must be rather hot.

Ali doesn't seem to wear socks but he is usually dressed in slacks and tee shirts, or short-sleeved cotton shirts (any colour). I think it is very kind of you to bring him something. He is very shy so I don't think you ought to give it him until the end of your visit when he has got used to you. He is about 7 years old and seems about average size.

I've tidied the spare room and washed the bed covers. It looks quite bare but by the time your suitcases are in there it should look better. I did think of letting you have our room, but then decided it would be difficult getting our clothes changed round etc. Also the spare room will be cooler.

Peter and Barbara Howarth gave a farewell party last Sunday. It was a small party but very enjoyable as we knew most of the people. The Normans said they'd pop in for a short while at 7.30pm so no one bothered to arrived until after 8pm. But the Normans came at 8.30pm instead, so we still had the pleasure of their company.

Peter and Barbara left on Tuesday. I was going to see them off if there was room in the car but Salim (bank driver) didn't come for me. Anyway we have their address and will see them when we come home. They live near Manchester and we will be going up that way to see John's relations and Jean and Derek.

I have shampooed the lounge carpet and put it away for the summer. We now have two slip rugs and the sheepskin down. Florence called whilst I was busy and left Stuart here for 10 minutes which stretched into 2 hours. Also she brought Whisky. I had to pop out for bread and felt worried about leaving the baby alone but he was still sound asleep when I came back. He seems prettier now and has a lovely smile. You just stroke his cheeks or tickle his tummy and he smiles.

Last night the Cate's (who live across the road) asked us for a meal. They are Americans and the husband teaches at the university. They had invited another American couple along and a friend who is staying with them for a few weeks. We had barbequed meat; yellow rice and some delicious sauces.

I have developed a cold and this morning my head felt ten times thicker than usual. I was meant to go to the beach whilst John was golfing but as I had a siesta from 12pm to about 2pm I don't know if Florence called or not. In fact I spent most of the day sleeping as John was out 'till 3.30pm and when he came back we both had an afternoon siesta. I think all this sleeping has done me good as I feel as if my cold is on the way out already.

I don't think Rupert has had a mention this week, but except for matching tics in each ear he seems okay.

Well, only 2 wks 6 days now.

Lots of love from us both, Jean XXXXXX

Letter No. 34 (Handwritten airmail letter)

Friday June 2nd 1967

Dear Mum, Dad and Diane,

Less than two weeks. We are both looking forward to seeing you so much.

Quite a few of us intend wearing long dresses for the Poppy Dance. I shall wear my long red one anyway, so your long one, Mum, would be fine.

John thanks you for his birthday cards. He had a lovely celebration, a summons to the Norman's villa for pre dinner drinks. The GM from London, Mr Findlay, has been out for an AGM and on Wednesday he took the bank expatriate staff for a meal at the Waddan. The Normans left after the floorshow but Mr Findlay asked the rest of us to stay. He kept the drink flowing and was jolly nice to us all. He seemed shocked that the bedrooms aren't air conditioned and questioned Mr Norman about it. Also Joanne mentioned in her cunningly jovial way that Mr Norman made important customers stand and wait, without refreshment, to see him. Mr Findlay was duly shocked so we hope another nail has been driven into Mr Norman's coffin. John has kept quiet about wishing to go on Eastern overseas staff but both Mr Norman and Mr Findlay were throwing out feelers and Mr Norman was asking John what prospects he'd have back in London. So it seems they are keen to have him. We didn't leave the Waddan until 2am so we were both tired yesterday.

Yesterday evening we had the Pughs and Neales for a meal. It all went well, but Susan left early as Julia's daughter, Catherine, was sleeping at the Pugh's and she wanted to check that everything was okay with the children. Julia's husband, Norman, had been taken into hospital with stomach pains and Julia had needed to spend time at the hospital with him, so Susan had taken Catherine under her wing. Well apparently Susan found Sally and Catherine awake and just as they were settling down and dropping off to sleep Julia came back and thus prevented Susan rejoining us. I saw Julia this morning but she still didn't know what was causing Norman's pains.

I went to a 'sewing morning' yesterday and met a girl who loves dogs and is also hoping to get a villa, so I brought her in and showed her Rupert. She really liked him and he seemed very affectionate with big licks for her. So if she gets a villa she may have him.

We were invited, along with Terry and Jenny, to Ortis's new villa in Giorgimpopoli. We had a mouth-watering escalope of veal and ate the vegetables from side dishes.

Ortis has two sons, 15 months and 2½ years. Both drink beer and the younger one also drank John's whisky, which was on a side-table. All around the lounge they had soft toys decorating shelves and chairs and in the dining room the sideboard was covered with them. The children stay up until midnight every night but they seem to thrive on their way of life as they are both very big and happy.

You asked about Nancy – well I think we are getting the cold shoulder from them. John and I have racked our brains for reasons but as far as we know we haven't upset them. I have a theory that Nancy, Alan, Jim and Flo prefer a foursome to a sixsome and I also feel sure Nancy fancies Jim. The whole affair is complicated, although Flo and I get along okay whenever she pops in. She is fine to talk to but you can't rely on her for being punctual. John and I still like them all but neither of us feel like inviting them round as we think it isn't our turn to be host. Anyway we will just wait and see what happens.

I met three girls (including the one who liked Rupert) at the sewing morning. The other two, Anna and Polly I've met before. Both the latter girls have overworked banking husbands so I think we will have a get together soon and let the menfolk moan to each other.

I gave John a book for his birthday called 'The Battles of Napoleon' by David Chandler and also a silly little toy man with ginger hair, wearing armour. I think Kay is going to ask you to bring John's present from her out with you. I daresay she will be calling on you, you lucky people.

I went to see Gwen last Monday and Eric made me a shift dress whilst I was there (4 hours). It is very nice and I hope he will make me some more.

Well better go, feel rather tired.

Love from us both, Jean XXXXXX

Letter No. 35 (Handwritten airmail letter)

*Monday 5th June 1967

Dear Mum, Dad and Diane,

I don't know when this letter will get posted but I hope soon.

We had been living with a sense of expectancy for some time now and this morning when Jenny Dowrick came and told me that war had been declared it came as no surprise. She was in rather a state as she'd been sent home from work but couldn't reach her flat as a huge mob was surging towards her. Fortunately she managed to reverse the car in time and ended up here.

Throughout the morning we'd been popping over to Susan's for the BBC World Service so didn't feel too out of touch.

Jenny managed to ring Terry from Mrs. Agosta's so he came here for lunch.

John was terribly unworried and calm but he's been fortunate so far in not seeing any of the mobs, still he took the precaution of arming himself with the metal meat tenderiser for his afternoon drive back to Giorgimpopoli. Terry had seen a lot of mobs and said that quite a few of the shops in Tripoli were burning.

Jenny and I saw about twenty school children marching down our road with placards but no stones were thrown.

Jenny went with Susan to the main road to meet the school bus (Martin and Sally's) and a man advised them to go home (for safety). When the bus eventually came Susan crossed the road to get the children and poor Jenny had a huge stone thrown at her, which luckily missed.

The boys both went back to work for the afternoon and it has been arranged that John won't have to go into Tripoli for cash and travellers cheques until it is safe to do so. Terry came back about 5pm and said cars were overturned and burning and a building near the bank was on fire. (We'd seen the smoke from our balcony).

Tonight the country is under curfew from 7pm to 6am, which puts our minds at rest.

I expect tomorrow things will be different. David Pugh thinks the police were just letting people give vent to their feelings today and will clamp down tomorrow, but John thinks that by tomorrow they will be better organised – so who can tell.

I have a good stock of food and have filled the bath with water in case it gets cut off.

To be quite frank I don't expect you to come out now.

BOAC are flying as many people home as want to go but as David hasn't heard of anything too serious I will stay until he advises otherwise. John will probably have to stay until the crowd come hammering at the doors.

I'm rather worried about Rupert if we have to go but think it best to let him go wild rather than have him put to sleep. I'll leave some money and food with Mohamed hoping that he might be able to keep an eye out for him.

I daresay Kay would be grateful if you gave her a ring. As far as we can tell providing one sticks close to home you are okay and we are fortunate in not living in town.

I do hope everything quietens down and you can come out otherwise it will be a long wait as July, August and September will be too hot for sightseeing and enjoying yourselves. I can't think of anything else to say except moan at the way our *anniversary was celebrated.

If you ring Kay to tell her how things are here perhaps you'd thank her for the anniversary card she sent. Also thanks for the one you sent.

Hoping to see you soon either here or in England.

Lots of love from us both, Jean and John

NOTES:

*The Six Day War. Monday 5th June 1967 was the day Israel attacked Egyptian planes on the ground and started the Arab-Israeli war. The Libyan King Idris did not join in the fight, thus causing social tension and unrest amongst his Muslim citizens.

'In Tripoli eighteen Jews were killed and 25 injured. The survivors were placed in detention centres'. Info. From Michael B. Oren. Wikipedia [http://en.wikipedia.org/wki/Six-Day_War]

'Libya – Muslims rioted in the Jewish Quarter of Tripoli. 18 Jews were killed. Homes and synagogues were burned to the ground and the mobs prevented Libya's Jews from returning to their communities. The Libyan government rounded up all the Jews, confiscated their property and expelled them.' [http://jewishrefugees.blogspot.co.uk/2007/06/how-jews-were-treated-after-six-day-war.html].

*Jenny Dowrick. Jenny's husband Terry worked at the main branch of the Commercial Bank of Libya, in Tripoli. Jenny worked as a secretary for the American oil firm, Haliburton. Their flat was in Tripoli.

*Our anniversary: it was our second wedding anniversary on 5th June 1967.

Letter No. 36 A Telegram

PLEASE CANCEL HOLIDAY SAFE DON'T WORRY JEAN

My parents and sister had been booked to visit us in Libya on my twenty-third birthday. We had been looking forward to their visit very much but had to cancel due to the unsettled atmosphere in Tripoli at that time.

Letter No. 37. (Handwritten airmail letter)

Thursday 8th June 1967

Dear Mum, Dad, and Diane,

I hope my cable reached you safely. I expect Diane has spent her fare money on a new wardrobe already. When things have calmed down we must sort out a new date. Don't worry about sending any presents, I can wait.

Terry and Jenny are staying with us as their flat is in town so we have a party every night. Actually the boys play chess or cards and Jenny and I read in between cooking.

We all have an emergency case packed but hope we don't ever have to make use of them.

The boys have been going into work as usual but have only been doing essential work so they are home between 3pm and 4pm.

John and Terry go shopping before leaving for work and get fresh bread. They also managed to get tinned milk this morning.

We have sufficient meat for five days but some shops in town are opening for a few hours each day now, so we should be able to get more before our supply runs out.

I do hope you are not worrying about us. David (Pugh) is very calm and is reassuring as many people as he can get round to. No general evacuation order has been made for the English but many dependants of American employees have gone.

I am reading 'Forever Amber' Vol.1 and thoroughly enjoying it. I can't really think of much else to say, we just stay quietly at home.

Rupert only gets short walks keeping the flat in sight. I have packed a string bag with his food, plate, rabies certificate, lead, tin opener and £L2. I intend leaving it in our garden and trusting someone will look after him, possibly

Mohamed, if it comes to the push.

It is surprising how people get together and try to help each other. One feels free to knock on any door and be sure of a welcome.

The curfew is still operating and is being upheld.

Terry and John went to Terry's flat this afternoon and came back with a record player, a pile of records, a Scrabble board, and some frozen and tinned foods. So we are nicely set up.

I expect you are following the news and know as much as we do of the situation.

Please ring John's mum when you get this letter as I expect she is in a state. I understand you are getting messages via the Bank that we are okay so I hope you are reassured.

I was so looking forward to your visit but at least the spare room wasn't tidied in vain. The weather has been very windy and humid so you aren't missing much sun. Actually if you check when John's people are coming (I've forgotten the exact dates) perhaps you can arrange a date shortly after. Don't come in July, August or September.

Well I must close, we are just starting a game of Scrabble.

> Lots of love from us both,
> Jean XXXX

Letter No. 38. (Typed airmail paper)

Wednesday 14th June 1967

Dear Mum, Dad, and Diane,

Thank you for all the cards you sent. Diane's caused a lot of laughter. As you can see it isn't quite my birthday but I opened the cards when they arrived. We are still under curfew so we will not be celebrating for a while.

Actually the curfew has been relaxed a little. It is now 8.30pm to 5am. It is a great pity about your holiday. I hope you haven't lost any money on deposits etc. Nancy and Alan had to put Nancy's parents off also as they were due out just before you were to have left.

Most of the Yanks have left and Giorgimpopoli is like a ghost town with hundreds of roaming dogs and a few horses tethered in gardens. Wheelus offered to take pets and put them in a rehabilitation centre on the base providing that funds and helpers could be found. All went well for a day or so until some British people went to Giorgimpopoli and rounded up as many stray dogs as they could find and proceeded to Wheelus with them. After that Wheelus closed down the pet centre.

John doesn't expect to be very busy in future as most of the customers have gone and the rest can't send money out of the country anymore.

Jenny and Terry are still with us so we have company during the evenings and Jenny has only just started back to work so I have had company during the day. *I am with Jenny at the moment as I didn't feel like staying in the flat this afternoon. I also wanted to practise my typing as I may be getting a job at the British Embassy. The job is very much in the air as they really want someone who can speak Italian or Arabic and type properly. Anyway I am not looking at the keys so you must excuse the over-typing.

I have been endeavouring to grow my hair but gave up on Monday and had it chopped off. It is very short and everyone except John seemed to like it. Terry is bringing his camera over this evening so tomorrow I hope to have a few photos taken with Rupert, and you will see my cropped mop.

Rupert has caused me more worry and upset than anything else during the crisis. At first I thought I'd let him go if we were to be evacuated, then I thought I'd give him an overdose of sleeping pills. I asked the Spanish doctor if he could get the pills but he said they wouldn't work and Rupert may wake up after a lot of sickness so he offered to get an injection but when I saw him yesterday he said the injection would cause pain and convulsions as it would have to go in through a limb and not the heart if we did it ourselves. So we are more or less back to square one. Terry and John think that whatever happens we should have time to get him to the vet's before leaving, so we have let the matter rest there. Rupert is the one reason why I don't want to leave as it would be impossible to find him a new home.

Poor Jenny was petrified of Rupert when she first came but after a couple of days she decided he was 'a poor wee thing' and he is now allowed to lick and climb all over her, in fact he is being spoilt and I feel I will have a lot of retraining to do once they move back into town.

I was going to give a coffee morning on Thursday but when I mentioned it to Susan she said she had one planned for Wednesday, so we combined the two and had a big one at her house this morning. There must have been fifteen people there so we all had a good natter and let the children play in the garden. Gwen came with her two girls and the little one, Winkle, was found curled up in the grass, sound asleep. It was lovely to get out and meet all the neighbours again. Lately I have only been popping to the local shop and exercising Rupert in the garden.

Yesterday I went to Giorgimpopoli with John and helped balance the current accounts. Then I visited the nearby supermarket but they had very little on the shelves in the way of tinned goods. I was the only customer in the place; it is usually crowded out.

Mrs Norman called and she only has two people left in Giorgimpopoli that she knows.

Well this letter is very disjointed but I am concentrating on the typing as much as possible.

The quick brown fox jumped over the lazy sleeping dog . . .

I don't know what to advise regarding your holiday, even if you can all change dates I won't be able to say for certain about re-booking for October until at least a couple of months have passed. If you do re-book why don't you try coming via Malta as John's people are? It seems a shame not to see a little of the island when you are so near.

Well must close and I must try to drop *Mrs Richens a line. She sent me a birthday card which she had very shakily signed herself.

Lots of love to you all,

Jean xxxxxx

NOTES:

*This letter was typed by me at the almost deserted Haliburton office where Jenny worked.

*Mrs Richens, a very elderly lady who used to endeavour to teach me piano. She moved from Beckenham to live with her son, a vicar in Liverpool, sometime before I went to Libya.

Letter No. 39 (Handwritten on airmail paper)

Saturday 17th June 1967

Dear Mum, Dad, and Diane,

Thank you for your letter which arrived on my birthday, along with a letter from John's people and one from Jean and Derek, so all in all I was very pleased. Now Mum, hold your breath while I tell you what John bought me for my birthday: a gold ring with a jade stone bearing a Buddha carving. It is beautifully mounted and the gold weighs quite a lot. The jade isn't a top quality stone as it is a mixture of light and dark green but nevertheless it looks and feels nice on.

I began work at the embassy today. The job involves typing letters; birth and death certificates; helping at the counter; making out new passports and doing renewals; and making coffee. I haven't yet discovered my way around the building let alone worked out which form is which. David drove me in and brought me home in his car (bearing CD plates) but later I shall use an embassy pick-up system (5/- a month). I earn £65 per month with no deductions at all. Last night Jim Deasy was here and as he speaks Arabic he managed to persuade Mohamed to come in and do the washing and cleaning for £3 per week. So I am as pleased as punch excepting two factors: 1) Having to leave Rupert out on a stinking hot balcony, 2) missing my coffee mornings. Actually I shall tell Mohamed to put Rupert in the kitchen when he has finished in the flat, so problem number one will be solved.

You know the old saying 'It's an ill wind' etc. Well Friday was cloudy and hot and today has been a scorcher with a hot wind and no sun. So as far as weather goes the first couple of days of your holiday would have been too hot to do anything as even a trip to the beach would have been unpleasant.

We have heard good news of *Angela and family. They are in Italy and managed to get all their belongings out through Wheelus. They won't be allowed back ever but I should think they have plenty of cash to set up a business again.

Terry let me borrow his camera and I managed to take lots of photos of Rupert and one with Mohamed holding him on the lead. I don't know where they will be developed as all the camera shops seem to have been burnt out. Tripoli looks depressing with half the shops shuttered and scorched and piles of rubble around. I haven't been into town on foot yet but yesterday we did a tour by car which wasn't too upsetting as the damage is now old and boards and bricks are being put up. I don't know when I'll venture out beyond our local shops though, as things are still unsettled. I was talking to a gaffer who tidies around the flats further down the road and he said 'Maybe trouble finish, maybe not.' We think and hope individuals are safe but we expect trouble in the oil fields and more large buildings belonging to the oil companies being damaged.

Terry and Jenny have gone back to their flat so John and I are alone, and housebound after 8.30pm, excepting a walk in the garden for Rupert. We occasionally see policemen patrolling our road at night but by day they are everywhere. *They have done a marvellous job in quelling the mobs even though they are their own people. Around the embassy you can't move for police and trucks so I feel pretty safe.

It was so funny coming back to the flat after work and having to search for things. I'd left a pile of washing for Mohamed to do and couldn't find it at first and then I discovered it heaped on the sideboard in the dining room waiting to be ironed. He'd also put the old cutlery away mixed in with the new, and tonight I couldn't find my pyjamas or housecoat for ages but eventually the housecoat was found hanging in the wardrobe and my pyjamas had been put in with my bras in my dressing table drawer. Anyway tomorrow being Sunday and my day off I shall show him around.

As I only work from 8am to 1.30pm the fact that John and I have different days off shouldn't make much difference as on Fridays John either likes to lie in or go golfing in the morning, leaving time to go beaching together in the afternoon.

We went to the Under Water Club for lunch on Friday at the Norman's expense but it was very quiet and no liquor was available. The country has now gone 'dry' and all English and American cigarettes are banned; and what with the stoppage of sending money out of Libya we shall have to invest in gold bangles and hope to sell them when we get home.

Well, I myself feel cheerful, John is very tired, but all in all we are just hoping for the best and managing to jog along. Oh, Yes, one more thing, all British and American imports are banned so we will be living on pasta and cous-cous (local dish) from now on.

Better close. Lots of love from us both,

Jean xxxxxx

P.S. Hope your touring holiday goes well. xx

NOTES:

Angela was Nenis Nahaum's wife.

Police patrols. Rumour had it that the government swapped the police over between Tripolitania and Cyrenica as there is not much love lost between those two areas of Libya.

Memories

FIRST DAY AT WORK AT THE BRITISH EMBASSY, LIBYA.
Saturday 17th June 1967

At eight o'clock on a bright clear day I climbed the wide expanse of stone steps in front of me, leaving the blue waters of the harbour to my back and a shiny brass plate at eye level to my front. 'British Embassy in Libya' was engraved on the plaque and today I would be entering the heavy wooden doors to the side of the sign for the first time.

A Libyan employee, smartly dressed in a dark blue uniform, pulled one of the pair of doors open and stood back, allowing my eyes to become adjusted to the indoor light and my body to the early morning coolness of the building. The lobby was spacious and two more uniformed Libyans stood by a sizeable desk in readiness to run messages for the staff and help visitors find their way to the various departments.

David Pugh, the Consul, standing at nearly six feet tall and with a broad body to match had driven me to the embassy in his car and now he gently guided me, in his paternalistic way, to my new work station; a desk behind the long counter of the Consular Section. Two men stood, with their backs towards me, at a small separate table making morning tea. They were introduced as Luigi and Isaam. Although they shook my hand in a friendly manner their smiles were unsure and Luigi's eyes, out of shyness I supposed, did not want to look directly at me. I was told that they were to be my work colleagues behind the polished length of the counter.

David said that I must have a tour of the building and insisted that he conduct it personally. With his arm gently placed on my shoulder he guided me back across the reception area towards a series of doors, most of which were ajar. He knocked on each in turn and introduced me to various members of the Commercial Section. The second in command swung round from his desk and looked appraisingly at me. Leaning back he boomed out his welcome and laughingly said that he wished I could be working for him instead of David. The two men threw each other quick knowing looks, showing that they appreciated my attractiveness. I picked up on this light hearted exchange and thought that I would be well looked after by these two if I ever needed help.

In another room a woman with iron-grey hair and home-permed curls looked up from her desk that faced the door directly. She peered disapprovingly at me over the top of her half-moon spectacles. Instinctively she knew it would be rude not to stand to shake hands with me (an itsy bitsy girl) but equally she didn't want to lose any of the status of superiority that came with age and experience. To her mind standing would show deference. In the end she compromised by half rising and extending her hand partially across the desk and typewriter. Even in her stooped posture I could see that the Commercial Assistant was a large boned, angular woman wearing a flared, dull brown skirt that came down midway on her calves with a looping, lopsided hem. I made up my mind to only have minimal contact with this critical looking woman; I did not expect any help from this judgemental quarter.

After a break for coffee, we went up the stairs that led from the main lobby to visit Chancery situated on the first floor. This was the section where the ambassador had his office and one or two others of the hierarchy worked. David, observing protocol, did not intrude on His Excellency although he did effect an introduction to his secretary. Carol was an approachable girl, shipped out from the Foreign Office in London. She was an attractive, slim, blonde with a cheery smile and gave me a warm welcome. I liked her immediately although I felt that there would be little contact between us due to our differing status within embassy confines.

With the introductions over David set me my first task of the day. I was to make him another coffee and take it across the corridor to his office. Luigi and Isaam watched me like hawks to see that I only used the instant coffee powder and milk that belonged to the consul; they guarded their own supplies jealously. When I re-entered the public consular area the two clerks seemed happier with my presence and Luigi couldn't begin to explain quickly enough what was needed when issuing passports, either to Maltese with a claim to British citizenship or British ex-patriots. And for his part Isaam proved invaluable imparting local knowledge and cultural customs.

At the end of the day I felt that I would enjoy working at the embassy in an incredible setting where my desk overlooked the glistening harbour and gleaming boats.

Letter No. 40 (Handwritten on airmail paper)

Friday 23rd June 1967

From: British Embassy
Tripoli
Libya
B.F.P.O. 57

Dear Mum, Dad, and Diane,

I am so glad you are enjoying your holiday. We had a letter from Kay today and she says you are having lovely weather. Actually, our weather here has brightened up considerably; a hot sun and cool breeze.

Mohamed has been at Homs since Monday so the flat is grubby and the ironing is piled onto the ironing board ready for him tomorrow. I have decided to be less house-proud and take every opportunity of going to the beach. The Under Water Club isn't allowing members on its beach yet, as the police warned them not to use it, but Gwen and Eric Neale have passes for Piccola Capri beach and they took me down yesterday. It is a small strip of sand with some disused beach huts and clubhouses. It was once owned by the British Army but is now waiting for a buyer. The beach was packed yesterday but was safe enough as we had a couple of Libyan Army personnel guarding either end with rifles. I think the Europeans must have deserted the other beaches.

We still have our curfew and John is hoping it continues for at least two more weeks to see him through the half year.

My job is still okay and everyone seems friendly enough. One chap, Geoff Bishop, lives in *Clock House Road and has a fiancée living in Hayes Lane. I haven't had time to see if he knows any of my old cronies but I expect one or two names will be familiar to us both when we get down to a good old reminiscence.

You asked about home leave, well John is on a two-year tour so we should be home in September 1968, but who knows. Jim Deasy was due home in July but it has been put off until December. It all depends on replacements.

The removal of Wheelus shouldn't affect us. They offered no protection for us during the crisis so I don't care what happens to them. It was very much a case of America for the Americans and let the rest stew. Loads of Yanks are still living it up in Europe on expense accounts after fleeing from here in a panic, yet the ones who stayed are having to do all the work with no praise or extra cash. I think it was a good idea to get the dependants out but the way the men ran makes me sick. They left loads of English secretaries here with no safeguards and virtually no bosses to work for anyway.

John had a couple of Yanks in the bank the other day and one of them wanted to transfer his account from another bank in Tripoli to Giorgimpopoli by writing a cheque for the balance and paying it into John's branch. But as you can't have two accounts in Libya John said he'd have to get a letter from his Tripoli bank saying he'd closed his account. Apparently they went out looking very worried and trying to decide if it was safe to go into town.

I haven't been into town yet but I think it would be okay to go by car and park near to where you wanted to shop. I don't really fancy the walk down yet as one may get abuse shouted and maybe a stone or two but if I really had to go I would. At the moment John gets meat from Giorgimpopoli and I get groceries wherever I can.

I have a new lead for Rupert awaiting collection in Tripoli. I hope I can get it soon as his present one hasn't a hand loop as he chewed it off.

Before I forget – my new embassy address is at the top of the letter so you can use it in future if you wish. I will try to find out if it is safe to send dutiable things using it, as I need those bras more than anything. I must also get some material as Eric has offered to make me some more dresses. The material shop was burnt down but we do have men pushing bicycles round the streets loaded with shiny materials. I plan to stop one and find out if he has any plainer cottons for sale.

Well, hope your holiday leaves you all fit and ready to try again for a visit here.

Love from us both,
    Jean xxxxxx

NOTES:
  Clock House Road was in Beckenham, Kent; about a mile away from where I was brought up in Pelham Road.

Letter No. 41 (Handwritten on airmail paper)

Monday 26th June 1967 (date may be incorrect)

Dear Mum, Dad, and Diane,

I am enclosing some pieces of paper showing materials. As all the material shops in Tripoli have been burnt out I wondered if you could send me three or four dress lengths, using the cuttings as a basic idea. If you see something you really think I'd like but not shown here then go ahead as I didn't have many magazines to take cuttings from.

I have a corded cotton dress, which has worn remarkably well so if you see any of that type of material I would be very pleased. Also I'm not too bothered if the materials are cotton or not as my synthetic dresses have kept their 'new' look much better.

Eric made my shift using 2½ yds. And he had plenty to spare. He would have had even more left over if the material had been a few inches wider than 36". So if you see any that is wider than 36" get 3½ yds. Then he can run something up for Gwen or one of his children.

I feel rather guilty about this order as it means a lot of running around and expense for you, but I hope you will understand my need as some of my dresses look shabby now and I need to look smartish at the embassy. As for the money, well as you know we can't send money out at the moment and John wants to keep the sterling account as it is in case we can't add to it. If the money situation is still the same when you come out we will pay you in Libyan currency so that you can use it for spending money.

Just one more thing – can you buy a reel of matching cotton for each?

There is quite an urgency about sending this stuff as the BFPO Box may be closing down soon and I don't want to pay customs, so if you can buy it all on Saturday and post it off I'd be grateful – also can you pop in my bras and petticoats (also urgent).

Thank you for your last letter, it certainly seems that you had a good holiday – how I envy you all.

I did a bit of beach wallowing yesterday (Sunday) when the Pughs took me to Wheelus. The beach was just comfortably peopled – but hardly any women as most of them had been evacuated. The sea was warm and clear and the sun hot with a cool breeze. Today I look like a beacon but I'm not too sore.

Work is still enjoyable but there is too much at the moment – fortunately my typing speed has picked up as well as my passport making speed.

Better close now but before I forget, on Saturday afternoon Susan, Pat and myself got a lift into town and walked down the *Istaklal and up *24th December street, without any incidents so things are brightening up I hope.

Looking forward to your parcel.

     Love from us both, Jean XXXXXX

P.S. We received an invitation to *Carol and Alan's wedding on the 29th in

Vancouver. We had to refuse though. Still I'm very pleased they've taken the plunge at last.

NOTES:

The *Sc. Istaklal and the *24th December Street were the two main streets in Tripoli.

*Carol (Nash) my best school friend had been my bridesmaid in June 1965. She moved to Canada with her boyfriend, Alan (Colton) in July 1965. They took their time making sure that the move was right for them before marrying in July 1967 and settling in Vancouver.

Letter No. 42 (Handwritten on airmail paper)

Sunday 2nd July 1967

Dear Mum, Dad, and Diane,

Many thanks for your letters, Mum and Dad, (hint, hint to Diane). Just for the record Mum's letter is post-marked 29th 8pm and arrived on 1st at 8am. Record time. Dad's is post marked 26th and was received in Tripoli on 28th and arrived this morning.

Now about your visit – unfortunately it would be impossible for John to get to Malta but I could come – but we think it would prove too expensive for you for such a small reward i.e. Just nine days and only myself. We think the best plan is to stick to the original idea of coming all the way to see us in October or, if it is still inadvisable, to scrub the whole idea and have a holiday elsewhere.

The other problem is our homecoming, as I explained in my last letter (which Dad hadn't received before writing) we just don't know. Our suggestion for this is to go ahead and have the party for your Silver Wedding and Diane's 21st when it suits you and to forget about including us. When we do get home we can just have a small get-together similar to our lovely send-off party.

I'm afraid I can't enlarge much on the 'Angela saga', just in case we are censored, but anyway what I told you in my letter was just a very good red-herring and we have only recently found out that they are still here but possibly leaving soon.

3.7.67. Today I received a parcel from Kay containing material and a tie from Aunt Edie, and a blouse, shirt and another tie from Kay and John. We were very pleased with it all. The only thing is that when one of the embassy chaps gave me the parcel he told me I'm not allowed to use the BFPO address as I'm only locally employed (not UK staff). So I told him your parcel was on the way and he said okay but to use David's name in future. So we are back to square one. You had better forget the BFPO number and if we want anything else sent out I'll ask David first. It doesn't matter about spending 30/- on postage as it is still worth it.

I'd love to send you some photos but our only equipment is one movie projector. If one of the photo shops opens up again I'll try to buy a cheap still camera and send some snaps. I did borrow Terry Dowrick's camera one afternoon but only took pictures of Rupert and one with Mohamed holding his lead – the reason for this was because we thought we might be evacuated and Rupert would have to be put to sleep.

Mum, you keep asking if Flo came back with her baby – well I'm not sure what you mean, as I could only think you meant had she come back from Scotland after having him, which I know I've told you and also the way poor Jim has to keep running about after her. Ohh – it's just clicked you must mean did she leave Tripoli because of the trouble. The answer is 'no'. It takes more than a few riots to frighten Florence.

The weather is marvellous and if only I didn't keep peeling I'd pass for a local. I've been so lucky with trips to the beach either with the Neales or Pughs. My swimming is gradually getting stronger and I enjoy every moment on the beach. It is a good job John doesn't like swimming or he'd be rather jealous of all the time I spend in the sea.

We have met some Yanks from Wheelus and on Saturday they all came for a barbeque at the Pugh's. John came and ate there and then went back to work. I was still there when he came home.

Well I can't think of anything else to write except that I'm very tired and looking forward to an early night. I am bitten to pieces and last night found the culprit – a flea in the bed. I now sleep nursing the Pif-Paf.

Much love to you all from us both,

Jean XXXXXXXXX

P.S. Please let Kay know her parcel arrived safely.

Letter No. 43 (Handwritten airmail paper)

Thursday 6th July 1967

Dear Mum, Dad, and Diane,

I received the parcel today and was absolutely thrilled. I loved all the lengths of material and feel sure I'd have chosen the same ones. Also the 'undies' are just right and the pyjamas really cute. I've run out of adjectives but I feel sure you know how pleased I am. I've had fun thinking about the materials and patterns. I think I'll have the cream one fitted and with a frill at the hem for dressier outings. Eric is making up the material Kay sent from *Great Aunt Edie into a rolled neck shift.

Well it's only a couple of days since I last wrote and nothing much has happened. The weather is very hot and sticky and it is difficult to sleep at night. I managed a snooze this afternoon and feel more perky now.

I think I mentioned a woman called Chips who has been getting friendly. At first I thought she was okay but after spending all Sunday with her I became fed up with stories of herself and boastful lies, so I decided to steer clear of her. Well on Wednesday morning she rang me up at the embassy and said she had nowhere to stay so could we put her up. I had little option but to say yes. Anyway, when I got home at lunchtime John told me that Jenny may be coming to stay as Terry's father had died suddenly and he was going home for the funeral. So when Chips arrived last night John told her she could only stay for one night so she decided to move into the Waddan instead.

Today John took Terry and Jenny to the airport to see Terry off and now Jenny is with us.

John's just come in from work with a letter from *Mrs. Lawson of all people. She sounds rather lonely and says she hasn't seen you since you moved. Archie is working part-time and Dorothy is getting on at Unilever. I must write back as she sounded very interested in our way of life.

I have so many letters to write at the moment as I've only been writing to you since the crisis. When you see Grandad or *Kath Jones do say they are on my list and not forgotten.

We have a three-day strike at the moment and John is operating his bank through the back door with a sub-machine gunned policeman standing guard. Tripoli office has three armed policemen inside with orders to shoot at the first sign of trouble.

Anyway I feel more relaxed and am keeping my fingers crossed.

Love to you all,
    Love Jean XXXXXX

NOTES:
  *Great Aunt Edie belonged to John's side of the family
  *Mrs Lawson had been our next door neighbour at Pelham Road along with her husband, Archie and daughter Dorothy. (Dorothy was about four years younger than me).
  *Kath Jones lived next to the Lawsons with her widowed father and unmarried brother. She worked for the Civil Service in London.

Letter No. 44 (Typewritten on airmail paper)

Friday 14th July 1967

Dear Mum, Dad and Diane,

Thanks for your letter. I hope mine has been received by now.

Guess what, a fellow here named *Geoff Bishop used to live in Clock House Road and was a good friend of *David Hall. They correspond and Geoff is going to tell him of my whereabouts. Apparently David is planning to marry soon. The old saying 'it's a small world' certainly applies here.

I was sorry to hear about *Mr. Holden as he was a nice man and so very homely.

As you can see I'm not too overworked here at the embassy. I have managed to catch up on the backlog of Consular Section work and I am now typing this to you. Once my typing speed improves I shall be able to type all my letters home in my spare time spent behind my desk.

I have written to John's Great Aunts (Agatha and Edith) which makes two less on my list of people to write to.

Rupert had a couple of nasty sores in his ear so I took him along to the vet thinking they were probably tick heads gone septic. The vet looked and said they were nothing and that he'd probably been bitten by another dog. Well as you know Rupert never goes out by himself but I sometimes let him run in the garden downstairs where Thorba, a huge alsation belonging to the Spanish doctor, has a railed-in kennel and enclosure. Rupert and Thorba are having quite an affair and they put their heads through the palings and lick and nip each other so now Rupert is a dog with love bites. The vet and I had a dreadful job holding Rupert still whist he tried to spray antiseptic in his ears. Eventually he had to make a muzzle out of bandages and be really strict with him. Needless to say he was sick in the car coming home.

This afternoon we are going to a beach with Ortis along with the Dowricks and Ortis's family. Terry and John are golfing this morning. I am hoping to buy a snorkel in Giorgimpopoli this afternoon, as it is brilliant to swim wearing one.

I haven't been to the beach since last Sunday as I got pretty burnt but I am going again this Sunday with the Pughs to Wheelus. It is one of the best beaches near to town but I can only get in if I go with a UK employed embassy person. (I am only locally employed).

I had a rise the other day and got £L2.25pts for back pay so I think my monthly salary should be in the region of £L70 p.m. Not bad for half a day and (thanks to Mohamed) no housework to do when I get in.

15th Saturday.

Today you should be getting ready for *your party. We were invited to a barbeque along with the Pughs (*so they can bring us back after curfew) but John is working late on purpose to get out of going. Instead we are going to an *all night one with the Dowricks and Jenny's friends from her office. (I know it is rude to get out of the first one but we don't like the person much). We shall probably set off half-an-hour before curfew and come home after 5am for a couple of hours sleep before John sets off for work and I set off for the Wheelus beach with the Pughs.

Yesterday at the beach with Ortis I had a spot of trouble from a Libyan whilst I was swimming. He dived under and grasped my calf twice. I shouted at him and told him to go away but he wouldn't go away and he said it was an accident (after denying ever having been near me). When we were leaving he started up again and Ortis held John's arm and steered him away (he was white with rage). Obviously the Libyan wanted to cause trouble otherwise he would have left the matter alone. It could have turned really nasty as the beach was full of Libyans and I think the troublemaker knew it.

By the way you can send John's parcel BFPO if you use the Pugh's name instead of mine. Don't mention our name on the outside and then it will be okay. John is thrilled as he is so short of collars and shirts.

Better close now, as I must write to Kay and John.

Lots of love from us both,

Jean XXX

P.S. Can you please pop four new face cloths in John's parcel as I haven't been able to get out to search for any. Also two packets of cold water dye about the colour of denim jeans. (Get two shades if you are not sure). Many thanks. Soon I shall be requesting food parcels.

Have just received Dad's letter and smiled all the time I was reading it.

Next May will be a good time for a visit as it is a recommended tourist month.

Yes, I received Mum's parcel and was very pleased indeed. I did write as soon as I got it but the letter must have gone astray. XXXXXX

NOTES:

*Geoff Bishop worked just across the corridor from me at the embassy. I can't remember his department, although I was in the Consular Section.

*David Hall had been my very first boy friend when I was about fifteen years old. David went to the Beckenham Grammar School for Boys whereas I went to Balgowan Secondary Modern School for Girls.

*Mr Holden, who had died quite suddenly, had held a high position at Battersea Power Station (now the Tate Modern) and I went out with his son, Ian, for a little while. I am, at the time of writing, still in contact with his daughter, Sue Logan.

*With reference to my parent's party. It was to celebrate their Silver Wedding Anniversary. They were married on June 13th 1943 and I was born on June 15th 1944. The party had been delayed as they had been expecting to be in Libya on the actual day.

*The reference to the barbeque party with the Pughs and the fact that they could bring us back in their car after curfew was due to David's embassy status and the CD plates on his car. During and immediately after the troubles some embassy staff removed their CD plates seeing them as a liability and not as a mark of privilege and identification.

*The all night party couldn't have been that lively as I remember taking myself off to a bedroom during the course of the evening and flopping down on a double bed. When I woke up there was a strange girl asleep next to me.

Letter No. 45 (Typed on airmail paper)

Tuesday 25th July 1967

Dear Mum, Dad and Diane,

Yesterday I received the parcel for John, which was very quick in arriving. He was very pleased with the shirts and collars. Mohamed is going to Homs tomorrow so young Ali will be able to have his new shirt for the visit. I think he will look really lovely in the blue. Dear Rupert thought the dyes were playthings and managed to bite through one whilst I was in the kitchen.

On Sunday the Pughs took me to a beach party on an American private beach about eight miles out. The beach had a club house where they barbequed steaks and gave out free drinks. The sea was rough though, with a terrific undertow. I did a lot of jumping onto the waves in an effort to ride them and managed to make my shoulders sore where my swimsuit cut in (worth it though). Then David and I took out his lilo and equipped ourselves with snorkels, masks and flippers. We had intended going out a little way on it and then diving off but it took us about half an hour to both get on the thing, during which time we abandoned the diving gear as being too cumbersome. Eventually I got on it and David managed to pull himself up backwards but instead of just floating along astride the lilo David's weight pushed it down in the middle so we were floating in a 'V' shape with us in the dip.

This coming Friday Jim Deasy is giving a curry luncheon party to celebrate the Norman's departure on a ten week holiday. As the curfew is lifted until midnight I am fully expecting to spend twelve hours over lunch. I have managed to get the day off so I shall get my hair cut and set before going.

John has a nasty cold at the moment, due to me. I woke up one night about 1am feeling so hot that I drew back the bedroom curtains and opened the windows wide. Then about 6am we both woke up chilled to the bone as a thick cold mist had descended. John got the worst of it as he sleeps nearer the window.

Eric has made up the material that John's mum sent from Aunt Edie. It is a shift style with a rolled collar and you would never guess it had been homemade. He has fitted it perfectly and finished off all the seams and facings. He is going to charge from £1 to £2.10/- for each dress but he does them so well that it is worth paying.

Well, Mum, you asked a lot of questions in your last letter so I will answer them. The curfew is now only active from midnight to 5am and should be lifted soon. The liquor situation is back to normal but I don't know if any English alcohol is getting in.

Mohamed is doing very well keeping the flat tidy. He doesn't do things quite as well as I would but considering the small amount of money he gets (houseboys usually charge £L5 a week for what he does, whereas I only pay him £L3) he is certainly worth every piastre. He washes and irons well and enjoys polishing the pots and pans. I think that when he goes to Homs I will borrow Susan's vacuum cleaner and have a good clean all round.

Your weekend sailing trip sounds great. Do tell me about it.

I have just sent Grandad a card telling him I will be writing soon but stupidly I sent it to his flat, still as long as you let him know he is not forgotten.

I met some Libyans on the beach through Gwen and Eric and one of them is meant to be getting John a cheap lightweight suit. This Libyan lives at Garian (the flat topped mountain) and has a house built down inside the mountain. They all seemed pleasant and so far I've not been troubled by uncalled for attention.

Well I can't think of much else to say.

Love from us both,

Jean xxxxxx

Letter No. 46 (Handwritten airmail letter)

Monday 31st July 1967

Dear Mum, Dad, and Diane,

I haven't had a letter from you so far so I'll just tell you my own news.

Yesterday, Sunday, the Pughs took me to the covered market near the suk before going to the beach. This market reminds me of the one at Peckham where they sell fruit, vegetables, meat and small animals. I got a small bird in a tiny cage for £2.14/-. I really wanted a canary but they were £6.00 without a cage.

I've just cleaned this little 'sparrows' cage so it smells better now, poor thing. He has only chirped three times so far but I'm hoping for improvement. It is still rather frightened but later I hope it will be tame enough to sit on my finger. Short of naming it 'Scraggy' I can't think of anything to call it.

I did some snorkelling yesterday and I saw quite a few fish. It is fun hovering over them and then diving down and chasing them (without success, I may add). Actually I was rather foolish as I've got a mild cold, with quite a bit of catarrh, and when I dived I felt as if my head was going to burst. Today I feel as if my sinuses are going to explode.

We had a letter from Kay saying no one had written for three weeks and 'what have I done to deserve this treatment.' I felt rather sorry for her but John usually writes to her from the office and when he can't find time he lets me know and then I write.

Eric has made the trycel material into a shift. It looks very pretty and is beautifully made (as usual). I wore the green dress he'd made to the curry lunch at Jim Deasy's place and both Joanne and Jenny were amazed and want him to make for them too.

I sometimes let Rupert run in the garden, as you know, but I check first that Mohamed isn't sleeping round the side. Well, this afternoon I peeped round the corner and saw a little bottom stuck in the air, a bowed head and bare feet. At first I couldn't think who it could be but on coming back from the shops there was little Ali watering the garden. He is as shy as ever but eventually I got a smile when Rupert started jumping up (on his lead and at a safe distance away).

I hope his little shirt fitted, I'll let you know if I see him in it. Mohamed left a bag full of eggs in the fridge for us on his return from Homs.

The curry lunch was rather boring as one of the guests got a bit tiddly and wouldn't stop talking, so I went outside and fell asleep in a garden chair whilst John spent the whole time talking to this woman's husband about history.

The next day we had a Chinese meal at Gwen and Eric's and John spent the whole time talking to one of his bank customers about politics.

Gwen and Eric had invited some Libyans and Italians to the meal. I'm afraid John and I didn't like the Libyans and one asked us to his party next week, so although we said 'yes' we have decided to pretend we got some dates mixed up and I have written a note for Eric to give to him.

Although we've been lucky with invites out, both the lunch and evening meal were rather dull and the annoying thing is that we had invites for other things on the same days. I only hope we get some more invites that turn out more interesting.

Tuesday 1st August.

Sorry about the delay. The bird is still surviving and my cold has eased off. We have been invited to another barbeque at the private beach off the Homs road but as it is a Sunday John can't go and the Pughs can't go either as they are entertaining the Queen's Messenger this week. So instead Terry and Jenny are taking us to the yacht club, with the possibility of sailing, in the afternoon. I wonder how you got on with your sailing effort in Norfolk?

Did I mention that we have air conditioners at the embassy now? They have just been put in but as the current isn't very strong they only switch on a few at a time. Once the electricity has been sorted out it should be very comfortable.

It is getting rather too hot to sleep well now but just before nightfall we get a coolish breeze which lowers the temperature in the flat nicely.

The Woman's Guild (remember the bazaar?) has broken up as the vicar's wife said the Guild didn't do enough for the church (a blatant lie). The Guild has run a lot of bazaars as well as seeing to flowers in the church and also making coffee after church for those that want it. I feel sorry for the vicar, Michael West, as he is such a nice person and it has spoilt things for him, especially as it is his first posting.

We haven't seen Nancy and Alan for a long time so I doubt now if I'll give her the baby jacket you knitted. They are packing up here as Alan's salary isn't very good and then they hope to emigrate to Canada.

Sorry I didn't write sooner. Looking forward to hearing from you.

Love from us both, Jean XXX

Letter No. 47 (Handwritten on airmail paper)

Monday 7th August 1967

Dear Mum, Dad, and Diane,

It is pretty well okay here now, although it will take me a long time to feel the same way about the place as I used to. John's people should be able to wander around all right, even in the suk, when they come in October. I am looking forward to their visit but as usual I'm getting in a state about *Kay, I even dreamt about her last night (a nightmare actually).

Of course Dad and Diane's sailing efforts couldn't possibly surpass mine. There I was lying on my back in the bottom of the boat with both feet in the air and the starting bell jangling away. Terry had to let go of the main sail to save us from capsizing but after that ghastly start we picked up and managed to come 5th out of seven yachts. It was only a small race of twice round the harbour but I really enjoyed it. John came 2nd in his boat and felt pleased with himself.

Rupert, once more, may be leaving us as we met a couple at the yacht club who live on a large estate at Homs. They are keen to have a dog but the only problem is that the estate manager has two large Labradors that are vicious. They are chained up but knowing Rupert he will try to be friendly and probably get chewed up before the introductions are over. They are coming for a meal on Wednesday so we should know definitely by then. In fact we had met the chap, Mike, before, at John's 21st birthday party at the Regents Palace, London (1965). He had come as Jean Lunnan's partner (*Aunty Molly's, daughter). We knew he was here but had never been able to trace him. He is now married to another Jean and the original Jean has just married a UN representative from the Mauritius Islands whom she met and wed in New York.

Last Friday we went with Terry and Jenny to Piccola Capri beach and as they have two lilo's we had great fun trying to get two people on each. Terry decided it was best to stand in the shallows and thread them through.

I have now got my own lilo and this afternoon David and I took it out to the first reef at Wheelus and we dived from it. My ears were still a little painful but not too bad. There wasn't much to see but it was fun.

I have found a person to give the baby's jacket to. Jill Robinson is having a baby in a couple of month's time. She has kept quiet about it as she doesn't want her son, Colin, to know just yet as two months will seem such a long time to him. Jill must be at least thirty-five years old and Colin is seven already. Apparently she had been wanting a baby for a long time so we are very pleased for her.

This friend of David Hall is named Geoff Bishop and he may come and see you. David is now married and Geoff may bring him along as well. Terry Dowrick has some film which needs developing so I will get Geoff to bring it over and post it to you (he leaves in about ten days time) then if you can get it developed perhaps you can send it onto Kay to bring out as she will be here before Geoff's leave ends. Some of the snaps are of Rupert and one is of Mohamed holding Rupert's lead, so if it is a good one can you get a print done to give to Mohamed?

Work is jogging along okay but I'm fed up with the Lebanese chap, Isaam who also works in the Consular Section. He is big headed and tells the Arabs I'm his secretary. He also tries passing me the boring jobs that he has been told to do. Unfortunately he is my senior although our jobs should really be separate.

Grandad nearly got a letter, I'm just typing it out so I hope to send it off tomorrow with this one.

Well nothing much to say now, so I'd better wash up before the ants get to the dirty dishes. Which reminds me, John found a large locust outside his bank this morning and his messenger and cashier cooked it for him and he ate it. He has survived 12 hours so I hope the danger is past.

Love from us both,
    Jean XXXXXX

NOTES:

My mother-in-law never considered that I was 'good enough' for her only son and had a way of undermining me that made me feel nervous.

Aunty Molly was a friend of Kay's who lived at Gravesend.

Letter No. 48 (Typed and handwritten on airmail paper)

Monday 14th August 1967

Dear Mum, Dad, and Diane,

Thank you for your last letter. As I am at work at the moment I will tell you my own news first and answer your letter properly when I get home.

Rupert has been in trouble once more. The poor thing was left on the back balcony one morning, as I was expecting Mohamed in later. Mohamed moves Rupert from the back balcony to the front as the sun is on the front in the early morning and moves round to the back later on. Well Mohamed never came that day (I think he has trouble at Homs) so poor Rupert was left on the tiny back balcony during the height of the mid-day sun. (Probably over 100 degrees and the tiles throwing up even more heat). The heat must have been unbearable because I arrived home at lunch time to find the whole of the kitchen window fly screen down and Rupert's food and water scattered over the balcony. Rupert was panting on the hall floor looking exhausted. He must have jumped and jumped to get the screen down and then leapt in the kitchen window. He didn't do any other damage but the mess outside was quite something and the smell from the sun baked dog food horrible.

I managed to hide the damage by pulling down the shutters before John came home from work. So after lunch I tidied up and broke the news to John in the evening. He wasn't too mad as it was pretty understandable why Rupert had done it.

John has been accepted by the board of directors for overseas staff and has an official looking contract to sign.

Terry has been posted to Calcutta and will be leaving at the end of October. It is great news for them as Jenny was born in India and has always wanted to re-visit. Also she has always fancied Calcutta. John's first reaction was 'who am I going to play golf with' but that question was soon answered as Alan and Nancy are leaving in October also, so Jim Graham will be wanting a partner. It seems funny that after so long of not seeing them we should suddenly get invited to their new villa this coming Friday. We have always liked the Grahams but they more or less dropped us when they became friendly with Nancy and Alan so it seems that now they are getting friendly again.

Mr Norman, who is on leave in England, promised to get John on Eastern staff and also to get Terry another posting so he has kept those promises and we only hope his promise of getting Tripoli made a two year posting instead of three will come true. At the moment we aren't quite sure what will happen. We may get a leave after our two years, or we may have to stay three, or we may get another posting come next year with no leave in between. Still we should be home for Christmas 1969 whatever happens. To be away for three years seems an age but I do hope you can visit us here next year.

On Sunday we went yachting again. Jenny crewed for Terry and John crewed for Geoff Taylor again and I managed to get a crewing job for an Italian. He didn't speak much English and he'd never sailed in the club's type of boat before, so after another hilarious start with us going round in circles just inches from the setting off point we eventually got going to come 5th out of seven again. It was very calm and we nearly stopped moving several times. After the race and refreshments Geoff Taylor took John, me and another Jean for a sail just outside the harbour and he let John take the helm. He is pleased with John's progress and John is now thinking of joining the yacht club.

I think, rather than writing more another day I will close now. We are booked up this week – Waddan with Ortis tomorrow, Gwen and Eric Wednesday, party Thursday, Jim and Flo Friday, Terry and Jenny Saturday. So I won't have much time to add to this letter.

Thanks to Diane for letter and photos.

By the way we can send you the money we owe but perhaps you had better check exactly how much. I know we have £2 postage to pay and my dress material money but I'm not sure how much we owe for the other things – collar, shirts etc. So if you can say we will send a cheque and a £1 for Diane.

Sorry I'm in a rush but Rupert needs a walk and we must get to bed soon as tomorrow will not be finishing until the early hours; we don't leave here until 9.30pm for the Waddan.

Love to you all from us both,
Jean XXXXXX

Letter No. 49 (Handwritten on airmail paper)

Sunday 20th August 1967

Dear Mum, Dad and Diane,

Once again Rupert is clambering all over me and has caused the smudges on the paper with his nose. I've just put him out so I can concentrate now.

In your letter it appears that you are gadding about as much as us. I went to see Gwen and Eric last Monday afternoon and we then all went to Jenny's nearby villa (Jenny Havy and her husband Ivan). Jenny has four children and is only 25 years old but as Ivan is French it explains a lot.

As you can imagine I had great fun with Gwen's two and Jenny's four (one is only a baby) clambering over me. Jenny has an Aunt staying with her who hasn't seen all their films so we went over again on Tuesday evening with the Dowricks and took our projector. We had an enjoyable time and didn't leave until 1.30am.

Thursday was really good – we went to Nancy and Alan's farewell party at Jim and Florence's. It was the best party I'd ever been to and Jim Deasy added to the fun by getting his car stuck in a 6ft. deep hole of loose sand. As the hole was near Jim and Flo's villa he left it there and walked to the party. But when we were leaving he was so drunk he was nearly in tears of desperation when we said we wouldn't help him get it out. Anyway we were only teasing so he got in the car and the boys pushed and he shot out like a rocket. The funny part was that when I saw him the next day he asked if I knew who'd helped him out. He couldn't remember a thing.

We are becoming friendly with the Bank of North Africa people (or the British Bank of the Middle East as it is called at home). There are three young couples – Anna (Italian) and John Whitchelow, they have a little girl, Gianna, about three years old. Then Polly and Garry John, Polly is dreamy and Garry is lively, then Monica and Ian McNab. Monica is German and really beautiful and Ian is Scots. His father is a stockbroker and his mother is German. I just thought I'd give you a general outline as we are all roughly the same age and we seem to meet them at various parties and get on well.

You ask if the shops are re-opening. Well I think about half are but the other half were burnt out and the owners are either in England or Italy.

We are having lovely weather and although humid we get a good breeze in the evenings. I went swimming today and was surprised at the coolness of the sea.

You must excuse my untidy writing but it is getting dark and I can't put the lights on as I am only in my undies.

The other morning we had a rush as John accidentaly re-set the clock an hour slow. I got up at what seemed a quarter to seven (I never hear the alarm anyway) but by 7am John's suspicions were aroused and he checked with his watch and found it was 8am. So I rushed over to the Pugh's and phoned Tripoli office explaining what had happened and asking them to send up some cash for Giorgimpopoli and then I had some toast at the Pugh's and John went straight to his bank.

I'm afraid I can't say when we will be home but September '68 will be the earliest and if we get posted elsewhere before our two years here (as is possible, being a first tour) it may be September '69.

I haven't much else to say so I will close now. Hoping you have received my last letter okay by now.

Love from us both,
Jean XXXXXX

Letter No. 50 (Handwritten on airmail paper)

Saturday 26th August 1967

Dear Mum, Dad, and Diane,

Instant reply this week having received your letter at lunchtime. Rupert is in a 'let's climb on Jean' mood and I'm in an 'Oh, for a siesta' mood so altogether this letter should be rather a mess. He's occupied at the moment with an empty cigarette packet, but as it's nearly shredded I shall have to light up and blow smoke in his face, which usually makes him go away. Actually I'm saved for a few more minutes as I've just Pif-Paffed a fly and he is chasing it as it buzzes erratically around, once caught he will eat it.

I'm glad Geoff Bishop called, I expect, through the years, you will get a few visitors as we shall be giving various friends our home addresses. Jenny warned me the film would be expensive as they are prints not slides. I think only ten are of Rupert, but you must forgive my extravagance as at the time I thought we would be evacuated and have to have him put to sleep. I don't know if Geoff is bringing other things from England to Tripoli but I'd rather you forgot about the lacquer, Dippity-Do and golf balls and instead asked Kay to bring them out in October, as she won't mind.

I got John to write a cheque for £10, which should cover everything, also to give Diane a belated birthday £1, Dad an early birthday £1 and a £1 for Grandad to buy some rum and cokes. I hope it is sufficient, if not let me know please.

Poor Ali. The other day he thought he'd help whilst I was getting the front door key out of my bag after popping to the shops, so he offered to hold Rupert. I had a vague feeling it would be too much for him but not being able to explain I thought I'd let him, rather than risk hurting his feelings. In one leap Rupert was off the path and down into the garden, Ali flying through the air after him, then Rupert ran round and round and swung Ali, arms outstretched, like a top. All this was suddenly too much for Ali so Rupert was let go. He wasn't difficult to catch and luckily it was only in the garden but Ali looked most upset.

You said that when Dad spoke to Uncle Terry he didn't seem very happy. Does that mean he has 'gone off' Josie already? Are Josie's sons living at home with them?

You asked about Jean and Derek. We still correspond but not very often. Jean hates letter writing but whenever I do get one it is very interesting and amusing. It was John's first birthday on 17th August so I sent him a card. I didn't bother with a gift as we can always buy a belated present when we see them again. Naturally all Jean's letters are centred around baby John but she writes in such a way that I am laughing at all his antics as if I were actually there and watching him.

Last night we went to Wheelus, as we and the Pughs had been invited by an American airman. The floorshow consisted of a mediocre comedian and a girl singer from Liverpool who sang 'Daun Taun' (Down Town) and took off her dress at the same time. Anyway John and I played the fruit machines and were losing heavily so we decided to put the last 22 nickels in one machine and hope for the best and blow me, on the very last coin up came three lovely melons which meant a 7½ dollar jackpot. So yet again we left with more than we started with. John had also won money on the machines at Sea-Breeze (golf course) in the morning.

On Friday we had a meal at Terry and Jenny's and on Thursday we played canasta with the Pughs. The rest of the week, Mon-Wed, was spent having early nights after the previous weeks' outings.

We suddenly seem to have a lot to do and we certainly know lots of people now.

I expect we will have a drinks party when the *Scotts come. (We were going to have one in June for you). Luckily the Normans won't be back until the end of their stay so we won't have to invite them.

Best close now,

Love from us both,

Jean XXXXXX

NOTES: *The Scotts: John's mother (Kay) and step-father, John Morrison-Scott.

Letter No. 51 (Typewritten on airmail paper)

Thursday 21st September 1967

Dear Mum, Dad, and Diane,

I rather took advantage of your being away on holiday and decided not to write for a little while. I have been pretty busy lately and tired with all the late nights. Still we had a good time.

I have been trying to work out how old Dad is today and if I have not made a mistake I think he is exactly twice my age now. Just think Dad, when you were my age you had the most beautiful three month old daughter.

I hope your holiday has been enjoyable and also that Kay didn't have too much difficulty in contacting you about the camera. You must tell us how much we owe you for it and then we can send you a cheque including the cost of Terry and Jenny's films. John (Morrison-Scott) is bringing his still camera so at long last you may see some decent pictures of us.

The Elizabethan Club is holding its Annual Dinner Dance on the 30th September so we have written hasty letters to the Scotts telling them to bring out evening gear. I am pleased at the choice of date as it gives us something else to occupy them with whilst they are here.

A trip to Garian, Jeffren and maybe Sabratha has been tentatively arranged for the 29th September along with four other people so we should have a giggle as the other four are very lively.

I work with a Maltese person, Luigi, who has promised to take them around the suk and old town. Other than these three ideas we are at a loss to know what to do with them. I did suggest taking Kay out to sea on my lilo and then tipping it over.

On Saturday we are having Moira and Dennis Webb for a meal along with Jim Deasy and Susan Pugh's nanny, Jackie. It should be interesting as Moira and Jim are Irish and Jackie, Moira and Jim are RCs.

Liquor is once again in short supply, without Ortis I don't know how we'd manage, as not only does he supply us with the stuff but also cuts the price. As John says he has been well and truly bought out by Ortis and is obliged to be lenient with his account. Still he is a pleasant chap and we only wish we could converse more easily.

We had lunch at the Underwater Club last Friday and the hors d'oeuvres cost more than a two-course lunch at the Lizzie Club. In future we shall eat at the Lizzie and then drive to the Underwater Club for a swim.

We had arranged to meet Ortis there and whilst we were waiting I went for a snorkel. I was 'miles' out and then I discovered another snorkel addict rather near, so I decided to swim off at an angle as it was not necessary to be so close. After a little while I had an uneasy feeling of being followed so I swam round in my own length only to find this person a few yards behind. He came alongside and pointed down, I thought he had seen something interesting so I looked down and the horrible man grabbed the top of my leg. All my muscles jumped at this, my snorkel was out of my mouth in a flash whilst I screamed 'Stop it'. He apologised in broken English and said it was an accident. I was too frightened to argue the toss as we were too far from the beach for anyone to grasp what was going on. I was petrified as the water was so deep and he looked strong enough to hold me under. Anyway he swam off and I headed back to the beach only to find I was quite a distance from John, which meant I had a long walk over sharp rocks. Unfortunately I couldn't recognise the man again unless he had his snorkel on so I sat down and decided it could have been an accident but why was he following me in the first place?

We went to a small party at Polly and Garry's last week. They had twelve guests and we made up two dart teams. By a fluke I scored the double needed to get started but in the end we were way behind the others. We met the accountant of the BBME (British Bank of the Middle East) named Geoff Smith and he invited us to his party to be held on the following night. We had a super time and Geoff, Garry and John (Whitchelow) put on a floor show consisting of themselves taking off Fonteyn and Nureyev (Rudy). You have never seen anything so funny as these chaps leaping around into one another's arms, then tiptoeing and sort of pirouetting with arms above their heads. The expressions as well as the footwork were marvellous.

On Saturday we went to a Lizzie Club dance with Garry and Polly. They held it outside and were serving Syrian nosh. Unfortunately it rained and by the time everyone was settled inside the food had gone cold. Still it did stop raining after an hour so we all went back outside and danced on muddy tiles.

Geoff Bishop is back from leave and said he was sorry he never called in to see you again. He had a bit of bother with his fiancé at the beginning because he dashed off to see all his mates without taking notice of her and towards the end of his stay they were only just making it up. It is rather a shame for him. Personally I think he is daft if he marries her next year, as planned, because once before he mentioned that he wasn't too keen.

How's Uncle Terry's love life going? You didn't say much about how Nan is involved. Is the affair blessed with her approval or does she really think he should go back to Eileen?

Jean and Addie Cate are an American couple who live opposite and they have been on leave for a while. (Jean was evacuated with their adopted son, David, when the trouble started). Addie joined her later when his leave was due. They came back a week ago with another adopted son, Jason. He is two months old but Jean has only had him for a little while. Anyway I decided they were a deserving couple as we had a gorgeous meal there once and I have been to some of her tea parties so I gave her the little white jacket you knitted. She was very pleased with it and went into raptures when I said that you, Mum, had knitted it.

Unfortunately the Fiat is in trouble. The exhaust system is welded onto brackets which in turn are welded onto the underside of the car and one of the brackets has broken at the right angle where it joins the exhaust to the underside. As far as John and I can make out we will have to get a whole new exhaust, which will prove expensive.

Talking of expense, John was rather upset when I said I was taking three days leave without pay to enable me to have the whole of his people's stay free. He worked it out that I would be loosing £7 and why didn't I go in for three mornings? (He managed to keep such a straight face that I'm still not sure if he was joking or not).

Susan Pugh is planning to visit Malta at the end of October for a few days shopping. I would have liked to have joined her but John doesn't think that air fares and hotel bills would justify the suit and dresses I need to buy. Perhaps we can get across together later on, as for John's sake it would be worth the money just to get him away from the Bank for a few days.

Terry Dowrick makes me laugh as he is always complaining of overwork and Jenny says how nervy he is since he came back from leave in February. They seem to forget that John has been going at full steam since September last year.

I don't really want to be away from home for three years but if by doing two short tours (say 18mths here and 18mths elsewhere) it would be worth being away from home for three years as opposed to doing two years here. John is really being pushed as he is having to finish at Giorgimpopoli by lunchtime and then go into Tripoli office in the afternoons. It means he only gets a short lunch break if he has been extra busy at his sub-branch.

To my mind John seems the only one working hard as Jim and Terry natter and fool around most of the time.

I am still quite contented here but the locals get on my nerves with the way they fancy themselves, but other than that I know enough people within walking distance to visit if I get bored during the afternoons.

I always take Rupert when shopping but the other day I called in at Anna's flat in the Istaklal and left Rupert on their balcony whilst I went out to buy some sherry glasses by myself. My goodness the trouble I had with the locals, two touches and several near misses, as well as being forced to walk in the gutter. Usually when they see Rupert they are the ones cringing in the gutter and I am the one with the pavement to myself.

I haven't got your last letters here to answer properly but if I have missed any points I will catch up when I write again.

I hope you will understand if I don't write too regularly whilst John's people are here but I'll let you know how we all get on afterwards.

I am looking forward to their stay much more than I imagined. John promised to stick up for me if I have any trouble with his mother, but I don't really anticipate any.

The weather has been wet and cool the past few days but today it looks cheerful so I hope it stays that way.

I am cutting my wisdom teeth once again. They have been coming through on and off for the past three years but not one has erupted fully yet.

Best close now although I can't see much that needs doing regarding work.

Love from us both,
Jean XXXXXX

P.S. Hope you are saving the stamps on the envelopes.

NOTES: This was a typewritten letter, obviously put together whilst I was 'working' at the embassy. (Consular Section).

Letter No. 52 (Typewritten on airmail paper)

Wednesday 27th September 1967

Dear Mum, Dad, and Diane,

My memory is getting bad, I can't remember when I last wrote to you so if I repeat any news please forgive.

This is my last day at work until 16th October. I shall enjoy having all the extra time especially as Mohamed will still be coming in.

I hope the camera business has now been sorted out. Kay said you didn't think we wanted it brought out. Be glad to hear your comments anyway, as she has a pleasant knack of twisting things and causing trouble.

We had Denis and Moira Webb, along with Jim Deasy and Jackie Leece (Susan Pugh's nanny), over for a meal last Saturday. I think they must have enjoyed themselves as Jackie, who was the first to leave, didn't go until 2am. Jim seemed quite taken with Jackie and is planning to take her out later on.

John sprained his ankle the other evening when we were taking Rupert for a walk. Rupert escaped and John tried to trip him up but instead Rupert charged at such a rate that he bowled John over. That night John woke up in agony and the next day (Friday) he hobbled to a chair that I had placed by the front door and he stayed there until I got home from work. The doctor came in the early afternoon and put a crepe bandage on it and said not to worry. Actually after the Friday and the Saturday it started getting better quickly and now it is more or less back to normal.

Jenny Dowrick drove me to Piccola Capri beach on Sunday and we had a pleasant swim. The water seemed cool to us but I expect to John's people it will be pleasant. Jenny has offered to take them next Sunday.

On Sunday John and I spent the afternoon in bed until 7pm then we got up, made some nosh and tidied the spare room a little, then by 11pm we were back in bed and, blow me, if we didn't still feel tired on Monday morning. In fact I feel better this morning and we didn't get to bed until midnight last night.

Tonight we have some friends coming round to discuss plans for a trip out to Garian on Friday. This trip was going to be so good but now the Dowricks and Garry John can't come so numbers are getting smaller. And just as a final blow John and Anna Whitchelow's car isn't going too well and they are having to see about borrowing another or going in with someone else.

Still I daresay it will work out okay. Just John and I could go but as the road is lonely and in poor repair it is better to take more than one car in case of breakdowns.

As usual we are lacking in work at the embassy so I have brought my address book along and I shall flick through and decide who to write to. I have written to everyone that I owe letters to and am now waiting for replies.

By the way I received Grandad's letter the other day, it crossed my one in the post. Unfortunately I had told Grandad off, for not writing for such an age, when I received his letter, so please tell him 'thank you' and that I was very pleased to hear from him.

Well suppose I'd better close now and have my early morning cup of coffee then perhaps I'll look around to see if anything needs doing. (*Three cheers for the taxpayers).

Will try to write as usual but we may have a hectic time but there again, we may not.

Love from us both,

Jean XXX

PS. Don't forget to say how much we owe you for the camera, film and Jenny and Terry's film.

NOTE:

*'Three cheers for the taxpayers' – I was being sarcastic about my lack of work at the embassy as my salary was funded by UK taxpayers.

Letter No. 53 (Handwritten on airmail paper)

Monday 2nd October 1967

Dear Mum, Dad, and Diane,

Many thanks for your letter. You had a lovely holiday touring, by the sound of things. John and I will be following in your footsteps when we have our six months leave in late 1969. It seems that we will be away for three years now, as we asked Jim Deasy about it.

Kay and John arrived safely on Thursday, although the plane was half-an-hour late. We had a quiet evening and received our gifts (thank you for dippity-do and golf balls).

On Friday we were up bright and early and I made twenty rolls ready for the trip to Garian. Jim Deasy, Anna, John (and Gianna), Polly and Garry all met at our flat and we set off about 10.30am. We had three cars and had a lovely day. I have filmed quite a lot of the trip so you will be able to get a rough idea.

On Saturday Kay, John (Scott) and I went into Tripoli and had a coffee at Anna's. John played with her little girl most of the time and made a big hit with her. We took quite a few snaps from Anna's balcony, as it is high up above the *Istaklal.

On Saturday evening we all got dressed up and went to the Lizzie Club's Annual Dinner Dance which was a bit of a flop for us as the group played the most awful tunes and they were too loud to allow for much conversation. We sat with Jock and Sally Alexander and they felt the same as us with regard to the band. Still it made an outing and we had snippets of conversation with lots of people, which meant that Kay and John saw some of our friends.

Jenny Dowrick took us to the beach yesterday morning. She only stayed until 11.30am but we stayed on until 3pm when John collected us on his way home from work.

On Sunday evening we saw the films and Jock and Sally popped in and watched them with us. I was very impressed with them all. I didn't realise you could take such fabulous close-ups with a movie camera. I shall try to get a proper screen to see them on, as I think the colours will show up better than off our cream walls. We laughed and laughed at Dad in his sailing outfit. I loved the shots in the garden of you, Mum, picking and pruning the roses – glorious colours. Hasn't Rosalind grown up – she seems to be the image of Dorothy.

Today we are sitting in the Lizzie Club garden drinking coffee and writing. (Kay and John are doing their post-cards). I will be writing again when I find time. Don't worry if my letters are few and far between over the next two weeks.

Kay and John think it would be nice if you see them when their pictures are ready. It may help you from feeling too cut off from us.

Kay and John are enjoying their holiday and like the flat and surroundings, so everything is going fine.

Rupert went to his new home on Saturday. He seemed quite happy getting into *Dick's car but looked a little puzzled when he realised I was outside. Dick said he'd come and see us soon and take us to his villa to see Rupert. I still feel sad and miss him a lot but I've already noticed how much tidier the flat looks, and by the time Kay and John leave I should be more used to not having him around.

Dick seems very kind and said that he was taking Rupert with him on Saturday evening, when he was eating with some friends, so that Rupert wouldn't be left alone in a strange place to begin with.

Kay and John thought Rupert was fairly well trained considering his 'pi' blood.

Well Better Close.
    Love from us both,
        Jean XXXXXX

NOTES:

*ref. *Istaklal. The Istaklal was one of two main streets in Tripoli. '…In 1948 the Independence (Istaklal) Party was formed as a breakaway from the United National Front. [Wright, John. Libya: A Modern History. p.52. Croom Helm. ISBN 0-7099-*

2733-9]
Dick Winter had answered my advertisement for re-homing Rupert.

Letter No. 54 (Handwritten airmail letter)

Sunday 8th October 1967

Dear Mum, Dad, and Diane,

Kay and John have popped into Tripoli and the flat is quiet and clean so I decided to sit down and write as we have been so very busy and there is a lot to tell you.

We have had the Pughs over for a meal which went well. I started off with a crab cocktail and made the sauce by mixing hot chilli sauce and mayonnaise. Then we had roast lamb, peas, sprouts, and sliced potatoes and onions cooked in milk with a white sauce over the top.

I have joined an amateur dramatic group called the 'Barbary Coast Players' and we read from a Noel Coward play, which they intend putting on. I would rather like a small part but the chap in charge kept telling me to talk from my stomach, which I don't think I can manage, so perhaps I won't get a part at all.

On Thursday morning John, Kay and I paid £L1 for a gharry ride into Giorgimpopoli. We spent from 9.30am to 2.30pm on the beach and the temperature reached 98 degrees Fahrenheit. I had the fright of my life when I went snorkelling over the rocks and what did I see laying in the bottom of a sea-weedy hollow but a fish about half my size. I screamed, spat out my snorkel and pelted back to shore. Kay apparently heard me panting from across the water a long way off. I must try to get a book on sea-life, as I would be foolish to turn tail at every large creature I see. If I had been sure it was harmless I could have observed it very well.

On Thursday evening we went to Dick's for drinks and I saw Rupert once again. I miss him so much but at least I know he is happy in his new home as he hardly knew me and didn't seem upset when we left. Apparently he had escaped that afternoon and Dick had toured round in his car trying to find him, to no avail, but when he finally gave up and went home Rupert was waiting outside the gate, so it shows how well he has settled down.

I am wondering whether to get a kitten as I miss the company of a pet. The bird is still too frightened to sit on my finger or anything. At the moment everyone is out and it seems so lonely not having any disturbances from Rupert.

Anyway John and I have more or less decided to get a pedigee dog when we get home and keep it with us, even though transport and quarantine will prove expensive.

We did a trip to Leptis Magna on Friday and John Scott took lots of pictures. As our Fiat is 'dodgy' at the moment Kay and John went in the Whitchelow's car and we travelled behind slowly. It took four hours to get there (can be done in 1½ hours). Unfortunately Anna and John got a flat and the spare was also down so they had to get a taxi back and John Whitchelow collected the car on Saturday. Sounds funny with the three men all being called 'John'.

We've had such lovely weather but today it has broken and we've had a spot of rain and the wind is blowing hard. I hope it gets better soon as Kay and John have some more sun bathing to do, and I'd like to top up on my tan again, I am getting quite brown now.

We went into the suk one morning and I bought a winter dress for £1; a cotton summer one for £1.16/–; and a jumper for £1.5/–. I'd say they would have been twice as expensive in town. Unfortunately the jumper must have spent a few weeks strapped on a camel as it stinks of dung. At the moment I am soaking it in water with a spot of cologne in it.

Yesterday was a public holiday. We lazed in bed in the morning and had lunch at 3pm. Then we visited Gwen and Eric and Ivan and Jenny. I was suffering from a fate worse than death once again. It seems the moment I eat fruit or strange food my stomach turns itself inside out. John has been so lucky, as he eats the most odd things and never suffers at all.

I went and saw the film of the ballet 'Romeo and Juliet' with John Scott one evening. It starred Margot Fonteyn and Rudolf Nureyev. I quite enjoyed it but found the camera work disappointing and also the fact that Rudy and Margot didn't seem to do anything spectacular. (It may have been cut though). I also thought it peculiar that the nurse in it looked younger than the supposed teenager Juliet.

Don't worry about the 'Jims'. Jim and Florence Graham are still together and Jim Deasy is single (John's manager).

The dreaded Normans are back and John won't be getting a marriage allowance for another year, so his salary on Eastern staff is less than it was before. Also there is a vague possibility that we may be sent to Benghazi next spring.

Anyway must close now, hope you are all well.

Love from us both,
Jean XXXX

Jean and John's Wedding, 5th June 1965 at St John's Church, Penge

5th June 1965 – Jean and her father

John and Margaret Brush

Kay and John Morrison-Scott

Rosalind Ashby
(aged 3 years)

John, Carol and Ian Brown

Diane, John and Kay, John and Jean, Margaret and John, Carol, Ian and Rosalind

Friends and Family

Carol and Alan Colton, Canada 1967

Margaret

John

Margaret and John

Diane

Jean Andrews and son, John

Libya

Mohammed and Rupert, Villa Agosta

Rupert

Jean and Rupert

Jean and Zena

Jean

Judy and Zena

Tracy and Adrienne

Postcard of the International Fair Building

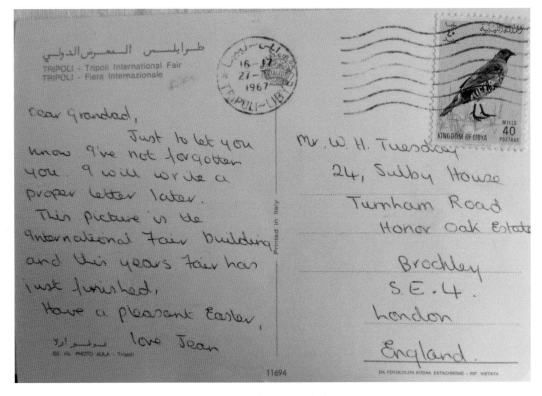

Postcard to Grandad

Postcard of the Royal Palace

Postcard of Leptis Magan

Tunisia

Postcard from Tunisia
(front and back)

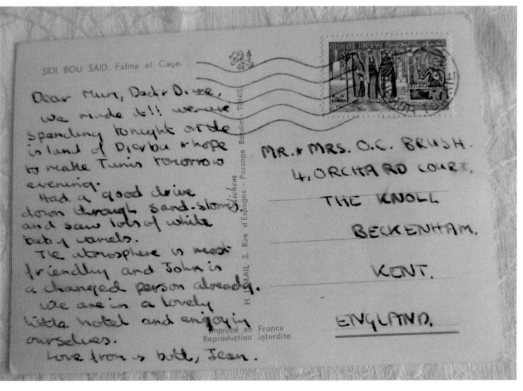

SIDI BOU SAID. Fatma et Cage.

Dear Mum, Dad & Diane,
   We made it!! we were
spending tonight on the
island of Djerba & hope
to make Tunis tomorrow
evening.
   Had a good drive
down through sand-storms
and saw lots of white
baby camels.
   The atmosphere is most
friendly and John is
a changed person already.
   We are in a lovely
little hotel and enjoying
ourselves.
   Love from us both, Jean.

MR. & MRS. O.C. BRUSH.
4, ORCHARD COURT,
THE KNOLL
BECKENHAM.
KENT.
ENGLAND.

Imprimé en France
Reproduction interdite

H. RAAIL 3, Rue d'Espagne - Passage Baldini - TUNIS

Telegram to John and Margaret

CONSULT TELEPHONE
LEX DIALLING CARD

GPO

POST OFFICE
OVERSEAS TELEGRAM

GPO

To send Telegrams—C
DIRECTORY OR TELE

JN 11   13 17

DFL819 C TPLT102 075

GBLX HI LATR 017

TRIPOLI LIBYA (17) 11 1120

ELT

BRUSH 4 ORCHARD COURT THE KNOL BECKENHAM

KENT ENGLAND

PLEASE CANCEL HOLIAY SAFE DONT WORRY JEAN

CO 4

POST OFFIC
OVERSEAS TELE

GPO

To send Telegrams—CONSULT TELEPHONE
DIRECTORY OR TELEX DIALLING CARD

GPO

OFFICE
TELEGRAM

Christmas 1969

John

John and Jean

Margaret and John

John, John, Kay, Jean, Margaret, Grandad

Letter No. 55 (Handwritten airmail letter)

Sunday October 15th 1967

Dear Mum, Dad, and Diane,

Thank you for your letters. I'm very 'cheesed' at the moment as it is past 9pm and no John yet. I get extremely angry at the amount of work he has to do especially as it is at Tripoli office. He now has to finish his Giorgimpopoli work at lunchtime and spend the afternoon and evening helping in Tripoli.

John didn't see much of Kay and John on their visit and I must admit I'm glad it's over. When Jenny and Terry stayed here in the flat during the trouble Jenny and I got on very well but with Kay I just couldn't get along. She and John (Scott) had very little conversation excepting what they'd been watching on TV at home. I found by the end of the day I was tense and boiling inside as she kept popping round me to see what I was doing and I felt I'd never get a moment's peace. After lunch John would sneak away to lie down and I used to feel so awkward sneaking away as well.

When they left at 6.30am she kissed us both goodbye. John gave a sigh of relief and said 'At least she only kissed me twice – 'Hello' and 'Goodbye'. He was as fed up as I and made another amusing comment after our evening out at the Waddan (us four and eight others). Apparently Kay had mentioned that she hadn't danced with him and John said to me 'If I'd asked her to dance I may have missed a chance of dancing with Monika.' (An attractive German girl).

The four pictures of Rupert are very good and I am always showing them to people. Mohamed was very pleased with his photograph and put it in his shirt pocket with a big smile on his face after I'd explained he could keep it.

He has a very bad cough at the moment and hasn't been in for four days excepting one afternoon when he came and did a pile of washing and ironing. (We were out at the time). He came in this morning though, but said he didn't feel too good so big hearted me sent him off and did three hours washing (four single sheets, one double, pillowcases, shirts etc.) by myself.

Kay and John gave him £L1 when they left which he was reluctant to take but then they gave him a car for Ali and his face lit up and ever since John and I keep hearing this wretched car being pushed around – the sort you hold and push and then let go of. Ali even pushes it up and down the outside walls.

The Spanish doctor and family from downstairs moved out last night to a villa in Giorgimpopoli, so we are now without their barking Alsatian and smelly boxer puppy. The puppy was sweet but it messed on their front balcony and it was rarely cleaned up. Needless to say they left the messes behind.

I think I mentioned that John Scott and I went to see the Romeo and Juliet ballet film at the Waddan cinema one evening. The Waddan seems the best place to go for films as I didn't see any locals there. (One tends to get molested in the other cinemas). Unfortunately they don't always show English films so the choice is limited.

I go back to work tomorrow so I will ask David about using the *Bag for Christmas presents. I suggest you send sea mail this time as it will cut the postage cost. I will check with John as to what we'd like and even if you send early I will make sure it is not opened until the proper time. I think I would like a tweed skirt (fairly smooth though) but will let you know definitely next week.

Rupert has been up to some tricks in his new home. Apparently he pulled all the washing from the line and dragged it around the garden making it filthy. We must have Dick for a meal soon and get him to bring Rupert with him. It will be fun to see the dog's reaction. I still miss him a lot, especially at times like this when I am waiting for John to come home and feeling fed-up. One consolation is the tidiness of the flat. Hardly a whisker to be seen now and the mats only need doing every couple of days.

The bird, Elvis, is fine but I had a surprise the other day as the cat from the Agosta's flat had been in whilst I was out and had knocked the cage from the windowsill to the sideboard.

The cage was on its side with birdseed and water everywhere and poor Elvis had nowhere to perch.

By the way I have an admirer. In the next block there is an elderly Egyptian and his family. I used to wave to him when I saw him and then about two weeks back he said he was going to Paris for a few days and wanted to bring me a present. I said 'no' and we argued a bit and came to an agreement that I would pay him for some perfume. I saw him the other day getting into his car and he said he had my present. He went to the boot and pulled out a parcel and said it was £L1, which I gave him. I came back upstairs to find that not only did the parcel contain a bottle of 'Femme' (an expensive perfume) but an electric hair curling tong and a beautiful rolled-gold letter opener. At first John said I was to pay him the full amount or give them back but I liked them too much to part with and as I couldn't afford to pay him we decided I should put them to one side and if he tries anything to give them back then. The trouble is one can't be sure he isn't after something or just feeling generous.

The Fiat is going in for a service tomorrow and we are borrowing Jock's Cortina whilst Felicity Fiat is being mended. (Jock is mostly in the desert). Well

must close. Will put a P.S. as to when John gets in as it is now 10pm.
Love from us both,
   Jean XXXXXX

P.S. 10 past 10pm!

NOTES: *the Bag refers to the Diplomatic Bag.

Letter No. 56 (Handwritten airmail letter)

Sunday 22nd October 1967

Dear Mum, Dad, and Diane,

Many thanks for your letter, Dad. I was pleased to hear you had been in contact with the Scotts and I hope you get to see the slides. There aren't many pictures of John but there are quite a few of me.

Now about your holiday. Personally I don't think your idea of renting a flat in Malta is necessary. Why don't you fly straight here by BOAC and spend as much time as possible with us and then stay in Malta for just two or three days on your way back. (Hotels are very reasonable and good by all accounts and we can give you lots of recommendations). I can have as much time as I like off from work so maybe I will come back with you to Malta and buy some clothes. I think the best time for your visit will be the two or three middle weeks in May as it should mean John will be placed in an easier position regarding work.

Also with regard to being shifted to Benghazi – we have an extra European coming out shortly and Mr Norman is thinking of sending him when things are straight here. So it looks as if John and I will spend the whole three year tour in Tripoli.

Obviously the way you want to plan your holiday is up to you but I think that taking a flat in Malta will entail a lot of expense and work for Mum, especially as we can put you up so easily here. (And I want to see as much as possible of you all as it will be another 16 months before we see you again after your visit).

I have done a stupid thing by writing on this air letter as John has written out the camera cheque. Anyway I'll write to Diane at work tomorrow or Tuesday and pop it in her letter. We have made the cheque for £23.14/- which is £2.15/- for case, £19/19s for the camera and £1 from me for Grandad.

I checked with David Pugh about using the BFPO 57 and he said it would be okay as long as the parcel isn't too large. I'm afraid it will have to be posted by 9th November to get here in time (according to David anyway) but don't worry if you post it a little later. We have been racking our brains thinking of ideas but all I need is a winter skirt (oatmeal tweed if possible, not mini though). Don't worry if you can't get the colour but bear in mind I have one mixed tweed skirt and one black and white one already. (36" hips). John decided all he needed was a few white hankies (his mother brought out socks and some shirts). So as the list isn't very extensive we thought perhaps a movie film as well, as the shops here aren't quite back to normal yet. Hope that is all okay and thank you in advance. Don't forget to send it sea mail as it is much cheaper.

Last night we had John and Anna Whitchelow along with Bob Ayres (embassy staff) and Dick and Rupert for a meal. They didn't leave until gone 2am and then we stood outside for another half an hour chatting to Bob. Bob didn't say much during the evening as I think he is rather shy but when the others had driven off he came out of his shell and had quite a lot to say, just to the two of us.

Rupert leapt around a bit when everyone first arrived and he sneaked into the kitchen and licked the dirty plates which had been stacked on the floor but other than that he lay down quietly and slept. The improvement is really noticeable and he certainly had no second thoughts about leaving with Dick. Dick really likes him and takes him everywhere. Apparently Rupert doesn't get car sick anymore as Dick pulls down the back seat and Rupert dashes from side to side poking his head out of either window on trips. Dick had taken two girls and Rupert to the beach on Friday and Rupert had the back of the car to himself as usual, leaving Dick and his two companions squeezed into the front.

It is starting to get chilly now in the mornings and evenings although the temperature reaches 75 degrees to 80 degrees in the daytime. I suppose it would still strike you as warm although John and I are feeling the cold.

We have fleas in the bedroom at the moment and I have over thirty bites on me. We took up the carpet and hung it over the balcony and then I washed everything with paraffin. But Mohamed (being industrious) brought the carpet in again, so once more it was dragged out and I had to paraffin the floors again. Anyway since the room was done the bites have got less. I hate to say it but I think they drop off Mohamed and also he only sweeps the carpet using a soft brush.

John discovered he was missing a golf club on Friday and even after a search of the spare room it couldn't be found but today it suddenly appeared in his golf bag. So obviously whilst I was out shopping Mohamed had sneaked up and replaced it. I expect young Ali had been digging the garden with it or hitting his baby brother, Salim. I think Mohamed has his wife or sister here as well as Salim. Salim is a miniature Ali of about 2½ years, but at the moment he is bald. I think they (Libyans) often shave their babies' heads to get rid of nits.

The Spanish people from below have moved to a villa at Giorgimpopoli as the flat must have been very overcrowded with a toddler, a new baby and a nurse, plus the boxer puppy and the Alsatian. I haven't seen much of the new people but the nameplate suggests he is a doctor.

Excepting for last night we have had a quiet week and after the first few days back at the embassy I am once again twiddling my thumbs or writing letters home. From November we have to work Tuesday and Thursday afternoons from 3-30pm to 6pm, which is a nuisance and to my mind unnecessary.

Must close,
Love from us both to you all,
Jean XXXXXX

Letter No. 57 (Handwritten airmail paper)

Tuesday 24th October 1967

Dear Diane,

You are lazy. What about a letter from you. Still I may be jumping the gun as you may be running true to form and have a letter at work which is being written over a period of weeks.

The main object of this note is to enclose the camera cheque which I mentioned in my last letter. I hope the ordinary mail is getting through your end, only I understand the post offices in England aren't accepting parcels at the moment due to strikes and what have you.

Thank goodness John's people have gone, it was a real bore having them. I was pretty disappointed as I'd been quite looking forward to their visit. Still I got a blue twin-set from them, which was a consolation. We arranged lots of outings for them and always went in a crowd but they just hovered on the edge, Kay looking miserable and John (Scott) beaming from ear to ear but with a vacant look in his eyes. John was as fed up as me so it wasn't just my prejudice. When we get home on leave John wants to spend as little time as possible with them, but I suppose we will have to stay there for a while in an effort to get organised, but we will be off touring as soon as possible.

Keep your fingers crossed that with the extra European staff member expected in the Tripoli office, John and I may get a few days in Malta before Xmas. We are entitled to local leave but as Mr Norman (the GM) is such a sod we never get a look in, although he takes enough time off himself.

Last night we popped in to see Dick as he had left his cigarettes and lighter behind on Saturday evening. Rupert bounced around and had dragged a tree branch into the living room to chew on. Rupert has also dug another deep hole in the front garden. Fortunately Dick takes it all in good part and the dog seems very happy and settled.

Tonight I am off to the Barbary Coast Players' meeting. They are hoping to organise Shakespeare readings so I hope I get a part to read. Probably not very interesting to you but I still like a touch of the 'Shakespeares'. (Remember those school plays?)

On Thursday we hope to go to a barbeque at the yacht club but, as the King's uncle has just died, a week of mourning has been declared, so it may be cancelled.

On Saturday Polly and Garry are coming for a meal. Terry and Jenny were meant to be coming also but they have to meet Terry's replacement at Idris airport at 7.30pm so they will only be able to manage drinks later on.

I might get a mate for my female goldfinch as it seems so lonely. I was even contemplating whether to let it go free but was told it would only be caught again or shot. There are very few wild birds in Tripoli. I don't know if the weather is discouraging to them or the fact that most of the local boys own air guns and take pot shots at them, therefore keeping the numbers down.

Well as I am writing about the oddest subjects you can see I am scraping the bottom of the barrel for material, so I will close.

Love Jean XXXXX

Letter No. 58 (Handwritten airmail letter)

Sunday 29th October 1967

Dear Mum, Dad, and Diane,

I hope my letter to Diane enclosing the cheque has arrived safely. I haven't had a letter this week so I hope the post is okay.

Sunday is now my busy day as Mohamed comes in on a Friday and has Sunday off instead. I make it my day for going right through the flat and finish off with floor washing. Mohamed is okay and does plenty of work for the money I give him but he misses quite a bit and never adds the final polish that makes the flat look sparkling clean.

We now have a good local milk 'Bon Lait'. It costs one shilling and ten pence for a litre and comes from France in a powder form. It is then made up here and the shops get a daily delivery. It is dated and lasts two days (I've used the same lot for five days though, and it has been okay). It doesn't come in bottles but polythene bags. They give you a jug with your first bag, which has a hole in the bottom to stop you using it for anything else. Then you fit your bag of milk in the jug and snip off the corner and you are all set. It is pleasant tasting milk and I use it on cereals.

The weather has been dull and wet the past week but it looks brighter today. I think I may get a little more swimming in before next summer but I've gone off the underwater lark idea with tanks etc. since I was told that poor *Lottie Hass got eaten alive by a shark. Do you know if it is true? And if so when did it happen?

I may take up badminton this winter as I know Susan Pugh is keen and she may be able to give me a lift to the Tripoli College where it is held. As the weather is cooling John may play golf Friday afternoons (so he can lie in in the morning) and I can go with him after work. I eat so much nowadays I must keep up the exercise to keep the figure in order, but my bottom is certainly getting larger. John says it is a good job I still suffer from 'Tripoli Trots' otherwise I'd be enormous. (Sympathetic husband). He never gets anything except occasional 'morning sickness' after a hectic night out. I must admit that although he likes his drink and has a couple every evening he doesn't go in for excess unless we are at a party. He drives home perfectly, but once he stands up to get out of the car he wobbles about and makes a lot of noise getting up our stairs. (Nice for our fellow flat occupants). I wish I could get it on film as he looks like Charlie Chaplin.

Terry and Jenny are off to Calcutta in three weeks and their replacement, Nigel Plummer, came out this morning. He was meant to be here last night but as usual Alitalia overbooked and several people had to spend the night in Rome. Don't use Alitalia when you come out, as overbooking is very common with them. I'm longing to hear from you and to hear what your plans are for next May. Do stay with us for as long as possible.

We had Terry and Jenny for a meal on Thursday and then on Saturday we had Garry and Polly.

I still have lots of people on my list to have round for meals but we have lots of things to go to so goodness knows when I will finish.

I think I mentioned about the ship HMS Scarborough with 32 cadets calling in to Tripoli on an official visit on November 9th. Well, on November 10th David Pugh is having a cocktail party with invites to 18 officers and cadets and John and I have been invited too. The ambassador and the ship's captain will be there also. Work at the embassy has been hectic (embassy hectic but a slack day compared to a commercial firm I expect). I even had to go back one afternoon. It has been interesting though as I have been stencilling lists of events and official calls to be made by the Captain. A lot of planning and then the lists have to be sent out to lots of people. On top of all this I have to make coffee and stop work for five minutes to drink mine. I could write a book about my job and I'm sure none of the nits (embassy staff) would recognise themselves as they are too full of self-importance. (There are some exceptions though).

I have been getting rid of some of my winter clothes as there are several things I never wore last year as Tripoli proved too fashionable. Luigi (the Maltese I work with) is taking them to the Father in the Old City who will distribute them amongst the poor *Maltese. It is surprising how many poor (destitute) Maltese and Italians there are here. I never realised until I started work and discovered a lot of them can't even afford £1-10s for new British passports. They have to have them even though they have never left Tripoli in their lives.

John and I are looking forward to an early night tonight as we were up late on Thursday, Friday and Saturday, although we managed a siesta Friday. I think we should manage to be asleep by 9.30pm.

Tomorrow afternoon I am going shopping with Monika and I hope to get a larger birdcage and another goldfinch, so that young 'Elvina' will have company. I hope she lays an egg.

I am also hoping to get some brown suede shoes. We have heard that Vatures (a reasonably priced Jewish clothes shop) is operating, but you have to creep in by the back entrance.

Well must close. Hope to get a letter from you soon,
        Love from us both,
            Jean and John XXXXXX

NOTES:

*According to Wikipedia, Lottie Hass was still alive in 2009. She was born in 1929. Hans Hass, her husband, died in 2013 aged 94 years.

*Malta was part of the British Empire until 1964, when it gained independence. Maltese residing in Tripoli held British passports and could continue to do so providing that they had evidence that an ancestor had been born in Malta when the island was a

colony. Part of my job at the Embassy was to check records and renew passports for the Maltese.

Letter No. 59 (Handwritten on airmail paper)

Sunday 5th November 1967

Dear Mum, Dad, and Diane,

Thank you for your joint letter. Yes, Dad, I now quite understand the Malta position. It sounds a good idea to take a flat if, as you say it is no more expensive than flying direct. When choosing dates do try to avoid the very beginning and end of May though. I hope to be able to fly back to Malta with you to buy some dresses but I doubt if John will be able to come.

I bought a much larger cage for the bird and today I went back to the suk with the old cage and got another goldfinch. The chappie wanted £L5 for it and he came down to £L2½ whilst I was still bargaining 'No, only £L1½'. Anyway he was still asking £L2½ and even picked the bird out and had it in my cage. He then came to £L2 and I said 'No. Take it out, I'm only giving £L1½'. And just as I was going to go up to £1.75pts. he said 'Okay, give me £L1½', so I felt very pleased. The poor bird had such long claws it kept falling over and getting its feet caught on the bars. Anyway the first thing I did on getting it home was to hold it and try to cut its claws with scissors but they wouldn't cut, so feeling frantic I carried him into the bedroom and managed to get John's clippers out of the drawer one handed, and after that it was easy. I have left him in the small cage and put the cages together so they can get used to each other. I can hear them chirping away so they should be okay in the same cage eventually. The new bird is older than Elvis and the man said it is female but I don't think it is, as it has a lot of red on its face and throat. Elvis is now back to being male, as he must have been very young when I got him and the red feathers are only just coming through.

I understand that Kay and John are coming on Monday for a slide session. I hope you like the views of Tripoli and surrounding areas.

On Tuesday I plan to play badminton. I have borrowed some shorts (white) and hope to get a pair of my own later on, if I can find any in the shops.

On Monday Dick, Jackie (she works with Dick) and Rupert and maybe another couple are coming for drinks. I am longing to see Rupert again. I am very lucky though because I saw him last Monday when we visited Dick for drinks. He is much thinner and more muscular now, in fact in tip-top condition. Dick takes him for long walks and lets him loose on the beach, he also gives him a drop of olive oil each day.

On Thursday we went to a party at Jim Deasy's, which was a drag. He had invited one girl whose father was visiting her, who wouldn't leave us females alone. He got very drunk and when he spoke (which was non-stop) we got spattered with whisky and chewed peanuts. Then he danced with Monika and she couldn't stand the way he held her so tightly. We spent most of our time avoiding him.

Friday was a lovely sunny and bright day and after I'd finished work we ate a quick lunch and took Sally (who's husband, Jock is in the desert) to Sabratha. We used Sally's Ford Cortina, which John loves driving and we collected Monika, Ian and Carl (a friend of Ian's) in their car and then onto Florence's to collect another load (Florence and baby, two visiting school teachers and another Ian). We had a lovely drive through the cultivated Zavia area and at one point in the journey had to slow down to let about nine camels pass. When at the ruins we split up into separate groups but at one point we all met at the ancient public toilets. We sat on the marble loos and admired the headless and armless statues that were facing us.

Down one of the 'streets' John and I found the remains of an olive oil shop. It had a deep stone storage room with only two openings. Then we explored the theatre, you could actually put on plays there today, as so much of it is intact and the seating is safe as well. It has about four 'box offices', which were easy to define. I took a lot of film but as so much of it has to be panned I am keeping my fingers crossed it comes out clear.

In the evening we rushed back to visit Jenny and Ivan. But Ivan was in the desert so we just nattered instead of playing cards as planned. Also the horrible Libyan captain was there, who we had hoped we'd seen the last of.

On Saturday evening we were feeling shattered, I'd been lucky enough to get a two hour siesta but John was very tired. However, we had to visit a Lebanese chappie, along with Ian and Monika, for a Lebanese meal. He had another five guests and one couple knew Dick and Rupert. The food was very good. Mixed hors d'oeuvres followed by parsley, tomatoes and other things finely chopped and then chicken and aubergines, finishing off with fruit. The Lebanese, Antonio, was so hospitable I had to eat three bananas for fear of offending him and John had to drink whisky, wine and arrack all in generous quantities.

This morning we both felt groggy and John nearly passed out at work with tiredness. This afternoon he didn't have to work and although it seemed a shame to miss such a lovely bright afternoon we both slept until 6pm, ate, and back to bed (where I am finishing this letter).

I don't know when the next dramatic club meeting will be, as most of the members are tied up with the 'Present Laughter' production. I didn't volunteer to do any reading at the last meeting as I'd just heard about Egypt bombing an Israeli ship and for some reason I felt sick and trembly. John says he wasn't frightened and thought the whole thing was a laugh but I'm too scared to think that way. I had more or less forgotten all about the six-day war but suddenly it all came back and I didn't want to go through it again. Apparently the troublemakers who incited the mobs are still in jail so if anything else does happen it shouldn't affect us this time.

You asked about my waist size, it is about 26" but hips are 36" so I'd rather you went by hips, as I don't want it too baggy and I can always squeeze myself in. I am hoping to lose a bit of weight at badminton anyway.

Well better close, I'll probably get a letter from you tomorrow, as Monday seems the usual day.

Love from us both,
Jean XXXXXX

P.S. Is *Nan's address 133, Ladywell Road. Lewisham. S.E.13? I will write to her soon.

NOTES: *Nan refers to my grandmother on my father's side.

Letter No. 60 (Handwritten on airmail paper)

Sunday 12th November 1967

Dear Mum, Dad, and Diane,

Thank you for your letter and for putting my mind at rest about Lottie Hass. Unfortunately swimming is finished now as the weather is cooling down. I have just sent a pile of winter clothing to the cleaners and am wearing jumpers and skirts. Jenny Dowrick sold me a new courtel dress that her mother had sent to her some time ago, as she won't be needing many winter things in Calcutta, so I am well pleased.

We had a letter from the Scotts saying how much they enjoyed the films and the giggle you had with my shot of John relieving himself. It was probably shaky as I was giggling myself when taking it. Kay said you were going over to see them for another film show, so I presume you get on with them better now. I hope so anyway as it probably cheers you to get first hand news of us, and next June it will help them when you see them on your return from here.

It hardly seems possible that Terry and Jenny are off next Friday. I shall miss Jenny as she is very good about driving me around and also we have nice little gossip sessions. She is the only person I gossip with as we just keep our opinions quiet in other company.

On Thursday we had a late session with Terry and Jenny's farewell party and a group of us ended up at Polly and Garry's for coffee until 3am. Jim Deasy was there but he went to sleep clutching his glass of cognac. Then John Whitchelow sat on Geoff Smith's knee and they played Archie Andrews and Peter Brough. After that Polly and Garry decided it was time for us to go so they said 'goodnight' and reappeared five minutes later in night clothes expressing surprise that we were still there, so on a highly jovial note we all left. Jim was just waking up.

Friday we went to the Pugh's cocktail party which had 18 sailors plus Captain Forrester and his wife, and the ambassador and Mrs Sarell. One sailor we were talking to said he'd been married for fifteen years but could count the number of years spent with his wife on one hand. It must be a horrible life for the wives.

We went over the ship, HMS Scarborough, on Friday afternoon and found a chatty junior rating who kindly took us round. He loves the life but gets annoyed with the cadets who aren't very practical although they know the theory.

Saturday found us eating at the Chicken on Wheels and onto the Mocambo for dancing and small floorshow. We were invited by Rocco along with Terry and Jenny. Rocco is an Italian as broad as he is tall with a scruffy appearance. He is a very rich man and owns a lot of land here as well as having control over the import of liquor (owning all the rights). Do you remember Nenis (the Jew) and Angela – who are now in Italy? Well Rocco is Angela's father and he and Nenis were in partnership with the liquor deal. They have a shop in Giorgimpopoli.

The Mocambo floorshow amazed me as they had a striptease artist. I expected her to go as far as a bikini, as is usual here, but she went down to a G-string and a few sequins.

Gosh, the weather is rough today. Very windy and draughty indoors but a bit humid as well.

You know the little bird I bought last week, Toby? Well a couple of days back his eyes were nearly gummed completely together with sleepy-dust. I left him for a day but as there was no improvement I had to take him to the vet. He was pitiful to watch as Elvis kept knocking into him and making him lose his balance. So Elvis is in the small cage at the moment. Poor Toby would get down to his food container but keep misjudging the height back to his perch. The vet said he'd caught a cold and put some drops in his eyes and wants to see him again tomorrow. He is a very kind vet and made no charge. He was very gentle with Toby as well. Anyway the bird can see much better already and his eyes are over half open so he can hop around as usual.

Rupert came last Monday with Dick and Jackie. (Jackie is a secretary at Dick's company and they go out together sometimes). Rupert behaved very well but accidentally broke a glass with his tail wagging. Dick told us that one early morning he was woken by a scratching noise and Rupert poking at him. He thought the scratching noise sounded as if someone was trying to open a window from the outside, so he crept around the villa with moonlight glinting on his rifle and Rupert cowering along behind. He tiptoed from room to room like this and eventually traced the noise to a mouse trapped behind a toolbox in the spare room. With relief he went back to bed only to discover that Rupert, suffering from nerves, had done a runny dollop under the bed.

I hope your evening with the Davis's, Len, Joyce and Albert went well. Do I know the Boakes? I am having Geoff Smith and his French girl friend Carole for a meal next Saturday, probably along with Jenny and Ivan Havy. (Ivan being French as well – although both he and Carole speak excellent English).

Well better close and do some cooking as we plan to be in bed around 8.30pm. (Much needed sleep – luckily John got this afternoon off).

Love from us both,
Jean XXXXXX

Letter No. 61 (Handwritten on airmail paper)

Tuesday 21st November 1967

Dear Mum, Dad, and Diane,

As we have had a holiday here I decided not to write on Sunday as I wouldn't be able to post it before Wednesday anyway.

Monday was a holiday in honour of the opening of Parliament, which was, as far as I can gather, celebrated only by our embassy. Tuesday, today, has been more widespread in celebrations as John got the day off as well. Something to do with the *UN declaration of Independence for Libya.

You must tell me how *devaluation affects you at home. It isn't so bad for us as we will get more sterling for money we send home from here. If only John had brought all our money from home here and then sent it back after devaluation we could have made on the deal. Still that is only speculation. It was a nasty shock though and left me feeling ashamed that *Wilson could do such a thing after saying he wouldn't.

Terry and Jenny set off to Calcutta on Friday. John went to see them off with Jim Deasy. They were all smiles, absolutely bubbling over to leave Tripoli. Jenny had been upset on the Thursday evening as she had to say goodbye to so many of her friends at the Yacht Club barbeque, but by Friday she was okay. With luck our September to March leave should coincide with their February to July one so we plan to do something together for a couple of weeks.

It is rather a shame that our leave will be a winter one but at least Christmas should be on a grand scale, and I fancy some skiing in the Grampians. I have just mentioned to John that a cruise to a warmer climate wouldn't be a bad idea either and he seemed quite keen. He mentioned South Africa but I think that would be expensive.

Garry's mother is here at the moment and although she has only been here a week he is fed up. Apparently she is a strict Methodist and doesn't hold with drinking although I spoke to her at the barbeque and she seemed very pleasant.

Diane is fixed up for her stay – I showed the photos of her to Geoff Smith (manager of the Bank of North Africa) and he said he'd look after her. He is 26 years old – good money and prospects – but shorter than me, chubby, glasses and ginger. Still for all his physical shortcomings he really is a nice person and has an identical twin in England. His mother had another set of twins (a boy and girl) and two other separate children. Poor woman.

The bird, Toby, went back to the vets on Monday for more eye drops and the vet was pleased with his progress. Judging by his expression of amazement I gather he had rather expected Toby to die between the first visit on Saturday and Monday. His eyes are still a bit 'odd' but he can see well enough now.

The badminton was good. I played four games but found the knock about before the matches more exhausting than the actual games. I was very stiff the next two days. I had to play in borrowed slacks and my own canvas shoes but Luigi (from the Consular Section) is getting me some white shorts and I must get some plimsolls. Diane, shall I get short or long white socks? I fancy long ones but not quite sure. Why do you need four racquets? (spellings carefully copied from Mum's last letter). Are they all the same or for different types of game?

Saw Rupert for a few minutes last Friday when we popped into Dick's to leave a juicy bone. He told us that Rupert was extremely well trained as he'd been driving along with him in the back of the car when suddenly Rupert took a leap out of the window and by the time Dick had screeched to a halt, Rupert was seen relieving himself by a tree. I think that story comes a close second to the 'mouse robber'.

Last night we had Gwen and Eric over for drinks along with Sally (from across the road) and Ken Neal (who works at the embassy) and his girlfriend Rosemary, also from the embassy. It was a good evening and our nattering ended on the subject of ghosts and unidentified flying objects.

Anyway must close as I'm finishing this at work and I've a 'death' to do in a minute. Certificates and what have you, my second one so far.

Will write soon, expect I'll get your letter today.

Love from us both,

Jean xxxxxx

P.S. Hope you are keeping the postage stamps.

NOTES:

Ref: *'Libyan independence was proclaimed on 24th December 1951 ... Early in the morning, the last powers held by the British and French Residents were transferred to the provisional government'. [Wright, John. Libya: A Modern History. Croom Helm. ISBN 0-7099-2733-9 p.73].

Ref: *devaluation – *Wilson is the Labour PM, Harold Wilson, who had promised not to devalue the pound.

Letter No. 62 (Handwritten on airmail paper)

Sunday 26th November 1967

Dear Mum, Dad, and Diane,

Thank you for your last letter. I bet you are fed up with cine film shows by now. John and I are looking forward to seeing the film and getting our techniques sorted out. We have another film here ready for developing. Luckily the Kodak shop has reopened so we don't have any problem. Films have rocketed in price though: £1.17/-, sorry £1.11/- taking devaluation into account.

Mohamed has gone off to Homs so I'm having to do my own housework for a few days. I save the dirty washing for him though. I usually do my own undies and woollies but the other afternoon it rained whilst they were on the line so they were left out overnight and the next morning, when I got home from work I discovered that they had all been ironed and put away. He had even put them in the correct places, bras in one drawer, pants and slips in another and stockings in another. I was most surprised and imagined him puzzling it all out.

We had a horrible evening yesterday as we were summoned to the Norman's for drinks to meet the Lee-Woods. The Lee-Wood family originally owned the Eastern Bank and Mr Lee-Wood is a Director. They were a charming couple but John really blotted his copybook by arriving late. It wasn't really our fault as originally we thought it was for 7.30pm instead of 7pm, and John didn't get home until 6.30pm. Then after a hurried change we had to collect Nigel (Terry's replacement) and Joanne before driving out to Giorgimpopoli. We were greeted by Mr Norman with a 'You're late' plus icy stare. During the evening John apologised and mentioned that he'd had to collect Nigel and Joanne, and Mr Norman turned very nasty and said he shouldn't have been late and to make sure he arrived on time for Monday (cocktails at the Waddan). John was fuming, especially as he'd apologised.

Anyway the 'do' ended just after 9pm and Joanne, Nigel and Jim Deasy came back for drinks. I made a plate of sandwiches, which pleased everyone as no one had had time to eat beforehand. Then we pulled Mr Norman to bits and drank to his death. (Really nasty and childish I'm afraid but as previously Mr Norman had boasted of 'breaking a man' at one of his earlier postings we felt he deserved it).

Did I mention in my last letter that on Tuesday (which we both had off) I bought some dangling black earrings? When I was buying them I was hard put to choose between them and a silver pair of danglers. Anyway John surprised me by getting me the silver ones the next day. I think they were meant to be part of a Christmas gift but he decided to give them to me early.

The weather is lovely at the moment. It seems to go in spasms; wet for a week followed by two weeks of dry weather with sunny warm days and chilly mornings and evenings.

On Friday John drove Sally and Nigel in Sally's husband's Cortina to Garian along with Garry and Polly and Garry's Mum. I had to work in the morning but he wasn't too late back.

I walked into town the other day and borrowed a friend's little dog, Vodka. He certainly kept the Arabs away. I didn't get touched once or forced into the gutter. John really took to him and for a while we were considering keeping him, as my friend already has a dog and she only took Vodka over when he was roaming around without a home. Anyway we decided against it as the flat really is unsuitable for a dog of any size. I shall definitely borrow him again though when I go into town.

Poor Terry and Jenny, I expect you have heard about the riots and curfew in Calcutta. I'm afraid everyone from the bank here thinks it is funny, excepting me.

Work is going fine except that yesterday we had a death to deal with. It is a complicated business as the body has to go to the hospital for analysing and then when it is certified free from contagious disease it goes into the mortuary. David, *John, or Luigi then have to see the body sealed into the coffin ready for transportation home. They suggested that I go and see it sealed but fortunately they weren't serious. John Keeling was lucky though, because it should have been his 'turn' but then Luigi came back from holiday earlier than expected and they sent him instead. As Luigi is Maltese and therefore a Roman Catholic he gets quite a morbid enjoyment out of it all.

I couldn't really see much point in sending the body back as it was minus various organs, which were still being analysed at the hospital.

I'll think of something more cheerful to write now. Next Thursday and Friday I have two children's parties to go to which I expect will be hectic. Unfortunately the mothers of these children, Jenny and Gwen, not only live next-door-but-one to each other but have fallen out over the parties. Jenny wanted to make it a joint one for her Paul and Gwen's 'Winkle' (Adrienne) but according to Jenny, Gwen grabbed all the children (those to be invited) and then decided to have her Winkle's party on the Friday instead of the proper day, Thursday. Anyway it seems to me that if I go to one I'll have to go to them both but although John can take me to Winkle's, as it is a Friday, I don't know how to get to Jenny's.

The situation is complicated as Jenny is a 'trouble-stirrer' but we both like her husband, Ivan, and enjoy a game of cards with them, so I don't really want to upset her. I think she is being silly as I'm sure Gwen didn't 'grab all the children' for Winkle's party. Gwen is so easy going and not at all like that. Anyway I have a feeling that I'm treading on dangerous ground but can't see a way out of it, I only hope it doesn't rebound on me. So far I haven't mentioned that I'm invited to both parties to either of them.

Gwen and Eric spent a lot of time in Africa where they had native servants who spoke only pidgin English. On one occasion one of Eric's workmates was asked to provide a 'dead body box' which turned out to be a coffin. Then another time Gwen asked a servant to bring a tin of flour to her, which she knew was on the top shelf of the cupboard. He came back saying he couldn't find it, so she sent him off to look again, telling him where it was once more. Still he couldn't find it so she went back with him and pointed it out, he then said 'Me see, but him no there' meaning that, although he'd seen it, the fact hadn't registered. I think the funniest one though was their friend who, having finished his main course asked his servant where the pudding was and was answered 'Wibble Wobble no go sleep yet' 'Pardon', he said. 'Wibble Wobble no go sleep yet.' Still puzzled he followed the servant into the kitchen only to be shown an unset jelly.

By the way Kay mentioned sending the film back quite a few letters ago and I said that a chap from the Embassy, Bob Ayres, who is coming home for Christmas would, perhaps, bring it back if she posted it to him, but I think your idea of putting it in our parcel is the best. If you see her and anything is mentioned tell her to disregard my instructions, as I didn't know at the time about your putting it in the parcel.

Did I tell you that I read 'Silent Spring' by Rachael Carson? I hurriedly checked the Pif-Paf ingredients and luckily it is okay as the insect killing part comes from chrysanthemums and isn't a man-made chemical. When shopping I turned down some disinfectant containing DDT, just in case the fumes affected us.

Well I can't think of much else. John had to go back to work this afternoon to clear up something Terry had made a mess of when he was at Giorgimpopoli, which is a shame as we'd been getting used to spending Sunday afternoon together.

Must get some Christmas cards soon, but haven't seen any decent ones yet. We had our first, from John's Aunt Molly at Gravesend, today. Ramadan is due to begin soon so we should get a day off.

Love from us both,

Jean xxxxxx

P.S. When are you going to write Diane? Naughty.

NOTES: *John Keeling was the Vice-Consul at the British Embassy

Letter No. 63 (Handwritten airmail letter)

Sunday 3rd December 1967

Dear Mum, Dad, and Diane,

Thank you for the letter which I received yesterday. I am writing 'big' as we have had a quiet week.

Last Monday the bank had an official cocktail party at the Waddan for the Lee-Woods. I think John and I exonerated ourselves as we arrived five minutes early and worked hard nattering to guests. I had my hair cropped and set so Mr Norman had to say something about it. He is jolly rude, he doesn't say it looks nice but mentions with a condescending air that he has noticed it. John is back in favour as well. Jim Deasy asked him to help out at Tripoli on Saturday afternoon and John said he couldn't as he was up to his eyes with work at Giorgimpopoli. So what happens, but Mr Norman comes snooping round to Giorgimpopoli office at 2pm just to check that John was telling Jim the truth. Anyway Mr Norman gets such a shock at the amount John has to do that he stays and helps for an hour and says that when he finishes he is to go home and not go into Tripoli. He got home at 8pm.

I went to two children's parties on Thursday and Friday afternoons. It was great fun. The first one was for Jenny's eldest, Paul, who was five years old. She has four children in total and Steve, who is nearly three, and quite tubby, got so excited that he wet his pants and was sent to his room in disgrace. I later found him sitting cross-legged on his bed like a little Buddha, stuffing sweets into his wet mouth and crying quietly. Anyway I blew some soap bubbles for him and he cheered up.

The next day was Gwen's Winkle's third birthday and Steve was missing. Apparently he had wet his pants again and Jenny had made him stay at home. Poor little chap. Gwen sent him a plate of cakes and later on he toddled up to join in.

Glad you saw 'The Knack'. John and I did see it ages ago at home and thoroughly enjoyed it.

You asked about Dick and Rupert. Well I had put an advert in the Lizzie Club about Rupert and someone told Dick about it knowing that he wanted a dog. Dick had been round several times apparently but each time I was out. Then one day Rupert was dragging me back from the shop when Dick was driving up our road after another fruitless visit. He pulled down his window and asked if I was the person who wanted to get rid of a dog. 'Yes', I said. So he came back to the flat and had a few beers and said he'd collect Rupert in two days. I was surprised he wanted him, as all the time we'd been talking Rupert had been sitting on the settee with me, chewing my arm. I kept smiling through the pain saying he was over excited and didn't hurt a bit.

Actually Dick has another girl friend who is Italian named Delia. They came round on Wednesday and we played canasta. Next Thursday we are going to Dick's for another game. Rupert came too and was very good.

I went to badminton on Tuesday and Thursday this week as John has been so late home. On Thursday I leapt up at the wrong time and got a shuttlecock on my forehead at two feet distance and with a load of power behind it. I felt groggy on Friday morning but by the afternoon I was okay.

Ramadan started Friday night. I nearly jumped out of bed on hearing the first cannon shot but by the second one I realised what it was for. We heard twenty-one shots in all at fifteen-second intervals.

Yesterday evening I was in Tripoli with a friend and by dusk the streets were practically deserted as the Libyans had all gone home to eat.

I hope I mentioned in my last letter that your holiday dates are fine. Five months to go so it's not too long I suppose.

We've just bought Christmas cards so I hope they arrive in time.

> Love from us both,
> Jean XXXXXX

Letter No. 64 (Handwritten on airmail paper)

Sunday 10th December 1967

Dear Mum, Dad and Diane,

Thank you for your lovely long letter Mum. I was very interested to hear about the pearl ring you hope to buy as I've been hinting to John about some earrings to match my jade ring We should look like a couple of dowagers come next May.

It's a shame about Mr Fisk and I agree with your feelings about it. If you get the push as well I daresay you could take over my embassy job in May whilst I enjoy your holiday here. I didn't realise Mr Stokes had died. I'm not sure but was he John Hughes' boss when he worked at ICT? Anyway I hope it all works out okay. Will Albert's removal be to a distant office? It seems a shame if he has to move house.

We were pleased to hear of Bob's promotion but it is a pity that they have to move so far away. I expect he will make a good profit on the West Wickham house and probably not have to spend so much on one in or near Birmingham. Rosalind sounds lovely, especially imagining her doing a recitation. I am looking forward to seeing both her and Jean and Derek's John when we get home.

By the way Winkle is a girl. She is Gwen and Eric's youngest. She is really Adrienne but when she was little they used to call her 'Twinkle Toes' but Tracy, her sister, who is five, couldn't manage the 'T' in Twinkle so she is now Winkle. Even when you ask her her name she says 'Winkle'. Both children's parties went off very well.

The other two children in the film are Catherine who is Julia's only child and Colin who is Jill's. (Julia and Jill are neighbours). Jill has just had another boy called Ian. He is lovely and just like his brother judging by baby pictures of Colin. Jean Cate's Jason (who I gave the jacket to) is also adorable and very handsome.

Is David Denman any better now regarding his split personality? I should think being away from home has helped a lot.

I hardly see the Egyptian neighbour now as I don't have to go onto the front balcony often. I used to have to go out there a lot to brush, feed and pet Rupert which was when I mainly saw him. The perfume has been used and I'm endeavouring to get some more but I have John's Christmas present to buy and I need at least two pairs of shoes for myself, as well as a coat, and on £6 a week spending money I'm not going to get far, especially as I've just lent the house-keeping £5.00. Oh Well.

I've been trying to get John a stick tiepin but I don't think they have any in Tripoli so I'm at a loss. I know he wants weapons but I'm frightened of getting the wrong thing, and I don't want him to choose as I'd like to surprise him.

At long last I've written to Nanny Brush and Grandad. I must write to Mrs Richens and Auntie Edie, as well as Jane and Barbara. We have had four Christmas cards so far. One was from the Lawsons showing a sketch of *St. John's which I was pleased with. We left our Christmas cards rather late but they were a bit behind with them in the shops. They are very 'Woolworthsy' and frightfully expensive. I hope you get your birthday card okay Mum.

We have also left our 'cheque sending' very late but we enclose one now with £1 for your birthday, Mum, and £1 each for you three at Christmas plus £1 for Grandad and 10/- each for Uncle Bill and Nanny Brush so I hope you can get something for them from us. If you can't manage it in time please apologise from us.

We've not been up to much this week, canasta at Dick's and drinks at Gwen and Eric's. John has been feeling very tired and is still working all hours.

Dick's Italian girlfriend used to try to persuade Dick to treat Rupert like a dog but things have worked in reverse and even she now makes excuses for Rupert's misdemeanours by saying 'Well, he is still only a puppy'. (All fifteen months of him). Honestly, that dog will never be trained with the way he gets soft owners. He apparently managed to get Dick's sheet off the clothes-line, drag it into the carport and chew it. Dick is now thinking of chewing Rupert's mat by way of revenge.

I've been trying to collect clothes for the Maltese, but on top of the recent church bazaar there's not much about. I've not much sympathy for the Maltese though. They breed like rabbits and extra money usually goes on wine and cigarettes. Even Malta won't have the British Maltese back unless they, and their fathers, were born in Malta.

As my hair is short I've gone in for a 'Twiggy' style, which involves sticking two curlers in on the crown and combing the rest flat before winding a wide crepe bandage around it. John reckons I look like a boy and hates it.

At work we can put the air conditioners onto warm but they tend to give you headaches so we sit and freeze and watch the wind whip across the harbour.

Did I mention that we treated ourselves to £8 worth of gas fire for the lounge? It keeps the room lovely and warm but I don't think the bank will repay us. We generally eat in the lounge now, makes it a bit smelly but at least it is comfortable.

Elvis is minus his tail at the moment and Toby only has one feather in his. Toby is dead scruffy; he is normally puffed out and has a drooping wing. I managed to get a special birdseed for them, made in Italy, so goldfinches must be caged there as well. I used to give them canary and budgie seed mixed plus lettuce and bacon fat. They sing quite a bit, especially when I put the cage outside or if I am frying food.

Talking of frying, I must get the sausages cooked ready for toad-in-the-hole.

Hoping you are all fit and don't have colds etc.

Trusting the cheque is okay.

Love from us both, Jean xxxxxx

P.S. We had a letter from Terry and Jenny Dowrick. They are very happy in Calcutta and the riots didn't really affect them excepting for one night which Terry spent sleeping at the bank. They have a cook/houseboy at £7.10/- a month, a 'sweeper' at £3 a month, and a washer or 'dhobi' at £1.10/- a month which means Jenny has nothing to do all day and is looking for a job. Lucky things!

NOTES: *St John's Church, Penge, where John and I were married in 1965.

Letter No. 65 (Handwritten airmail letter)

Tuesday 19th December 1967

Dear Mum, Dad, and Diane,

Thank you for your letter. Sorry to be a bit late this week but unfortunately your letter got rather held up in the post this end. I think they just put the new day's work on top of the old at the post office during Christmas and busy seasons.

I'll get my sad news over first. Poor Toby died during Saturday/Sunday night. I think he must have hung onto the cold that caused his eyes to stick shut some weeks back. I didn't discover him until 1pm Sunday as I'd gone back to bed after getting John's breakfast. I took the cage over to the Pugh's and David took him out for me. Elvis looks a bit miserable without him but Luigi is getting me a canary soon.

Now onto the best news this year. MR NORMAN IS BEING RETIRED. We don't know how soon and so far only his secretary, Joanne, is meant to know. I can't say how happy the whole bank feels.

We will be celebrating Christmas on 24th, as we did last year. I have bought an eight-pound turkey (£3) and Nigel and Alan are lunching with us. (The new chaps in Tripoli Office). I am expecting between seven and nine for tea and between four and seven for supper, so we should enjoy ourselves. I am hoping that Nigel will help prepare the nosh as he has taken a Cordon Bleu cookery course. John has just spent over £12 on drink, and that was at discount from Ortis.

We have received your parcel, which I have hidden away in the spare room. Christmas shopping isn't much fun here, poor selection, fantastic prices and I have had to do it all by myself this year as John has been working well into the evening just lately.

When you said in a previous letter that Uncle Terry had been seen coming out of his old house I thought perhaps he was living there occasionally, so I sent the Christmas card to Mr and Mrs T.C. Brush.

Talking of Christmas cards I have seen some here of the design you described John Smaldon as having sent, but they are very expensive so I didn't buy any.

I will be spending Christmas Day at Julia's and John is going to pack in work as soon as the bank shuts so he should make it for lunch. In fact we will be having two Christmas's.

We went to a big company's party on Saturday. It was packed out but we managed to get a table with Moira and Denis. A lot of people seemed to know John from the bank and he was described by one fairly important chap as being a 'jewel'. The food was delicious, countless turkeys; beef; ham; etc. Everything you could wish for.

Last Wednesday Rupert came at 3pm to save Dick having to go back home for him after evening classes, before coming here for cards. He was very good but still a handful to manage when on the lead. He cut his paw on the way round the block and was so funny to watch as when he didn't think you were looking he'd use it normally, but as soon as you showed the slightest interest he'd limp. Dick was rather worried in case he'd have to carry him to the car.

We went for drinks at Ian and Monika McNab's on Sunday evening and stayed 'till gone 1am. Mostly we sang but the other Bank of North Africa chaps can be so funny that most of us ended up with strained stomach muscles from laughing at their antics.

Sorry this letter is such a mess but am writing it at work now. On Thursday Alans' fiancée may be spending a day or two with us. She is Dutch and as they plan to get married in January I won't be the only wife (except Mary Norman) in the bank any more.

Received your Christmas letter this lunchtime. Pleased to hear the cheque arrived safely.

I'm stuck for words at the moment. Oh, I know, Luigi is following up the case of an eleven year old Maltese boy who has been deserted by his parents and is now in an orphanage. Well, I bought him a little present for Christmas and then David Pugh suggested that we make a collection for all the children in the home. Luigi checked to see how many children would be there over the holiday and discovered that only the above mentioned Carmelo and another little boy were going to be left. So as it wasn't worth collecting for, David gave two plasticine kits and John Keeling gave 10/- for Luigi to buy something with. So they should have four gifts each as Luigi is buying something as well. It seems such a shame that they will be the only ones in the home over Christmas but I don't think it would be a good idea for an English family to take them in for the day because of the language difficulty.

Well must close, wishing you all a very Happy Christmas and don't forget to toast Christmas 1969.

Lots of love

    Jean and John XXXXXX

Letter No. 66 (Handwritten airmail letter)

Tuesday 26th December 1967

Dear Mum, Dad, and Diane,

Thank you very much for the skirt, hankies and films you sent, all were perfect. Our 24th celebrations went off very well. We had to go to the Norman's for drinks first but met some pleasant people there. We then rushed home and when the time came to get the turkey out of the oven the legs just fell off as it was so well cooked. After lunch Alan, John and I washed up and Nigel cut sandwiches for tea. Tea was followed by supper and by this time the boys were rather intoxicated as they'd been here all the time whilst the other guests had only been to either tea or supper.

Christmas Day. John went to work and I tidied up. Then I went to Julia and Norman's and John joined us just before lunch. It was a pleasant enough Christmas Day but John and I had really had our celebrations the day before.

Ortis gave us a lovely gift – four bottles of drink (brandy, prunella, cherry brandy and Italian) and a cut glass ice bucket with silver tongs with silver edging to the bucket. Ortis is the only customer who seems to give gifts, unlike in England where the cashiers do very well.

David Pugh had four gifts sent to him from a Libyan and he kindly shared them out. I chose a box of kirsch liqueur chocolates. This was to do with embassy work.

The Pughs gave John 200 cigarettes and me an attractive red leather cushion. I certainly hadn't expected anything from them and the small gifts I gave to them were really a 'thank you' for the lifts they give me and the shopping Susan does for me in emergencies. The ambassador's wife, Mrs Sarell, sent all the ladies connected to the embassy a little gift. I got a hanging calendar tea towel.

We went to the Drysdale's cocktail party on the 23rd and had the misfortune to arrive fractionally behind the ambassador. We felt rather like the dustcart following the Lord Mayor's show.

Alan's Dutch fiancée, Anika stayed with us Thursday and Friday night.

Fortunately John and I were out both evenings as they were pretty 'lovey dovey'. Alan is going to Holland in three weeks time to get married and then they will be coming straight back here. Alan is lucky as his father and the London GM are buddies and he was especially transferred here so that he could get married during his first tour. Anika is okay but I don't think I will be as friendly with her as I was with Jenny. She's rather a bouncy type and I should imagine enjoys having her own way. She is much taller than me and speaks perfect American (learnt from boy-friends).

Mr Norman's leaving is now public. He hopes to go in April. According to him he resigned, as he wasn't getting any co-operation from London. But, thanks to Joanne, we know he has been retired off. Alan knows the new GM and says he is a family man and very approachable. He isn't meant to be very generous with furnishings though, but John and I have got used to our rough stuff by now.

I've just been thinking. It's only four months before you come out. Hooray. With luck Mr Norman will be well away, so John may have more time for trips with us. It will do John good to be unworried by him as he was so much better during the Norman's ten weeks holiday away during the summer.

Elvis is quite used to being alone now. I've just cleaned his cage and popped bacon fat and lettuce in as extras. He is jumping from one to the other, having a nibble at each, and now he is on the floor cracking bird seed. He sings an awful lot when alone but as soon as I come into the room he stops.

Alan is hoping to get a dog as they will be living in Peter Howarth's Colina Verdi villa. If he gets it before the wedding I've offered to look after it for the two days he will be away.

John had some bother with a shop-keeper (Libyan) yesterday, who tried to get into the bank when it was closed, the shutters being half-way down. After a shouting match this chap threatened 'to see John later'. I'm a little worried as John will be working very late for the half year and the area around the bank will be deserted, so I hope this person forgets about it. Incidentally, he wasn't even a customer.

Today Mohamed and I cleaned through the flat. He stayed about three hours, which was very good. Still he won't have much to do tomorrow.

I hope to go into Tripoli tomorrow morning as the walk will do me good and I need a cover for the ironing board.

I stuck a lot of our Christmas cards on the lounge window, as they look very effective with the dark shutter pulled down behind them, but the condensation has caused the Selotape to become unstuck so some are falling off. I had a card from Mrs Richens, but no letter. By the way the one you forwarded on was from Alrene Benson whom I haven't heard from or written to for years.

Sorry this letter is rather late. Still you fare better than Kay and John. I will have to write to them as well today, as John hasn't written for ages.

Dorothy (Lawson) wrote and told me about the forthcoming baby, so I will be writing to her shortly. Just think though, the baby will be fifteen months old before I see it. You miss quite a few things being here.

Happy New Year,

Love from us both, Jean xxxxxx

Letter No. 67 (Handwritten on airmail paper)

30th December 1967

Dear Mum, Dad and Diane,

We received your letter at lunch time and as requested I am answering quickly but as Ramadan is due to end tomorrow or the next day I am not sure how long it will take reaching you.

We really don't know what to suggest about your holiday. You see, John couldn't possibly get leave as none is given locally here and I couldn't spend more than two days with you in Malta as it wouldn't be fair on John. It would be too much of a strain after a very long day at work for him to have to bother looking after himself. If you could see him when he eventually gets home from work I know you would understand.

Do PLEASE make it to Tripoli. We really want you here and I am so looking forward to showing you around. Just one other thing, we certainly don't expect any 'board and lodging' so you will only need a little spending money.

We haven't done anything since Christmas. John is up to his neck in work and has managed to balance as far as possible but Tripoli office with the GM, manager, and two other chaps is in the mire, so he is having to help out. Jim Deasy's replacement 'Slosh' Irving arrived yesterday, drank until 3am and overslept this morning.

Tomorrow we are meant to be going to a supper dance at the residency but I think I will be going alone as John is so busy. Hopefully, by the 6th when they have their charity ball he should be able to make it.

Young Elvis is pretty intelligent. He saw me cracking a walnut for him, watched it drop into his food container and without any hesitation hopped from his perch, picked it up and hopped back to his perch with it, where he held it in his claws and pecked at it.

We still seem to be troubled by fleas. Not only do we keep getting bitten but I have found two on me. My feet are in a very itchy state and today a flea hopped out of my furry slippers, onto my foot and proceeded towards my knee. Unfortunately I didn't manage to catch it. The slippers are now on the balcony, well pif-paffed and I am wearing my plimsolls.

At long last John has just driven up. I recognise the car by the exhaust rattle. It is 10.30pm.

Well must close as he fancies fish and chips and I must hurry so that he can get some sleep. He certainly looks in need of it, poor thing.

Happy New Year to you all
        Love from us both
            Jean xxxxxx

Letter No. 68 (Handwritten on airmail paper)

Monday 1st January (Probably)

Dear Mum, Dad, and Diane,

Thank you for your letters Mum. I'd better answer some of your queries first. Our home address is:- Villa Agosta, Sciara Di Rossi (off the Ben Ascuir), Tripoli. For my swim suit I need bust size 34" hips 36"

Geoff Bishop is still at the embassy and has broken off his engagement to the girl in England but is now going 'steady' with a nanny here. I have enclosed a cheque for £2, which is on Geoff's bank (I gave him Libyan money for it). If you could pass the money onto Grandad – or if you think it better to buy him something he needs with it, please do. I decided not to tell John as he'd only moan. I suppose he doesn't quite appreciate grandparents as he never saw any of his. Yet the funny thing is the other day he was wondering how to give his little Libyan clerk £L10 to get a new suit, without offending him. Still Grandad needn't know, which is the main thing.

Mohamed and Ali are the same as ever. Ali has grown taller and is not quite as chubby but he still has a lovely face. He smiles, waves and sometimes manages a 'hello' but basically he is very shy.

Mohamed was a great help on Thursday, when we had our party. He helped get the room ready in the morning and the following day he washed everything up and put all the empties away. The biggest surprise was Jim Deasy's engagement. He had mentioned before that he intended getting married on leave, no one in mind though. We had all expected it to be an Irish girl. Anyway he popped the question to a secretary who works for Esso, who he had been out with a few times. She is about his age and seems the type to keep him in order; quite sophisticated and good-looking.

The party was very good. Everyone more or less knew each other so John and I didn't have to bother introducing and fitting newcomers into groups. We got most of them helping themselves to drinks and our punch disappeared in no time. (2 bottles of apple-champagne, 1 bottle brandy, 1 can orange juice and bits of fruit). The food also went quickly; sausage rolls; baked potatoes stuffed with cheese; bits on toast and biscuits; an onion and garlic dip; and scotch eggs.

We had stocked up on scotch and gin especially well but we had loads left and instead the 40 bottles of beer ran out about 11.30pm. We never thought the beer would go, as it is quite cold weather.

We had to get a permit for the party and we could only have music until midnight, but as every one seemed more interested in talking than dancing it didn't matter.

Susan Pugh only had one punch and a little apricot brandy so we were trying to get her to have something else when David said, 'Perhaps a glass of milk would be in order'. I exclaimed 'You're not, are you?' and she nodded with a self-satisfied smile on her face and said 'Just.' The baby is due in September and both of them are as pleased as punch. Susan had been in two minds ever since she came here. Sally and Martin will be going to boarding school next year and she had been undecided about having another child as, on one hand she would like a baby to stop her missing the other two, but on the other hand she thought it would be nice to have no more worries.

We were meant to have a rehearsal for the 'Chalk Garden' (by Enid Bagnold) on Friday but it was cancelled, so goodness knows when we will begin as we only have a month. I even got my name in the local paper (The Ghibli) last Sunday as it gave a list of the parts and the players.

I felt really mean today as John Keeling (Vice-Consul) is giving a farewell party in two weeks time. Unfortunately he is doing it jointly with Isaam and also inviting a lot of Libyans. I didn't want to go as soon as I found out, and John isn't keen either. So today I told him that we couldn't make it and he asked if it was because of Isaam and the Libyans. I had to say 'Yes' but felt so nasty. Anyway I went and talked to Geoff Bishop about it and he said he agreed with us and although he was going (he and John share the flat anyway) he had advised his girl friend against it. The thing is that John and I like John Keeling a lot and don't want to offend him. Perhaps we will have him round here for an evening to make up.

John Keeling is a very nice chap, just 24 years old but to sum him up he is as innocent as a babe. He never understands a smutty joke and thinks of all girls as just friends. I sometimes wonder if he has ever even kissed a girl. It is a shame he is leaving before you come out (hoping Diane could teach him a trick or two) as he is very pleasant and easy to talk to.

Rupert came on Wednesday with Dick and Delia. He flopped onto the sheepskin by an opened box of chocolates. I said 'Isn't he good, he's not even prodding the chocolates with his nose'. We all looked round, Rupert looked up and then prodded the chocolates with his nose.

As you know the Whitchelows (John, Anna, and Gianna) and the Johns (Garry and Polly) live above the Bank of North Africa on the Istaklal but because of the Turkish PM's visit here they have been told by the police that they are not to have any visitors during the processions or take photographs.

We had to leave the embassy early today because the roads were being closed off. As far as I can make out, not having seen a newspaper, the PM arrived today and was driven about through hardboard triumphal arches, which had been stuck up in the middle of roads. On Monday the 24th December Independence processions take place. They are late because of Ramadan.

I haven't got to work on Monday – nor has John, but all the UK based embassy staff have to go in.

Well I'm afraid this letter won't be posted until Tuesday when I go back to work, but I'll close off now as I owe about eight other letters.

Don't forget that you mustn't mention the cheque but I'll know if you received it okay if you say you have got our address for your visas.

Lots of love from us both,

Jean XXXXXX

PARTY GAMES: Moriarty. At the mention of the above name my mind slips back fifty decades and I can still see Jim Graham sprawled on the tiled floor of our lounge, blindfolded, and banging a rolled newspaper towards a similarly equipped adversary. Each would call out 'Where are you Moriarty?' and bang the newspaper down hard where they thought their antagonist might be. I think that a 'hit' meant a change of players.

NOTES: Polly John wrote a weekly cookery column in the local paper (The Ghibli) and also baked a cake each week for Mrs Sarell that she delivered to the residency.

Letter No. 69 (Hand written airmail letter)

Friday 12th January 1968

Dear Mum, Dad, and Diane,

Thank you for your letters. We received Dad's today and are very pleased that you are getting booked up for your stay with us. We are looking forward to your next letter, with definite dates and times, very much.

Sorry not to have written before but since the embassy ball on the 6th we have been out every night. The ball was great. We made our own group and had lots of fun on the dance floor by forming circles and joining up for highland flings during twist numbers. Some of the hats were really mad, we had a flashing light house and a model bird with flapping wings in the battery operated group; a couple of birthday cakes, and lots of Christmas trees complete with baubles.

Last night we went to Garry and Polly's party at their own flat and later a smaller group ended up at the villa where they have been staying for the past week looking after the Cate's children. Ian McNab strummed away on the guitar and we quietly sang folksy songs (not to waken the children).

I had Rupert last Wednesday afternoon but as I was working he had to stay in the kitchen. Dick and Delia came for cards later in the evening. We gave Rupert his belated Christmas gift, a squeaky rubber toy. He enjoyed opening the parcel but was frightened every time the toy squeaked. When it was time for them to go he picked it up and carried it downstairs and took it partway down the road before dropping it in preference to an exciting smell. (Well I suppose it was exciting to him.)

The lights have just gone out. I am fed up with this, they went off yesterday just as I was getting ready for the party, so I had to do my make-up by candlelight. It is hardly surprising that we have these cuts as at the moment we are suffering a terrific sand storm with raging winds. I suppose a tree has fallen down on a line and broken it.

We are both fed up with the weather. It's not so much the cold, as the other discomforts it causes. Sand everywhere; a constantly gritty mouth; no lights; creaks and groans as the wind pounds on the shutters; and draughts which cause the bedroom door to keep banging open and shut. (The lock is broken). Also the doorbell isn't working and last night (when we were out) David Pugh apparently had to knock on the back door of the people downstairs, then come through their flat into the stairway before hammering on our front door.

I had a nice letter from Uncle Nobby. Thanks for forwarding it on. Sending Christmas cards seems a fairly good way of keeping in touch, although this Christmas we didn't send quite as many home.

Garry and Polly had to do some shopping one afternoon so they left the Cate's children here for a couple of hours. David is three years and Jason 4 months. As it happened Josie turned up with her seven month old Michael. Josie and I coped all right, but the mess I had to tidy up afterwards was unbelievable.

Jim Graham's tour finishes in March and Florence is going back with baby Stuart at the end of this month. She is going house hunting as Barclays give house loans and they plan to let it out when they are away. They will be coming back to Libya for another tour but not to Tripoli. They are lucky as they only do 21 months here as opposed to our three years.

Carol wrote and she and Alan are planning to buy a house. She sent two wedding photos, which are lovely.

Mr Norman's replacement, Mr Green, is due out soon and I met Jim Deasy's replacement (Slosh Irving) for the first time at Garry and Polly's party. He seems okay.

Have just received your Very Important letter. Hooray. *What a way to spend your anniversary though, up at the crack of dawn. You will find that the air trip will only take three hours because of the time difference. John thinks that Terry and Jenny used the 'City of Tunis' and weren't very impressed. I just thought I'd mention it, as if you expect the worse it doesn't come as such a shock and you will probably find it better than expected.

Tell Dad we won't be getting up at 4am to meet the boat; probably 5am will do as it is only a ten-minute drive. In that time you will see the Castle Museum; 24th December Street; the harbour road; and the New Mosque.

Your dates are very convenient as they don't involve an end of month and you will be gone by the time John has his half-year balance.

As for nosh, butter here is 3/- for half-a-pound, so I daresay it would be worthwhile your bringing some. We'd love some proper bacon as well, not those tissuey frozen packs. Also fresh Maltese mushrooms. I'll let you know what else as time goes by. Don't bring drink from England but make use of your quota on the plane, and for cigarettes as well. (200 Rothmans here cost £1.14/-). For my birthday gift I'd like a two-piece swimsuit with a heavy looking top piece and tiny tight fitting shorts as opposed to briefs. I imagine stretch denim would be the material used. Don't worry if you don't see any though, it was just an idea.

By the way I now have a 'Silver Wing' Dunlop badminton racquet. But this Tuesday I will be going to the Barbary Coast Players' meeting instead of badminton.

June can't come quickly enough.

>Love from us both,
>>Jean XXXXXX

P.S. Glad you are better now, Mum. John and I have been lucky so far, even though the weather is mostly cold and damp.

NOTES: *My parents were booking to visit us in Tripoli by flying to Malta first and then sailing to Tripoli on their wedding anniversary, 13th June.*

Letter No. 70 (Handwritten ordinary lined paper)

Friday 19th January 1968

Dear Mum, Dad, and Diane,

Thank you Diane, for your letter. I will answer it as soon as poss.

I am feeling rather sorry for myself at the moment as I have a cold. No sense of taste or smell and a wheezing chest. I am annoyed as in my last letter I remember saying how well we both were. I was meant to play hockey this afternoon (for the first time in years) but this morning when I ran from the car to the embassy to avoid the rain I realised I'd never last for more than two minutes on the hockey field.

Guess who's an actress? Amateur though. Me. I went to a casting meeting of the Barbary Coast Players and landed the third smallest part. I am the little lady in 'The Chalk Garden' and am first on stage with a 'Good morning. May one sit?' and finish on page four, with a few lines in-between. Actually I am very pleased as I don't have much to learn and if I make a hash of it it doesn't matter too much, but if I turn out okay it will give me confidence for next time. Susan Pugh, who has done a lot of amateur dramatics previously, has a fairly large part and is meant to be pregnant in it, which caused a few knowing chuckles.

We visited Jenny Havy last week. Ivan is in the desert, and her small dog is expecting puppies, due in about a week's time. Jenny not only has four children under five years, and the expectant bitch but has also taken over a little stray dachshund type puppy. I don't know how she copes. I found just having Rupert a full time job. We are visiting her again this Sunday, as Ivan should be back by then. We both like Ivan and although Jenny is a friendly chatty person she is rather a gossip and we have to watch what we say, especially about people she knows.

We had our weekly canasta game last night at Dick's. Rupert was very affectionate and tried to climb alternately on either John's lap or mine. Silly great lump.

Eruptions took place at the embassy today. Dick's girlfriend, Delia shares a flat with an English girl, Christine. Christine associates with a Libyan who knows Isaam (the Lebanese clerk in my department). Anyway Christine invited her Libyan friend and Isaam round for drinks when Dick and Delia happened to be there. During the course of conversation Isaam said that I was his secretary. This really annoyed me as I've had suspicions about Isaam and his lies relating to me before, and also a certain amount of proof from a horrible Libyan air force Captain who once told me I was Isaam's secretary. Anyway with all this 'evidence' I wrote a memo today complaining. I presented it to Mr Drysdale who passed it onto David. David was sympathetic and later spoke to Isaam. Isaam then challenged me and said he had said I was a 'consular section secretary'. I immediately called him a liar, as all three 'witnesses' (the Captain, Dick and Delia) had told me that he had said I was his secretary. Anyway we had quite a shouting match and Isaam was so mad that his eyes turned pink in anger. I didn't give in and am dreading the atmosphere at work tomorrow. Still it has all added spice to life and at least it should stop anymore of his nonsense.

Alan Smith, from the bank, gets married tomorrow. He flew to Holland on Thursday afternoon and gets back to work on Sunday. I plan to hold a Sunday coffee morning in a couple of week's time to give Anika a chance to meet other bank wives.

Florence and baby Stuart leave on Tuesday. I saw her last Tuesday, which I expect will be the last time for a good many years. These 'goodbyes' are always rather sad, as you can't hope to meet everyone again, although you always say you will.

John's people sent us a lot of prints, the colours seem wishy washy but apparently they were better on the screen. Still it was thoughtful of them and a pleasant reminder of the hot summer. Today it is wet, windy and stormy.

Well, better get on with the washing up.

> Love from us both
> Jean XXXXXX

Letter No. 71 (Handwritten ordinary lined paper)

Monday 5th February 1968

Dear Mum, Dad, and Diane,

Thank you for your letter, which I received today. You asked quite a few questions which I shall endeavour to answer.

Jim Deasy is leaving on Friday, which was why we gave our party. He gave a party last Friday and has another coming up on Wednesday. We didn't arrive at his party on Friday until 9pm thinking it was starting at 8.30pm but people were leaving when we turned up and we later found out that it had started at 7pm.

The birth announcement that you read in the Times was for Peter Bull who is First Secretary, Commercial Section. He is a pleasant chubby chappie but I don't see much of him.

I can't do much for Diane about Geoff Bishop as he is going steady with a nanny here and he is leaving in March anyway. I'm not sure if he is coming back or going elsewhere.

We gave Isaam a shock the other evening, as we were playing cards at Delia's when he called to take her flat-mate, Christine out. He didn't know what to say and he couldn't get out quickly enough. Unfortunately he is not leaving but seems to have crawled in on John Keeling's farewell party. John is too nice to see how Isaam uses him to build up his reputation. Obviously Isaam's idea is to tell his friends that he is high up in the embassy and therefore can use the embassy flats whenever he wishes. He must feel upset that his 'secretary' can't be there to help his image along.

Dick and Delia took me and Rupert out to some pre-desert land on Sunday afternoon. We three sat squashed in the front of the car whilst Rupert had all the back to himself. We stopped where the road ended and let Rupert off the lead. The sand was as smooth as silk between thousands of beetle tracks and the odd camel print. It really was an unforgettable sight. We walked and ran over the dunes until we came to a cultivated patch of land with some black Bedouin tents on the far side. We then put Rupert on the lead and walked around the field until three white desert dogs spotted Rupert and came pounding across, growling fiercely. Dick did the only thing possible and let Rupert off the lead. He trotted towards them and they all stood in a circle growling. We were petrified that they would set on him. After a little while Dick suggested that we walk away and hope that Rupert would follow us. He did. We were so relieved to have him still in one piece.

Today at work Miss Baldock (the lady with the poodle that I sat next to on the plane) came in. I told her about Rupert and the desert dogs and she said that she and some friends had been attacked by a wild looking brown and white dog at 12 kilometre beach a few weeks back. One of her friend's dog had been bitten and she had only managed to lift her own poodle up in time. Also this wild looking dog with mad yellow eyes had chased three Libyan women across the beach (barracans a-billowing in the breeze I expect). Well I said 'That was no wild dog, it was Rupert'. It really was, because Dick had told us about 'three silly women' on the beach complaining that Rupert had frightened their dogs.

We have been out practically every night last week and this coming week looks like a repeat. Anyway John has complained to Mr Norman about having to do Tripoli's work as well as his own and Mr Norman was very understanding and said he had noticed how 'Slosh Irving' (Jim's replacement) palmed off his work. So from now on John only goes to Tripoli when he can and not to do a set job there but just to help out generally. I still think it is too much but John seems happy enough.

Well I've told you all the general news first to make sure my writing efforts were not just skipped through before telling you my big news: I AM COMING TO ENGLAND FOR A FEW DAYS IN APRIL AND MAY.

Jenny and Ivan Havy were discussing the problem of finding someone to help look after their four children on their trip through France and two weeks in England. I jokingly said I would, and they thought it a smashing idea. John needed persuading, but not too much. So I have fixed leave without pay at work and should be arriving at Pontin's Holiday camp, Christchurch on April 20th.

Our arrangements are to leave here on 30th March; sail from Tunis to Marseilles, then drive up through France spending time with Ivan's family at their hotel. Then onto Cherbourg where we sail to Southampton. So I shall be in Christchurch from Saturday 20th April to Saturday 4th May.

Jenny and Ivan have a huge car (£50 off the base, it was left in June) and they have a lot of calls to make in England. We will definitely call in to see you but I am also hoping you will be able to spend some time in Christchurch. They haven't planned all their visits yet and as they are paying all my expenses I can't just go off as I please. I think it will be best to leave our own arrangements until we arrive and then I will ring you up.

The only other alternative is for you to cancel your holiday arrangements for coming to Tripoli and booking up in Christchurch instead. The only trouble with that is that you won't see John and I really want to show you around Tripoli and give you a good holiday. But on the 'for' side we have to consider the considerable saving it would be for you all. Anyway you must decide but do bear in mind that Ivan and Jenny must come first as they are paying for me.

I am not sure whether to tell Grandad or not. I would love to surprise him but then I thought it might be rather a shock for him. I will let you decide about that and then you can tell me and I will know whether or not to mention it in letters to him. I am particularly pleased at the thought of seeing Grandad again as in his last letter he got rather morbid and said he didn't think he'd ever see me again. So this flying visit should cheer him up. Also I'll just be in time for his birthday.

Well better close now, but please don't make arrangements for me to visit people as I just won't have the time, but anyone who is able to come to Christchurch (perhaps on a Sunday) I would love to see.

Love to you all, from us both,
    Jean XXXXXX

Letter No. 72 (Typewritten and handwritten on airmail paper)

Wednesday 14th February 1968

Dear Mum, Dad, and Diane,

I have been holding back on this letter hoping to hear from you regarding my visit to England. Anyway I will relate all the latest news and hope that John brings a letter from you this evening.

The play has been held up owing to the producer being ill but all being well the first rehearsal should take place this evening. Unfortunately we can't get the theatre until 9.30pm so after finishing work this evening I am hoping to sleep until 8pm otherwise I'll never keep going. Luckily I can kip down anytime and sleep soundly, so I will be getting in my eight hours per day but rather split up. However, as my part isn't too big perhaps I will only have to attend a few rehearsals.

Today I was asked if I'd like to earn about £40 by working at the Tripoli International Fair. In total it involves about six afternoons from 4pm to 9pm and one Sunday morning. John was rather dubious as he is afraid people will look upon me as being no more than a shop assistant but after pointing out that the girl who I would be replacing is the daughter of the head of the British Council here (she has just recovered from pneumonia and her mother didn't want her to over-tax her strength) and all the other women doing it have husbands well up in businesses, he relented. I think he was a bit worried as Florence Graham once took a job in a chemist shop and Barclays told Jim that she must leave.

We've been gadding about as usual. David Pugh has a craze on playing games (Monopoly, Careers and Risk) and we are more often than not the unfortunate couple picked upon to play with him, and lose. He always wins. A lot of it is luck but also he practices by himself during the afternoons.

We still play canasta but I'm afraid badminton has been given a miss lately, although I hope to go again next Tuesday.

We discovered some lovely rock structures at 12-kilometre beach (just before the popular 13-kilometre beach). It will be ideal for snorkelling and I am getting John a fishing rod so he won't get fed up whilst I am swimming. These rocks stretch right along the beach and some of them form caves. We had great fun climbing down into them from the beach and coming out just above the water line and then scrabbling up to the top again.

We met Ian and Monika on the way to the beach, just by chance, and then Dick and Delia appeared, so it was quite a jolly outing.

The weather is smashing, lovely and warm and bright. When I got home at lunchtime I opened all the windows to let the warmth in. It still gets chilly at night but not too bad. I daresay it is too good to last but might as well make the most of it.

As I'd hoped John brought your letter home this evening. I am so pleased everything seems to be working out well.

We should be seeing Jenny and Ivan on Friday. The only thing not really settled is the Pontin's booking but it is only a matter of writing to Christchurch. I should think our dates will be okay with the holiday camp, as it is rather out of season. Anyway as soon as I know they have definitely booked I'll let you know.

I have written to Jean and Derek and Jane and Alby hoping they can get to Christchurch as well, but they are the only people beside yourselves that I have made the suggestion to.

It will be great seeing you all and the middle weekend sounds fine. With luck we may get an extra visit to your flat but as I mentioned before it really depends on Jenny and Ivan. Their children are:- Paul, 5 years, Greta, 4 years, Steve, 3 years and Debbie Monic, 9 months. Paul is the least trouble; Greta is a cunning little minx; Steve is naughty, but my favourite; and the baby is a happy little thing. I think I will have to ask Jenny if I can smack them from time to time if they are difficult to control. Up to now I've always made a fuss of them knowing it was only for an hour or two but if it went on for six weeks I'd end up a wreck.

I shall write to Grandad as soon as possible and look forward to telling him the news.

We will be staying at Pontins for the whole two weeks but they will be gallivanting about for odd days visiting. I suppose it will depend on who they are seeing as to whether the children and I will be left behind at 'camp'. Naturally I shall make every effort to stay in Pontins with or without the four 'little devils' during your stay. I don't think there will be any trouble on that score as Jenny and Ivan understand that I want to see you all. We shall probably pop in and visit John's people as well, as the Havys have some friends near Cobham.

I can't think of much else to say – I will let you know when the Pontins booking is definite.

Since typing the first page John has been mulling over the Tripoli Fair proposition and has decided that on top of the play it will be too much, so tomorrow I will say goodbye to £40. I can't say I'm too disappointed, I just thought the money would be useful.

I went along to the theatre with one of the other actors this evening but there was no sign of life. Goodness knows when the rehearsals will begin. I'm getting disgruntled with the whole thing.

Dorothy and Bob's new house sounds lovely. I'm pleased to see that they have a spare bedroom!

Well I'll close off now, and say once again how happy I feel about everything.

Love from us both,

Jean XXXXXX

Letter No. 73 (Handwritten airmail letter)

Saturday 17th February 1968

Dear Mum, Dad, and Diane,

I just don't know how to write what I have to say, so prepare yourselves for the worse.

We went to see Jenny and Ivan last night and they had just received news of a posting to Beirut so all the holiday plans are dashed. Luckily, although I'd written to Grandad, I hadn't posted the letter so at least one person won't be disappointed. As if the above isn't enough we received news today that John is to be posted to Benghazi (Ben Ghastly as it is known). So unless something drastic can be done your visit to Libya is also ruined.

We should be leaving Tripoli in six to eight weeks time and probably driving to Benghazi where we will complete our tour in much anguish.

Now the only way to save your holiday that I can think of is to re-book the sea trip from Malta, going to Benghazi instead of to Tripoli. And believe me – I am keeping my fingers crossed that it can be done without too much trouble and extra expense.

Going to Benghazi has a few compensations e.g. we will have a villa with, presumably, a garden. Also we will have a vacuum cleaner and washing machine. John will be the accountant there, which is a big step up, also the manager sounds helpful. We may also be buying a larger car. I have heard of a two year old Humber going for £500 but the customs duty of about £350 will have to be paid as it belongs to an embassy chap who was exempted from duty. Anyway the car is still very much in the air but we think it will be worth it if it is in good condition as we can use it here for eighteen months and then drive home in it.

Jenny and Ivan have their original dog Brandy and her three puppies in addition to a three month old cross-dachshund to dispose of. John and I decided last night to take the three-month-old Zena as she is small, affectionate and very pretty and we intend to take her to Benghazi as the villa will be suitable for a dog. (I did think of having Rupert back! I could just imagine him being car sick all the way to Benghazi).

We intend taking two days to drive to Benghazi, so with Zena, Elvis, and the canary (which is coming soon) we shall enter town like a circus.

Although Benghazi is pretty dead I think we are looking forward to the change as most of our friends have left or are leaving Tripoli so it means starting up again here (socially) anyway. Apparently there are no places to eat out but the British community seems close knit and good at arranging their own entertainment. There is also a yacht club; golf course (of sorts); tennis and squash; and the beaches are meant to be nice.

One other big thing is that the embassy there might be interested in taking me on, but apparently there is no shortage of other work if they don't need me.

Well I'll round off by saying how sorry I am about all our arrangements but here's hoping you can manage Benghazi without too much trouble.

Lots of Love,

Jean XXXXXX

Letter No. 74 (Handwritten on airmail paper)

Saturday 24th February 1968

Dear Mum, Dad, and Diane,

I received your letter today, which sounded so cheerful about everything, but I expect you have got my other one now telling you of all our disappointments. As a final blow the Humber Sceptre fell through too.

I have just written to Len and Joyce telling them about the cancellation. Thank goodness Grandad wasn't told.

Today we had a ghibli with a temperature of ninety-four degrees Fahrenheit in the sun. Fortunately it wasn't too windy but the atmosphere felt really heavy and headache making.

Before I forget could you please tell us how to make your famous Arundel punch. We will have to have a farewell party and as we don't want to stock up on fancy drinks I think a punch would be a good idea for those who don't fancy scotch, gin or beer. John is hoping to arrange with Ortis to sell back any full bottles of drink but as you can see it will be quite a problem. We managed to get about twenty-five people into the flat before but this time the numbers will be doubled so the drink will have to be kept in the kitchen and we will need a waiter (one of the embassy messengers I expect), and probably Mohamed on the washing up. I think that for 'eats' I will do a lot of cold meat and pickles etc. and loaves of bread, leaving it out in the dining room on a help yourself basis.

We saw Jenny and Ivan last night and as Ivan is very fond of the little dog Zena, that John and I are taking to Benghazi with us, we arranged to give her back to them on our way driving home from Benghazi – that is if we are able to do the long trip through Egypt and the Lebanon. Actually six months leave is a long time so we will probably take our time driving home and also keep in the warm as long as possible. I can't bear the thought of an English winter. Still all our plans so far seem to be falling through, so I expect we will end up flying home direct. Pessimist me.

I played badminton on Tuesday after two weeks of not going and on Wednesday I was exhausted and am still as stiff and achy as anything.

Last night my wisdom teeth were playing up and when I woke my jaw was very stiff and painful. I just happened to mention it to David Pugh and he said he had a dream last night about pulling out one of his own wisdom teeth that had a four-inch long plastic root. How peculiar.

Thank you Mum for offering to make Susan's baby something but as I doubt if I shall ever see it or them again, not to worry. I suppose they may visit you next January, as they have a house in Bromley. I'll give them your address anyway. Also John Keeling and Geoff Bishop may pop in. If you don't want them to let me know – only I thought perhaps it might ease the gap a little.

John and I have bought a board game called 'Oil Prospecting' to take to Benghazi. Apparently you have to make your own entertainment there. Still we do here really, as the hotels and restaurants are pretty expensive.

Food is very dear in Benghazi, 18/- for a cauliflower and £1½ for a kilo of meat. The World Health Organisation did a cost of living census throughout the world and Benghazi was the second highest. Perhaps I may grow a few vegetables in the garden, if it is big enough.

John has just brought home your other letter. It's such a terrible shame that nothing seems to be working out right.

Yes, I will come to Malta, all being well. What I suggest you do is make you own three bookings and I will sort out my dates this end. Nothing is settled yet. If only we knew our dates for going to Benghazi I could find out about another embassy job and fix up leave.

What might be a good idea is for you to book your rooms and make a provisional booking for me to be confirmed in, say, the middle of May. You see not only is everything awkward to arrange because we haven't any set dates but also I don't know what the flights are like from Benghazi. I may even have to come to Tripoli first and then onto Malta.

I'm afraid there's no chance of John making it, especially so close to the half-year balance. I am looking forward to doing some shopping but my funds will not be as vast as they would have been had my trip to England not been cancelled. Still I shall be very happy to get some summer dresses and a couple of cocktail outfits.

I'd better close now. I can't express how sad I am at everything falling through, but Malta is better than nothing and the people are friendly there, which will certainly make a change from the locals here.

Love from us both,
Jean XXXXXX

(75a) Copy of the programme of the invitation to –

Tea at the Residence for Her Majesty the Queen of Libya

Wednesday 6th March 1968

3.00 p.m.	Embassy ladies assemble
3.15 p.m.	Diplomatic wives arrive
3.45 p.m.	Ladies take their places in hall in order of precedence to await Her Majesty
4.00 p.m.	Her Majesty arrives, is greeted by Mrs Sarell, is presented with bouquet by Alan Drysdale and enters hall to be greeted by diplomatic wives and ladies of the Embassy
4.20 p.m.	Her Majesty sits in drawing room and talks to Mrs Sarell
4.30 p.m.	Tea is served and Her Majesty goes into dining room
5.00 p.m.	Her Majesty returns to the drawing room. Ladies are taken up to talk to her for five minutes at a time.
6.00 p.m.	Her Majesty leaves

Letter No. 75 (Hand written on airmail paper)

Thursday 14th March 1968

Dear Mum, Dad, and Diane,

Thanks for your letter, Mum. What a good idea to take a flat in Malta. Though, now, of course, we don't know if we are going to *Benghazi. I'm furious – we've been messed about so much – not only have we a second-hand car lined up (fairly large in order to take our belongings with us), Zena lined up and a small stock of unusual food stuffs ready to take but also I've washed the ruddy curtains. I may even lose my job because David has found a shorthand typist to replace me. Words fail me (except unprintable ones).

The trouble is the friction between Mr Norman (who left today) and the new GM, Mr Green. Mr Green is doing everything he can to undo Mr Norman's efforts. Because Mr Norman was prepared to obey London's letter about transferring John, Mr Green is not. Because Mr Norman gave certain over-drafts Mr Green is making the people pay them off etc.etc. The worst aspect is that because John ended up being Mr Norman's blue–eyed boy Mr Green dislikes John on principal. (Still I should be in favour as Mr Norman hated me.) Oh well, enough of our muddles.

*Tea with the Queen of Libya went off very well. She seemed very sweet and not at all formal. I didn't talk with her though. In fact the drawing room was very crowded and, as there weren't enough seats, about eight of us had to stay outside. Afterwards we had a share out of the leftovers and I ended up with half a huge chocolate gateaux (about eighteen inches in diameter). I had great fun carrying it home up the street to the flat as all the Arab children started shouting 'gimee, gimee'. Ali was out playing further up the road and his eyes shone when I told him to follow me into the flat. I gave him four huge slices and made it clear that it was for him and Mohamed, but about two hours later John and I heard Mohamed giving Ali a big telling off – so I presume he ate the lot.

I had a letter from Jean Andrews and just as they had arranged to buy a new house to go with Derek's promotion Derek cracked up, after three days in his new job, saying it was too much for him. He is now on sick leave until further notice and has to see a psychiatrist. I hope Jean is exaggerating, as usual, and things aren't as serious as they appear to be.

We managed to make Tunis. We left here on Friday morning and had to waste a couple of hours at four separate customs posts (fighting our way through Arabs and Americans). We took the car on a converted rowing boat to Djerba, spending just the one night on the island and leaving for Tunis at midday. We had driven through a sand storm on the Friday and the car's accelerator pedal stuck at ninety kilometres an hour but once Dick had unjammed it the car was fine excepting for one puncture. On leaving Djerba and heading for Tunis we took a second-class road as it was less mileage. The road was constructed of hard-packed sand and in places it had been eaten away, leaving great long cracks from one side to the other. At one point we had to drive through a stagnant stream and on the other side we came upon a herd of camels. I have some lovely film of them, as I could get really close. After leaving the camels we sped on until Dick shouted something about the road disappearing and slamming on the breaks. Unfortunately we went head first into a hole and Delia cut the bridge of her nose and knocked herself out for a few minutes. Luckily the car remained upright, although well bedded in the sand at the front. It took us an hour and a quarter to dig ourselves out and we didn't see another car or person in all that time. I took a few shots of the accident once things had got back into perspective. It could have been nasty, but we were lucky.

We arrived in Tunis early evening and booked into The Claridge for two nights. On Sunday morning we browsed in the suk and then drove to Carthage to look at the ruins. We had a lovely fish lunch in a restaurant on the coast. The Carthage ruins were reasonably interesting but there isn't much left of them to get a full picture – just a few clumps of stones here and there.

In the evening we ate in the suk at a local Tunisian restaurant. The speciality starter was an egg cooked in a sort of crisp batter/pastry. As you bit into it the yolk ran out and the waiters came forward, prepared, with damp napkins to mop you up. All the meals we ate in Tunisia were excellent and very reasonably priced.

I forgot to mention that when we left Djerba we met a couple from Ireland; I don't think they were Irish though. It was obviously their annual holiday so you can imagine how bigheaded I was explaining that we had just driven over from Tripoli where John was working.

I only managed to buy one ordinary dress in Tunis mainly because we didn't have very much time for shopping, so my trip to Malta is essential.

We left Tunis about mid-day on Monday and drove through rain and storms to Gabes. We couldn't find any rooms in the big hotel at Gabes and so the four of us ended up in one large room in a small hotel. Luckily we were so tired that no one minded.

We spent a lot of time in the Gabes market place and bought a few odds and ends. We were impressed by the cheapness of everything and wouldn't mind going back with a truck some time to get some of the wickerwork furniture and woven carpets.

After our shopping we headed home. We were in the flat at 6.15pm and had to be out at 7pm for a bank cocktail party. What a rush.

It is now Sunday and the holiday seems a long way behind. John seems to be getting on better with Mr Green now. He came to see the flat yesterday and said we can get lampshades and kitchen equipment as soon as we like. He also said we can get two carpets and new china. But we think we ought to price them first.

Yesterday evening Ortis took us to the hotel ship, that is in the harbour, for a meal. (It is here for the TIF). John and I were so tired that after eating and a little dancing Ortis had to bring us home. We felt pretty bad about it but as we were in a party of ten (eight Italians) and he intended going back afterwards I don't suppose it mattered too much.

John was sick when we got in (surprisingly not drink) and had stomach-ache this morning. I sneaked back to bed after breakfast and didn't get up again until nearly 11am. We are in for yet another full week. I am out every night, or else entertaining here, until next Saturday. John has Tuesday free though, as that is badminton night for me.

Well must close, sorry this letter is much belated.

Hope you are all well,

    Love from us both,

        Jean

PS. I'm starting on a diet today.

PPS. John not working this afternoon, he has gone to bed – I hope it isn't the flu, which has affected 40% of the population.

NOTES:

   *Ref: *Benghazi. Plans had been set in motion to transfer John to the branch in Benghazi. In the end it fell through and we stayed on in Tripoli.*

   *Ref: Tea with the *Queen. The Queen of Libya, married to King Idris. She was Turkish and a lot younger than the King.*

   *Ref: *Tunis. There was a five-day public holiday that we took advantage of, travelling in Dick's Renault 4 car along with his Italian girl friend Delia.*

   *Ref: * I shall always remember the loud low pitched grunting of the camels as I walked amongst them filming. I had not realised before just how noisy they could be.*

Post Card No. 76a

March 1968
A postcard from Tunisia

Dear Mum, Dad and Diane,

We made it. We are spending tonight on the island of Djerba and hope to make Tunis tomorrow evening. Had a good drive down through sandstorms and saw lots of white baby camels. The atmosphere is most friendly and John is a changed person already. We are in a lovely little hotel and enjoying ourselves.

Love from us both

Jean.

Letter No. 76 (Handwritten airmail paper)

Monday 31st March 1968

Dear Mum, Dad and Diane,

I am sorry I didn't write last week but I was so tired that I only managed one scruffy page, which wasn't worth sending. Mind you, I had a good time getting tired.

We have now got Zena, who is a dear. She just snuggles up to you when indoors and when out walking she usually stays close. She only goes on a lead when on a main road, so is really no trouble. Her only fault is that she isn't completely house-trained. I just can't get her to understand that she must scratch at the door when she needs to go out. She isn't a patch on Rupert for mischievous behaviour and character but for the flat she is ideal.

I've also got Geoff Bishop's noisy budgie. But as I can't really keep three birds Geoff suggested I sell it at the Spring Fair to be held in the residency in a couple of weeks time.

John and I have been to three farewell 'do's' for John and Geoff – they left today. Last night we went on from the residency 'do' for the boys to Jim Graham's party at his villa. We are also going to another one for him at Cindy and Geoff's on Tuesday.

Just lately we have been going to one party after another as well as fitting in a couple of evenings at home entertaining. John has had the past two Saturdays off due to Arab holidays and I had yesterday off as well. We took Zena rock climbing at 12 kilometre beach but by the time I'd helped her up and down (owing to her short legs) John was miles in front. It was completely deserted excepting for two policemen on horseback who asked if our car was locked. The sea was the deepest blue I'd ever seen it.

Last Sunday Jenny and Ivan left three of their children with me whilst they went shopping and when they came to collect them they all wanted to stay, so I kept the eldest, Paul 5½ years, who managed to break most of John's model aeroplanes whilst playing. He, Paul, was a changed boy once the others had left, and wanted to go home. He was so quiet I didn't know what to do with him so in the afternoon we went to the Old Castle Museum with Zena and looked at stuffed animals. John and I took him back in the evening and then went for a lovely meal in a new Giorgimpopoli restaurant, The Caravan, with Jenny and Ivan. Afterwards we went to a nightclub and watched fat, ugly girls prancing around, and a skinny stripper writhing on a box with film slides projected onto a screen behind her explaining her dream. The show was saved by three chaps playing South American music, they were excellent and the audience kept them there for encore after encore.

I liked the brown swim suit very much but think I will have the turquoise colour if possible. If the sizes are 'busts' I'll have the 34" but if hips I'll need 36". I'll have to squeeze into it, my bottom is getting immense.

We received your letter this lunchtime. In answer to your question about Rupert – he was left in Dick's garden when we went to Tunisia and a neighbour came in to feed him. Dick said he was fine when he got home. According to Dick Rupert is pretty wild and enjoys being out all the time. Dick even lets him right out now as apparently Rupert has an alsation 'girl-friend' who calls round for him some-times, and they trot off together. What a difference - Zena is no bigger than a cat and so sleepy.

I hope your visit to Sue Webb goes off well. Are they still at 'Thirteen' or have they somewhere larger now?

By the way, perhaps it would be a good idea to knit Susan Pugh's baby something after all, if you have the time, as it doesn't seem so likely now that we will be going to Benghazi.

I met the Maltese, Joe Lewis (who runs the badminton) last night at the residency 'do' and I asked him about quarantine for dogs in Malta. I have been worrying about Zena being left alone for most of the day when I am with you. He seems to think it would be three months. But then his wife kindly offered to look after her for my holiday with you. Zena is so affectionate it would really upset her to be left alone all the time John is at work. She cries and trembles when I get home at half-past-one and it takes me at least five minutes to calm her – yet I think she is reasonably happy on the balcony.

Poor John has been summonsed to Tripoli office once he has finished at Giorgimpopoli as, apparently, Nigel's work is so up the creek that they want him to help out. I'm so annoyed as he didn't get home for lunch until 4pm today, as it is the end of the month, so I don't expect him back before 9pm this evening.

One last favour to ask – could you please get the book 'The Defenders' by Geoffrey Cousins (Muller, 35/-). It's a secret for John, as I know he would like it.

Must close as he has just arrived home – only 8.15pm – Big Deal.

Love from us both,
Jean XXXXXX

Letter No. 77 (Handwritten on airmail paper)

Saturday 6th April 1968

Dear Mum, Dad, and Diane,

What a rotten day today. I've been sneezing my head off and we have had a vicious sandstorm. Now I think it is going to rain, so I expect the electricity will be cut off too.

My newest pets have been causing trouble. As you know Geoff's budgie was meant to be sold at the Residency Fair but 'dear' Isaam found out and said he'd have him for £L2. So I hastily said he'd been promised to Susan for her stall so Isaam bought entrance tickets and said he'd get him there. I just couldn't let Isaam have 'Budgie' as he poked pencils at him when Geoff first gave him to me at work. Anyway I told Bob Ayres (Radio and Communications Department at the embassy) and he said he'd think about having him. So I came home, changed and broke the news to John that the budgie wasn't going. He was furious so I said that Bob was definitely taking him. Well, after the Fair we collected Bob, who was to have a meal with us before taking John to the embassy basement for a game of snooker. Bob was not really interested in the bird but said he'd think about it.

When they had gone I sneaked off to bed and pretended to be asleep when John got back. But the next morning I was really in the dog-box. So I told Bob about the rumpus in the Tungate household all because of one little budgie and he said he'd take it. So next week, all being well, he goes.

Now it's Zena's turn. We (Zena and I) had walked into town and back and she seemed tired on getting home so was snoozing peacefully on the sheepskin. John came back from work made a fuss of her and then washed his hair. He came into the lounge for me to check that his parting was straight and went to stroke Zena again when he noticed that her face was puffy. I said it was probably to do with her loosing her puppy teeth. After five minutes I went and had a good look at her and saw that her nose was swollen and one eye nearly shut. 'Quick, John' I shouted. 'She's got mumps or rabies or something'. We drove to Giorgimpopoli and found that the vet was still open. He took one look at her and said she was suffering from an allergy. He then dosed her – a pill in her mouth, an injection in her leg and a pellet up her bottom. Poor little thing.

This morning she was her usual self.

We played cards at Dick's on Thursday and I was astounded at the size of Rupert in comparison. Zena is probably only as big as his head and neck. Still he is a lovely dog and really my favourite of the two, not John's though.

The Residency Fair was quite good and we met lots of people we hadn't seen for some time. I took Zena along and she behaved well.

We went to *Cindy and Geoff's party on Tuesday but didn't enjoy it very much. John was tired and the people weren't very lively.

Susan Pugh's mother is out for three weeks and Polly's parents came on Thursday. Susan's Mum seems a dear old soul and the children won't leave her alone, which pleases her, I think.

I'm not sure if I mentioned in my last letter about a game called 'Risk' that we have tried to get here. It is a Waddington game and the board is quite large so even if you see it, it may not be convenient to bring out. If you think you can manage it please let me know and we will call off the search here. Anyway do get one for yourselves as it is first-rate. David Pugh has got John and myself trained up, as well as several other neighbours and he plays nearly every night.

It was funny the other evening as he came to see if we would like a game, but we were already going out so we gave him a whisky and then we all left the flat together. John and I got in the car and passed him calling on Sheila and another lady, Pat, from around the corner. He really is addicted to the game.

Not very much news this week I'm afraid. The tour here may be cut to two years for us, but I doubt if we will be home in September even if it is. Perhaps we will get away in February. It will be good for John if it is but not so good for our savings as I doubt if I'll get such a well paid job elsewhere.

I hope to make my booking next week and will let you know. I must be out on 13th June though, for your anniversary. We still haven't heard from London

regarding Benghazi.
  Love from us both,
    Jean xxxxxx

NOTES: *Geoff Humphries was Jim Graham's replacement at Barclays Bank, Tripoli. They had moved into Jim and Florence's flat. Cindy found a job at the embassy and we became good friends, working just across a corridor from each other.

Letter No. 78 (Handwritten on airmail paper)

Saturday 13th April 1968

Dear Mum, Dad, and Diane,

Thank you for your letter. I am sorry you are all a bit under the weather but in two months time all should be well.

I have made my air booking. Unfortunately on Wednesdays they only have Kingdom of Libya Airlines flying to Malta and as I want to be with you for your anniversary I have put my life in the hands of a two-engine, forty-seater plane with a French pilot. HELP.

The flight leaves Idris Airport at 7.45am and reaches Malta at 8.05am (only 20 minutes). I intend leaving Malta on Thursday 27th at 3.45pm and get back to Idris at 5.50pm (2 hours 5 minutes). I suppose the actual flight is about 1½ hours each way as the times quoted are local times. Perhaps you could tell me whether you will be able to meet me at 8.05am or if I should take a taxi to your flat (which will probably be our best bet as I expect you will be very tired).

Do you want me to bring a sheepskin for you, or will it be too bulky to take back?

Surprise, surprise. John has got Easter Sunday off. The first Christian holiday he has had here. I expect we will have Christmas off this year as well. Mr Green, the new GM is very good in my opinion, although John doesn't like working with him much.

It was so funny on Thursday afternoon as John had decided to take it off so that we could look at the new Morris cars which had just arrived in Tripoli. He said he hoped no one would ring up Giorgimpopoli as he hadn't told anyone he was sneaking the afternoon off. Well, we passed 'Slosh' Irving on the way and then, as luck would have it, we bumped into Mr Green at the actual show garage. Mr Green was looking at sports cars for his wife and he came across to us as we were clambering in and out of a Mini-Traveller. He was very pleasant though and reckoned the Traveller was a good buy.

John and I decided on an off white Traveller without the wood trim. It is roomy in the front but any rear seat passengers would be cramped as a) I couldn't get my knees in straight and b) my head was touching the roof. Still, with the back seat collapsed there is heaps of room for luggage. Cars cost a fortune here. This one was £L642. Still, we hope to get £L300 for the Fiat.

Zena is doing well and her house training is coming along nicely. The people downstairs gave me a tennis ball for her so I can exercise her without exercising myself too much. She will only eat fresh meat so I have to get her cheap stewing steak and have it minced. It is a good job she is small otherwise she would prove rather expensive to keep.

Yesterday an Australian neighbour Sheila, along with Zena, Ali and myself had a good game round the back of the flat with the ball.

On Monday I had helped Sheila bath her new five-week old kitten. I had noticed a couple of fleas on it but once it was in the water about fifty came to light.

This morning I have washed our 'numdha' lounge carpet and feel exhausted. Zena has also been bathed so the flat is wet from one end to the other.

Yesterday, Sunday, we went to a curry lunch at Dr and Mrs Lass' villa. John was busting for a wee on the way home so we popped in on Gwen and Eric's as we were near their villa.

Our social life has come to a standstill now. We just have a card evening on a Wednesday and an afternoon trip on Friday arranged. It is funny how some weeks we have lots of things and others we have nothing much. Still I enjoy reading at home and going to bed at a reasonable time so I don't mind these 'slack' weeks.

The weather seems to be brightening up again. We seem to get chilly winds, though.

I can't think of anything else to say so I'll close now.

Love from us both,

Jean XXXXXX

JEAN SHELDON

Letter No. 79 (Handwritten on pink airmail paper)

Thursday 25th April 1968

Dear Mum, Dad, and Diane,

Thank you for your letters. Just lately I haven't been in a letter-writing mood so that is why mine are later than usual.

It was so funny as the same day that Dad's letter arrived with the newspaper cutting about a fart expert, we had a letter from Kay enclosing a filthy rhyme. John and I decided we had a right lot of parents between us.

Zena is still okay. I'm trying to train her to 'sit' and 'stay' when I say so, and not just when she feels like it.

Last night we had Garry and Polly round with Polly's parents and the Pughs with Susan's mother. Susan's mother so took to Zena that she may get herself a little dog when she is home.

Garry was the last one to have a 'pee' at our place as the loo broke when he flushed. It was a good job that David was here as he rushed home, taking the inside of the toilet cistern with him and fixed it up well enough to stop it over-flowing. Unfortunately we daren't use the toilet properly until it is mended.

Friday – Toilet now mended (£L4½) so crisis is over. Actually it is marvellous to have a quiet flat after so long of putting up with continual broken plumbing noises from the bathroom.

Some of the prices you quoted came as rather a shock as a small loaf here is only one shilling. Your meat is still cheaper but our sugar is only one shilling a kilo (you buy it loose). Mind you, our frozen foods put the bill up - about six shillings for four servings of frozen vegetables. The thing is that the Libyans have put huge import taxes on all the foodstuffs that they know only the Europeans use.

Enclosed is a cheque for Grandad for his birthday. I'm sorry I haven't sent him any extra for ages but by the end of the week all my housekeeping and my own £L3 seem to have disappeared. It is amazing how I get through £L18 (£L3 for Mohamed and the rest on food). Also you must prompt me when Valerie's 21st is due.

Sorry my writing is so appalling, I hope you can understand it. I will close now as excepting the usual jaunts nothing much has happened.

Hoping Dad's knee is improving, and you are all well,

    Love from us both,

      Jean XXXXXX

Letter No. 80 (Handwritten on airmail paper)

Friday 3rd May 1968

Dear Mum, Dad, and Diane,

You may even get an early letter this week, providing I finish this today.

There's a bit of trouble at work at the moment. The embassy is expecting a visit from the inspectors in June and they have therefore arranged that we work longer summer hours i.e. 35 hours per week. The idea is that we go in from 8am to 1.30pm and come back for two hours on Wednesdays. Well I think it is fine that the UK based staff do so but not us locally engaged. You see, some of the oil companies only do 37 hours and the secretaries get full pay (about £L150 a month) whereas we only get paid for part-time, £L70 a month. Also our letters of appointment state that summer hours total thirty-three. Anyway us six 'Embassy Ladies' have all written minutes protesting about working Wednesday afternoons.

Zena was so funny today. John was out when I got home from work so I took her for a walk during which time John arrived home. Well, Zena must have picked up John's scent outside the main front door as she started wagging her tail and yelping excitedly. She pounded up the stairs and threw herself at the inner door and made such a fuss of John you would have thought he'd been gone a year.

Susan's mother went home yesterday and on Wednesday we went over for drinks. There were quite a few other people present and John got on very well with my 'enemy' Rex Mowforth from the embassy. According to John conversation started off in the normal way tapering off to slurred comments and fixed grins by the end of the evening. John was in a very bad way and after helping him home I stuck him on the front balcony to watch whilst I took Zena out alone. (Something I hate doing after dark here). Still, I don't object to him getting sozzled when we haven't got to drive home.

We washed and polished the mini once more today and as Dick had helped John mend the Fiat's brakes, thus saving us about £L10, I have nearly persuaded him to buy a car vacuum cleaner. I think we will come to a sharing arrangement with the Pughs – they use ours for their car and we use their larger one to vacuum our flat.

These car cleaners run off the battery and with our journey home in mind I think it would be a useful thing to have.

Sunday 5th

Thanks for your letter which I received yesterday. Last night we went along to the British Council where they were showing 'The Card'. It was quite funny in parts. The Council get these films every few months under the heading 'Educational'. The last one we saw was 'Genevieve' but they had trouble persuading the Libyan authorities as to its educational value.

It's very hot today and I have pulled most of the shutters down to keep the flat cool. I think, though, that it will cool off a little before May is through but will build up again for June and July.

The birds have just been cleaned out and true to form Elvis has immediately bathed and messed the cage up. Zena is waiting for her lunch to get cool (mince and baked beans today). The other day I was cooking her mince with potatoes and greens, when John came home. He lifted the lid and commented that it 'smelt funny'. I laughed so much as he had thought it was ours. Poor chap, it shows what a great cook I am.

Just in case I don't have time to write to Diane could you tell her not to worry too much about presents for us – perhaps I'll see something in Malta that takes my fancy.

The shops in Tripoli seem a little better now regarding clothing. I even saw a pleasant summer frock for £3.8/- and, of course, some of the *British made things have gone down in price.

I am finding letter writing more and more difficult now as everything seems so normal nowadays. It is a shame that you won't be seeing how we live here but we will be going to other Arab countries in the future I expect, so if they prove nice postings it may be worth your while to visit us then.

Dick was saying the other evening how he accepts things here now but that he still likes looking at the sun setting behind palm trees and how he always feels amused seeing an Arab riding a donkey. This is true enough but I can't keep writing about the same things.

I have put an advertisement in the Lizzie Club to sell the Fiat. I hope someone comes soon as we made it look nice and shiny on Friday. I felt rather sad when John drove it into a spare carport; it seemed unkind in a way.

Love from us both, Jean XXX

PS. Dad, I hope your knee is responding to treatment as I want to see you water-skiing in Malta.

NOTES: *British imports had gone down in price due to sterling devaluation.

Letter No. 81 (Handwritten on pink airmail paper)

Sunday 12th May 1968

Dear Mum, Dad, and Diane,

This is not toilet paper Mum but best British Embassy scrap, paid for by the British tax-payer.

This last week has been one ghibli after another taking the temperature right up to 107 degrees Fahrenheit last night. I reckon 100 degrees has been the average lately. Fortunately it has cooled off today and I am able to let a breeze through the flat.

This morning I went shopping at 8.15am hoping to spend the rest of the morning cleaning and washing but I discovered I'd stupidly locked myself out. Mohamed wasn't to be found so I went to see a neighbour, Pam, who has a broken ankle and likes Zena. I came back to the flat at 11am and still Mohamed wasn't around and all three neighbours in the road that I felt I could ask to drive me out to Giorgimpopoli were out by that time. So poor Pam had to accommodate me again. Anyway I lunched with her and went back when John arrived home, what a wasted morning though.

With much borrowing of china and cutlery from Nigel I managed to invite six people for a meal on Thursday evening. We began with shrimp cocktails, then chicken casserole (one can of condensed celery soup and two of condensed mushroom soup – very good) and for pudding I made a choice of jelly and fruit or apricot pie, both with cream. I was surprised when nearly everyone asked for a bit of each of the desserts. An odd mixture.

Zena has had two severe 'telling-offs' for chewing our carpet. It now has three holes in it – one hole is about six inches long and three inches wide. Fortunately it is only the old Numdha that we got from Terry and Jenny for £L1 but it could have been the new one we've been promised.

The embassy 'strike' worked and we six ladies have been told that we need only come back on Wednesday afternoons when our heads of department think it necessary.

It hasn't been very happy at the embassy this last week as Peter Bull in Commercial Section lost his three-month-old baby son. Peter was in Benghazi when it happened and had to be rushed back. He was a lovely baby and I felt so sad typing out the death certificate; it only seemed a short while ago that I'd written the birth certificate.

I managed to buy a cotton dress in town for £L4, which isn't bad for here. I bought sandals as well. One pair cost £L2 and the other pair £L1.2/-. They were in a Bata shop.

We haven't managed to sell the Fiat yet but I intend putting an advertisement in a daily paper on Tuesday.

I have just had my hair cropped really short and the hairdresser made a good job of it. I feel rather penny-pinching though, as I just go in for a cut nowadays because he usually sets it too tight.

I am hoping to do a spot of water skiing soon so I shall be able to show off to you in Malta. Only a month to go, I am so looking forward to it. Fresh mushrooms and take-away Chinese food I hope.

By the way I have to get an entry permit for Malta, so I expect you will need one as well. It isn't taken too seriously and if you can't get it Luigi assures me that you will be given one at the airport on arrival. The only problem is that the airline may not want you to travel without it.

Polly is going to make me a dress for June 8th (Queen's Birthday). I chose the pattern and material yesterday. The dress has a fold down the front, or should I say pleat. I hope it turns out okay.

This letter has been hanging around for several days, so I will close off now,

Love to you all,

Jean XXXXXX

PS. Have just received your letter. I'm pleased John Keeling is going to visit you, he is a very pleasant person with no airs or graces. Thanks for all the news about *Judith Scandling. I love hearing how people are getting on. What nice names she chose for her baby.

Poor *Eileen, they seem to be having a very rough time. I hope the treatment works okay.

Do give my love to the *Ashbys and say we look forward to seeing them when we get home.

Yes, I will be bringing my movie camera. I want you, Mum, to take some films for me as the ones we saw that you had taken were excellent. Mind you our Tunisian one was pretty good – seem to have learnt by our mistakes.

Well I'll go and finish cooking lunch.

Love Jean.

NOTES:

Judith Scandling a neighbour from Pelham Road.

Eileen. My Uncle Terry's ex wife. She had been diagnosed with breast cancer. Terry

had left Eileen for Josie (who was his sister-in-law by marriage)
*Dorothy and Bob Ashby were good friends of the family. Their daughter, Rosalind
had been our bridesmaid in June 1965 when aged three years.*

Letter No. 82 (Handwritten airmail letter)

Monday 20th May 1968

Dear Mum, Dad, and Diane,

Yesterday I went to the beach for the afternoon. I didn't swim as the water
was too cold. The warm Mediterranean from last summer has spoilt me, so I
intend waiting another couple of weeks. Zena had a lovely time and got filthy
racing around with three other small dogs.

On Wednesday we went to Polly and Garry's for a meal and when we got
home I was ill with a stomach upset. This upset still hasn't left me and last night
I was up twice with it so today I decided to skip work. I have been trying to
contact a doctor but when I went across to Susan's to use her phone she was
asleep in bed so I will have to go over later.

We went to Gwen and Eric's on Thursday and they are very annoyed with
Jenny and Ivan, as the mother of the pups, Brandy, is still roaming around
homeless - poor little thing. Yesterday, though, I met some people and discovered
that they had originally said they would take her but they aren't very keen now
as she has been wandering around and hasn't had any rabies injections. So it
seems that nobody wants her. I wouldn't mind having her as well as Zena but
John says 'NO'. I feel pretty bad as everyone says they like Zena as she is quite
attractive but no one wants ugly little Brandy. But I couldn't give Zena up and
take Brandy instead although I wouldn't mind her as a 'second'.

Eric brought a Libyan over yesterday to look at the Fiat and he is coming back
this evening to discuss the price with John. I hope we sell it soon as it is wasted
just sitting in a spare carport. John is using it today though, as the Traveller is in
for its first service.

Can't think of much to write about really. The weather has settled and is
building up gradually for the summer now that the ghiblis have died off.

The gaffer that I arranged to clean Piccola Capri beach has apparently been
scraping the seaweed from the water's edge and burying it in shallow holes on
the beach. I will have to get him to burn it instead. Also, judging by the crowd
there on Sunday, I think I will have to give him a pay rise and get him working

three days a week instead of two.

I give out the Piccola Capri passes at the embassy and collect about 10/- each time towards paying the gaffer. These passes are only for British subjects so it is a bit awkward where you have mixed marriages.

We had three noisy little children in Consular Section the other day and I took them into Harry Hogarth's room as he likes children. But just as they were settled around his desk H.E. walked in to see Harry. I was pretty embarrassed but Harry said it didn't matter.

Zena managed to completely ruin the carpet on Friday by chewing a gigantic hole in it. John and I were having a siesta and she must have got bored. I only hope she doesn't get up to any expensive tricks when I'm in Malta.

Well I think I'll see if Susan is up now and try to contact a doctor. I hope you are all keeping well.

Love from us both,
    Jean XXXXXX

PS. Tuesday. Fit as a fiddle today, thank goodness.

Letter No. 83 (Handwritten airmail paper)

Sunday 26th May 1968

Dear Mum, Dad, and Diane,

Thank you for your letter. I am so pleased that John Keeling visited you. He wrote and told me about the pleasant evening and how he liked the flat.

Don't worry about bringing mushrooms from the UK as you can get them in Malta easily. In fact Polly is thinking of growing some. You may well laugh at my cravings but I love mushrooms and Chinese food and they seem to be two more of the things you can't get here.

Kay wrote and told us of the lovely time they had with you last week. I am so pleased that you get along well (in small doses I expect).

You must tell me about the barn dance, was it easy to join in? What did you wear?

We managed to sell the Fiat but only for £L250, which was less than we'd hoped. Still it will be a bit more when the money reaches UK, and John is relieved of one more problem.

The Morris went in for its first service during the week and it came out filthy dirty and with the back bumper smashed into the bodywork. We were so angry and upset. The garage said they would mend it free of charge today but John couldn't take it in as the bank's electricity was off yesterday and he had too much to catch up on.

I had three tries at water skiing on Wednesday but still couldn't get up on the wretched things.* I must admit that the boat wasn't pulling away quite fast enough, but others seemed to managed it.

It so happened that John had come to the beach to watch the skiing and was standing beside an army major as I made my attempts to get up on the skis. The major was exasperated and said to John 'I've told her a hundred times to keep her arms straight and legs bent, not the other way round'. John diplomatically kept quiet about the fact that I was his wife.

Actually I had made myself feel quite poorly when trying as I had bounced along so far on my bottom that I had almost given myself the equivalent of an enema. I will have to wear plastic pants under my costume next time!

I seem to have a psychological problem at the moment regarding swimming in the sea. It all stems from the big fright I had last October when John's people were here and I saw that huge fish. Ever since then I have had little inclination to swim. Anyway I couldn't get to sleep the other night for thinking about it but I think it has worked its way out of my system now and I feel a little braver. I was so frightened on Wednesday that I had to wear a life jacket in case I panicked.

On Friday afternoon we went with Zena to Joe Lewis's villa where she will be staying when I come to Malta. I am a little worried as they live on a busy road but Pat said the gates are always kept shut. The children seemed fond of her so she should have a happy time. I bought a special brush for her and her coat is like a mirror now. Two people I know who have kept dachshunds say that there is no dachs in her and that she is a terrier mixture. Still it doesn't bother us at all; she is still attractive and lively.

On Friday evening we had a meal at Sheila and Owen's with another couple (they live down the road). We had a great time and didn't leave until nearly 3am. I only had three hours sleep that night. Luckily I managed to sleep on Saturday afternoon as we went to Bob's (from the embassy) in the evening.

We have another busy week ahead and on Friday, John's birthday, we are going to a drinks party given by the Wildes (John Wilde, the new Vice-Consul and his wife Jeanette). I have been threatened with murder if I mention that it is his birthday (24th) but I thought it would be good fun if I did as we could give him the bumps on the embassy roof. (John and Jeanette have an upstairs flat in the embassy building).

Better close, I'm very tired once more, even although I've had three hours sleep this afternoon.

Love from us both,

Jean XXXXXX

Letter No. 84 (Handwritten airmail paper)

Sunday 2nd June 1968

Dear Mum, Dad, and Diane,

Thanks for your letter. I hope Eileen will be all right after the operation, poor thing. We had a death in Tripoli last week caused by cancer. He was a dear old man who had made his money here and was planning to retire to the Lebanon. Actually we had two deaths last week, the other was very tragic involving a twenty-five year old Canadian who drowned. Apparently it was very rough in the sea and this chap went in up to his chest and got bowled over by a large wave and dragged out by an undertow. It was all so stupid as he couldn't swim and should never have gone in in the first place. Swimming here is generally the safest you could ever wish for and if he could have swam he would still be alive today.

Anyway Luigi was happy – he loves death and all the pomp and ceremony that goes with it. Two in one week was too good to be true for him.

By the way if we meet the Pughs in Malta don't mention anything about the embassy that I have told you, just in case I shouldn't have said anything. (It's hush hush.)

John thanks you for his birthday cards. I gave him a 'paint by numbers' Chinese scroll. It is on a sort of gold cloth and should look lovely when finished. I can't stand the plastic models he keeps making and I thought the scroll would be more use when finished.

Guess what – Anika (who's husband Alan works in Tripoli office) is having a baby in December. It should coincide with their first wedding anniversary.

I have made a grave error. Without paying any attention to dates I have invited several girl friends for tea on Wednesday. Wednesday happens to be June 5th, not only our wedding anniversary but the anniversary of the Six-Day-War. Rumour has it that the troubles will flare up once more. The funny thing is that I had planned a tea party on the same date last year. (No one turned up, naturally.)

Zena had her allergy again yesterday, a poor swollen faced little creature. John says I have caught it today, as my nose is twice its normal size and beacon red owing to three insect bites. If it hasn't gone down by tomorrow I shall turn my desk round at work so that my back is to the counter and I shall refuse to serve anyone.

I went for a casting meeting for a play-reading last Tuesday and came away disappointed. The rehearsal reading takes place next Tuesday so I shall go along and learn how it should be done.

Antigone is being put on in the residency grounds whilst I'm away. I have been lumbered with forty tickets to sell and when I asked this girl, Thelma, if she wanted any she said she wasn't that hard up for an evening out. Oh, Well.

I went into town yesterday and saw some lovely towelling beach dresses for only £L3½ and with matching bags, plastic lined, for the same price. We (Sheila and me that is) actually went in for tennis racquets but they were all too expensive. Anika said that she has one that I could have so I think I will take her up on that and bring Sheila one from Malta.

Zena has developed a charming habit of eating her food then waddling to where you are sitting – flopping down at your side and burping twice. She is a very sturdy dog and getting rather plump. I think she and I are due for a diet soon. My weight has gone up to nine stone and it is all on my bottom (and nose at the moment).

Will close off now – love to you all,

From us both,

Jean XXXXXX

Letter No. 85 (Handwritten on airmail paper)

Sunday 30th June 1968

Dear Mum, Dad, and Diane,

I hope you had a pleasant journey home and not too many difficulties with the trains. I was lucky as Alf insisted on coming out to the airport with me and intended waiting for my plane to leave. As it happened though, I met some more embassy people, the Mowforths, and I managed to persuade Alf that I would be okay. They were so kind to me that I hope to see them when on leave.

John met me alright and I was through immigration and customs in ten minutes. He was so pleased to see me that he had not even had any lunch. As far as I can gather he was out nearly every evening and only cooked one proper meal for himself.

We have been out every evening and are booked up until Wednesday. Monday should prove interesting as we are going to a Canada Dominion Day celebration at a Canadian's villa. We don't know our host but he invited all the Consular Section.

We collected Zena on Friday*. She must have been very happy with Thelma and Dave as she was not even excited enough to dribble wee, as is her wont, when she saw us. Still she came away happily enough and headed straight for her favourite spot in the garden. She had a bit of trouble with the stairs to begin with (like she did when we first had her). She looks so funny when she trips up them, as her tummy hits them before her legs have regained their balance.

The birds are also back, in tip-top condition and Polly loved her Maltese Cross present.

John liked all the dresses I bought excepting the natural coloured one from Marks and Spencers which he isn't too keen on.

Well I must close off now, but before I do, thank you very much for the marvellous time I had and for putting up with my countless shopping expeditions.

Lots of Love,

Jean XXXXXX

Added by John in his handwriting:

I must just add a few lines to thank you very much for my presents. I am surprised that Jean allowed you to give me the scotch, as she complains enough about my drinking habits. Still, thanks also for looking after her for me,

Love, John.

*NOTES: *ref. Zena. I must have had a change of heart about who was to mind her whilst I was away.*

Letter No. 86 (Handwritten on airmail paper)

Monday 8th July 1968

Dear Mum, Dad, and Diane,

Many thanks for your letter Dad. Glad to hear that your journey home was a good one. I take it Diane made her lunch date with Geoff?

Please give my love to the Clarks when you see them, I expect John and I will see them when on leave.

We hadn't heard from Dorothy and Bob so your news about their baby was new to us. I am so pleased for them.

As you probably gathered from my last letter, our social life has been 'all go'. Unfortunately we had to drop out of some as John had been so busy at work with the half-year end.

We have sent off all our invitations for our party on 25th. We have asked 38 people but I doubt if they can all come. Anyway it was the nearest I could get to the 26th*.

Quite honestly I can think of very little to tell you. I will try to finish off the film and send it to you soon.

When you mail back all the films I would be pleased if you could let us have 20 or 24 invitation cards. We have more or less got to hold a more formal party in October for some of the more elderly people we know and owe invitations to. I would like some really nice cards. Not flashy but perhaps a gold edge or crinkly edge. I expect they will cost about six pence each.

Many thanks.

Well I'll close now, sorry about the shortness of the note,

Love from us both,

Jean xxxxxx

NOTES:
*26th July, Diane's twenty-first birthday.

Letter No. 87 (Typed on airmail paper)

Friday 19th July 1968

Dear Mum, Dad, and Diane,

Thank you for your letter which I received yesterday. The news about Valerie* has set me thinking as it makes you, Mum and Dad, a great aunt and uncle. By the way do you know what it makes Diane and me? Some sort of cousin, I suppose.

*Pleased to hear about Vivien and Bruce. I haven't heard a word from Dorothy and Bob regarding Duncan, so I don't know whether to drop them a line or sit and sulk because they didn't let me know personally.

I think I told you that our party is all fixed for the 25th (It will continue into *26th I expect, so I shall be thinking of Diane). We have asked just over 40 people and are expecting them all to come. I shall stick to those mushroom and chicken pasties and buy some pizzas. Then cook some chicken limbs and lay out bread, cheese, ham and pickles. The beer is going in the bath with slabs of ice (5/- a metre) and the kitchen will have all the other drinks, along with an ice box filled with cubes of ice from the Wheelus hospital.

I always get the jitters before having a party in case it flops but I am looking forward to this one as Sheila has said that she will help me get the food prepared and John will probably take the afternoon off to make up the punch.

We went to one of the Green's cocktail parties last night. He held it in his garden and due to insects bothering the ladies he spent most of his time crouched down squirting 'Off' over bare legs. (I wouldn't have any on mine as I couldn't find the magic word 'pyrethrum' on the can). We are going to another cocktail party on Saturday, which is a farewell one for the Munros, to be held at the residency. I shall probably wear my beige dress with the frill round the collar.

Last Sunday I went swimming with Polly at the residency pool. As it is very small but quite deep I spent most of my time diving from the springboard. I certainly don't improve, as the next day my lower ribs were just one big ache due to diving incorrectly.

The other evening we were driving, on our way to Polly and Gary's for a meal, when another car cut across our path to go down the Istaklal. John just kept going causing the other car to swing over to the wrong side of the road and I saw the girl passenger (who was nearer our car) move right over in her seat for fear. I nagged John for not giving way, even though he was in the right, as the couple looked English. He said he'd teach the b...... a lesson. Anyway we arrived at Polly and Garry's bank* and another couple joined us in the lift. Being typically British we travelled up in silence and didn't speak until we discovered that we were all going to the same front door. It was only when we were eating that I remembered that the b....... in the car had fair hair and his girl friend black hair. So, very nicely, I asked him what sort of car he drove. Needless to say it was the same couple. John told him off and after that we all got on very well, which was surprising.

I had to work on Wednesday afternoon as Luigi is away and David thought I should go in as Isaam has to work extra afternoons. Therefore I have managed at long last to write to John's great aunts and Grandad. I am also typing this at work.

Malta seems far behind me now and I don't know how John manages to keep going without a break. Mr Green has asked Nigel to check around other banks and companies to find out their length of contract and holiday arrangements so I am keeping my fingers crossed that the tour may be cut. Whether we will benefit I don't know. I would really like to finish the tour next March or April so that we have a summer leave.

Zena is still bouncing around and getting quite naughty when I take her out in the morning without her lead. Her favourite trick is to find a nice smelly old bone and either run all around people's gardens with it whilst I chase her shouting 'Drop it' (which she never does) or else she will take it under a parked car to munch it. She seems to pick up a lot of tics in her ears and I often get out as many as four in one day. She is very brave though, as it must be painful when I am pulling them out. She had one the other day right down in the ear which I found difficult to reach, even with the tweezers, it must have been tender for her. John makes a huge fuss of her and spends a lot of time picking her up and generally teasing (she loves it). Whenever she meets a man who she takes to she will roll on her back waiting for her tummy to be tickled.

The weather has been very hot these past few days and yesterday I kept going quite dizzy with it. It seems funny that you are worried in case the weather for Diane's party is bad whilst I am worried in case it is too hot for ours.

Can't think of much else to say (Malta seems to have spoilt my regularity in letter writing, as now I realise it is so much easier to talk and don't feel like writing everything down). We will have to get a tape-recorder each and do it that way!

Love from us both,
Jean XXXXXX

PS. I am enclosing a postcard which you could perhaps forward on for me to Maureen and Alf.

PPS. Determined to use up that film this afternoon so that I can post it to you. By the way, Diane, I managed to get you a lipstick but couldn't get the pink one, neither could I get those stockings.

NOTES:
   *Valerie was my first cousin, daughter of my Uncle Terry (my Dad's eldest brother). She was a year or so younger than me.
   *Vivien and Bruce were family friends.
   * Dorothy and Bob were also family friends who had just had a son, Duncan – brother to Rosalind.
   *26th July – my sister's 21st Birthday.
   *Polly and Garry's flat was above the British Bank of the Middle East in Tripoli where Garry worked.

Letter No. 88 (Handwritten on blue airmail paper)

Monday 29th July 1968

Dear Mum, Dad, and Diane,
   I hope you had a lovely birthday Diane. I expect you are really getting excited about your party now. I do hope the weather is fine.
   The weather was extremely hot – ninety-five degrees when we held our party but I managed to get quite few people to dance. It was a smashing party and I thoroughly enjoyed it. Mrs Agosta sent up a huge bunch of flowers from the garden, which I thought was very kind of her. The chicken and condensed mushroom soup pasties went down very well. I used nine packets of puff pastry on them.
   At the party Anna and John, and Polly and Gary were persuaded to perform their well honed 'ballet' to (I think) Johannes Brahms' Hungarian Dance No. 6 in D major. They pirouetted holding ridiculous poses whilst keeping their faces dead-pan throughout, finally finishing with Polly and Anna leaping into the air to be caught and cradled in their respective spouses arms – most impressive.
   On Friday we helped Mohamed get the flat tidy before going to Nigel's curry lunch. Nigel did wonders – chicken curry; beef curry; fish curry; vegetable curry

and all the trimmings. Also barbequed lamb with garlic sauce (which he is still eating apparently.) John and I then collected a tennis racquet from Alan and Anika's and then home to bed by 6.30pm.

We went to a barbeque on Saturday and although the food was really superb we didn't enjoy ourselves as much as we'd hoped. There were so many Americans there that it put me off for a start.

On Sunday morning Zena got the devil in her and wouldn't come when I called her during her early walk. I eventually caught her and gave her a little smack and she behaved for a short while, then she ran off again and this time I couldn't catch her. I was mad as I was meant to be going into town with John. So I left her and came back and got our breakfast. John was jolly annoyed as he hates the thought of her rummaging around in the street. She eventually turned up by our downstairs dustbin and was so excited to find us again that it seemed a shame that she was in disgrace.

Big red watermelons are in abundance at the moment. Little donkey–drawn carts stand at the roadside laden with them. I feel sorry for the donkeys standing in so much heat but the stallholders must get hot as well.

Thanks for posting my card on to Maureen and Alf.

Can't think of anything else to say,

> Love from us both,
> Jean XXXX

Letter No. 89 (Handwritten on airmail paper)

Sunday 11th August 1968

Dear Mum, Dad, and Diane,

Many thanks for your letters. I am very pleased about the party going so well; it makes all the work and worry seem worthwhile.

I am sorry about this ruddy pen. It is a Parker and it has never written properly since the day John got it.

We are pleased that you, Diane, like your gift. Kay is good at choosing things and she sent us a sketch of it.

Yesterday was Sennusi Army Day so we took Zena and Sheila to Leptis Magna and Nigel came in his car with two other people. It was very hot at the ruins and we only stayed an hour before driving to a nearby beach. The sand burnt our feet but the water was glorious; clear and wavy. The trip had made us spend £L10 on equipment beforehand including spanners, in case we broke down, and an icebox.

The other evening we went to Pat and Bob's villa on a farm and had a barbeque. They had some fresh grapes from the farm, which were sweet and firm - really good. They are looking after a small, fluffy, white Maltese terrier - rather like a Pekinese.

We had Polly and Garry, and Rosemary and Peter round for a meal and had a lovely evening. Rosemary and Peter are so brave and Rosemary now even talks about when she went into the Moasat Hospital to have her baby.

Susan Pugh was given a baby shower by Jill Robinson and Rosemary came along to it, which I thought was extremely courageous of her. Susan had some lovely gifts. Sheila and I had bought our things in the suk. I got a knitted cotton top and leggings for £L1 and Sheila got a cotton dress for 17/-. We also both treated ourselves to twin-sets at £L2.5/- each. Very good value. One week I got John three shirts for £L5 and two of them were Raelbrook. I love beating the shopkeepers down and save quite a bit of money that way.

I wrote another minute about Isaam at work the other week. He said he'd been sick when returning to the office after four days absence. So I wrote complaining the he looked too well tanned to have been very sick and a chap at work said he'd seen him on the beach. I also complained that although he was doing the embassy's translating due to Mr Tibi's leave it wasn't fair that everyone else had to do his ordinary work whilst he was being paid £20 a month extra for translating.

Did I tell you that Luigi found himself a suitable wife whilst he was in Malta? He gave me a bottle of 'Femme' to celebrate. He is going back to Malta later on to get officially engaged.

By the way I have posted off the films, suit, and two lipsticks for Diane. They should be with you soon. Brian Ives is the Post Corporal at the embassy and he sent it in his name for me (cost me several cups of coffee.)

I'm sorry you didn't get engaged Diane, I was looking forward to attending your wedding when I'm home on leave. Still perhaps it may work out that way yet.

By the way I want to send Valerie a pound for you to buy the baby something. John doesn't want to though, so unless I persuade him this evening I will get someone at work to give me a cheque. If I do this then please don't say anything unless the cheque is signed by John. I realise that Valerie is a bit of a slut but the baby is, after all, the first one in the family for years.

The weather is so humid and horrid. I can stand anything up to 100 degrees but not when it is humid.

Better close off now,
    Love from us both,
        Jean XXXXXX

PS. John Wilde (British Vice-Consul) gave me a pound note so I have wrapped it in carbon paper to stop the Post Office discovering it.

Letter No. 90 (Handwritten airmail paper)

Monday 26th August 1968

Dear Mum, Dad, and Diane,

Thank you for your newsy letter Mum. I am glad that Maureen and Alf had a pleasant time at the flat. Well-done Diane. Let's have a picture of Richard. How old is he? What does he do for a living?

Poor Susan Pugh has been suffering lately as the baby is pressing on her sciatic nerve and giving her awful backache. One of the 'batch' has arrived. Linda, an American, had a baby girl. (Three to go now.)

I went bonkers last week doing stencils for the new beach passes, trying to find enough of the right paper etc. (Believe me it was hectic.) A notice was then put in a local newspaper telling people to come to the embassy for new passes, then at midday on Saturday the Libyan Army said that they would issue their own passes. It was too late to take out the newspaper notice so this morning I had seventy-five people to turn away and put on a waiting list.

We had 'Chinese' food at the Greens on Thursday consisting of boiled rice, a few prawns in an orange sauce, bits of chicken with walnuts and grated cabbage with a few sultanas. To my mind it was a disgrace to serve such measly food. For pudding I had five raspberries and some sherbet ice cream.

We went to a Military Mission Ball at the Piccola Capri, but unfortunately there were a lot of Libyans there who annoyingly kept repeatedly asking me to dance but other than that we enjoyed ourselves.

On Saturday we took John and Jeanette Wilde and Pat and Bob Rumph to a Lizzie Club barbeque. It was very good except that it packed up at 11pm.

On Friday we were meant to go to a party at Ken's. He told us to arrive between 10pm and 10.30pm. We decided to sleep from 7pm to 9pm in readiness but needless to say we slept right through and missed it.

The other morning some of us found a poodle outside the embassy and eventually we took him to the Blue Crescent. Five of us are chipping in to keep him there for two weeks and we have put a 'Found Notice' in both the local paper and Lizzie Club. I do hope he is claimed as he is very loveable.

I have just fed the birds and they have stuffed themselves silly and now they are dozing on their perches. Zena is running around snapping at a fly. I hope she misses in case it is full of worm eggs.

Dr.Zhivago is coming to the Waddan soon. I expect there will be a mad rush for seats, but we'll try to go as it is meant to be good.

We heard from Jean and Derek and Jenny and Terry this week. Derek is practically recovered from his nervous breakdown and they now have fitted carpets throughout their new house. John, two years old, is fine but had to have his stomach pumped after eating some of Derek's pills.

Jenny sounds rather fed up with Calcutta. Apparently the English people there are very snobby and class conscious. Still, they have some local leave due and hope to go to Darjeeling or Kalimpong.

Polly had three stitches in her thumb go sceptic last week and this week it is my turn, as I managed to prod a fish fin under my thumb nail when scaling it ready to cook. I am hoping it clears by itself as I'd rather go water skiing than visit the doctor. (His surgery days are the same as skiing days.)

Must close now,
        Lots of love
        Jean XXXXXX

Letter No. 91 (Handwritten airmail letter)

Undated

Dear Mum, Dad, and Diane,

Many thanks for your letter. I was getting rather worried about you.

Sorry the parcel hasn't arrived. I can only assume that it missed the boat so it will be another month's wait I should think.

Susan Pugh is fine again now. Thelma's is due in a day or so and then Pam's at the end of September.

Glad to hear you are meeting your cousins. It is nice to keep in touch, though I can't see Di and I keeping in with our cousins. I do hope Valerie's baby is born on Dad's birthday. Any idea of her plans for it?

Last Friday I had to have half my thumb nail off because it had gone sceptic underneath. It was caused by a fish bone going under it when I was cleaning some fresh fish. John came along and watched the 'operation' and nearly fainted. I had my thumb frozen so it didn't hurt very much. I had to wear a sling for a couple of days to keep the thumb up to stop it throbbing. John was very gentle when he changed my dressings but now the skin has hardened up so just an ordinary plaster does the trick.

Yesterday a secretary from the embassy, Carol, said she'd have the poodle, so John took us to collect it from the Libyan-run kennels. We took one look at it and I said 'Let's have it put to sleep'. The poor thing had several sores and stank to high heaven. Carol decided to give him a chance, so we took her to her flat with him. Afterwards I disinfected the car and John and I showered.

Today *Carol told me that 'Paddy' cocked his leg all around the flat and had diarrhoea in three places; also he squealed and whined the whole time. She is going to give him a few more days to settle down and improve, if not he will have to be put down. Poor dog – he was fine two weeks ago – so it must have been the effect of the kennels.

Little Zena has been chewing things lately so she has been in disgrace. So far it has only been envelopes and cigarettes but I think she will have to stay outside on the balcony when we go out in future.

On Tuesday I am hoping to hold keep fit classes at the flat with a few friends. I am hoping it will catch on and that about six of us will take it in turns to hold weekly meetings.

I bought some smashing beige bell-bottom slacks in a sale. John really likes them, so I am especially pleased.

My 'friend' Isaam from the embassy got married last week.

Mr Green, the GM, has asked us to re-do the inventories and comment on the condition of our stuff. Most of ours says: old; unusable; worn; cracked etc. Also he told us to put down anything we need. My list was very long.

John and Jeanette Wilde gave a barbeque the other week, which they held on the embassy roof; but it was so blowy that eventually we had to come inside. We played indoor bowls which was jolly good fun and Nigel and I danced vigorously to 'Hey you get off of my cloud'. I was quite out of breath with jumping around.

Hope Di and Richard last, he sounds rather nice. I'll be home in time for a Christmas '69 wedding and want a white fur muff to go with my maid of honour outfit.

Give my kind regards to Alf and Maureen on the 14th.

    Love from us both,

        Jean

NOTE:

Carol worked in Chancery Section at the embassy as a career secretary. Although she was about my age (and very attractive) I was slightly in awe of her due to her higher status. However, I happened to be in the corridor on her upstairs floor one afternoon when she came careering towards me riding on a tea-trolley, pushed by one of the young male staff members. So far so good, but I don't think her antics were meant for the ambassador's eyes as he unexpectedly entered the hallway from his office. He, fortunately was not about to chastise a spirited young lady and so, with a half-smile and slight nod of his head towards her he passed on his way. Diplomacy par excellence.

Letter No. 92 (Handwritten airmail paper)

Undated

Dear Mum, Dad, and Diane,

Thanks for your letter and enclosures Dad.

I was most surprised that Valerie* had a baby girl. I was positive it was going to be a boy. She will be over a year old before I get to see her. But perhaps by then Valerie will have had her adopted. Is the baby's father paying maintenance?

I hope the films are good. I am longing to see them myself and promised Luigi a viewing. We bought him a lovely fluffy blanket for £L3 in the souk. It is Spanish and has a muted pattern on each side.

What sort of course are you hoping to go on Dad?

On October 19th Tripoli is having another Naval visit, similar to last November. The ship is HMS Torquay and is roughly the same as last year's Scarborough - an anti-submarine frigate. John and I intend inviting a couple of junior ratings for dinner one evening, just to show willing. Fortunately there isn't so much work involved for me at the embassy this time, as David has learnt how to type his own stencils (complete with correcting fluid) and also we have all last year's 'gen' as a guide.

I'm in trouble again, this time with a couple of 'old dears' at the embassy. To start at the beginning: I checked with two oil companies on the salary they would pay a locally engaged clerk/typist and the hours involved. (Not because I was thinking of leaving but just to find out). I discovered that working for the embassy was the better option. Anyway the Head of Chancery, Mr Goulding, called a meeting of all locally engaged staff, six women like myself and Libyan clerks and messengers. He told us about the forthcoming visit of the inspectors and said that they would have little or no money to allocate to pay rises; their main object was to cut down expenses. Then Mr Goulding invited our comments as he wanted to give the inspectors an outline of grievances. No one spoke and the poor chap kept looking from one to the other so I piped up, 'I'm quite happy'. He then said that if any of us wished to see him we could go to his office before Monday. The meeting broke up and once outside the door Margaret Clarke turned on me and said sarcastically, 'You're quite happy are you?' 'Yes' I replied 'Aren't you?' 'No I'm not,' she bit back. So I asked her why she hadn't spoken up and she said she wouldn't say anything in front of the messengers. All the time her friend, Muriel, was standing beside her nodding in agreement. So now I send Luigi to their office if I want any photocopying done.

Keep-fit this week was worse than last – only me. Still Sheila and Cindy should both be able to come next week. Susan was meant to come today but hasn't turned up so far. *(She's just arrived, this minute.)

As you know John bought 100 Schweppes shares some time ago and they are climbing steadily. We got some Pontins about two weeks back and they have gone up as well. And John Scott is getting the 'Westland' shares for us soon. We only poke about £100 in at a time but it is interesting. Actually I'm finding it difficult to keep track as we have a Swiss account now and have just joined *OIS with their IIT scheme (30 dollars a month). Also John has heard that Luxemburg have the same lack of restrictions on their banking accounts and that by joining the IIT scheme we can get money to Luxemburg by devious means. Also John has a current account here, plus one in London and I have a small savings account in Giorgimpopoli (thirteen pounds). So we have eight 'cubbyholes' to date with the possibility of nine. I will have to get John one of those Twinlock filing cases soon.

The IIT scheme is based on the idea of a unit trust. You put 30 dollars a month in for ten years and then you should be able to sell your shares back for double. The limit is governed by the amount (30x12x10 in our case) and not ten years as it first appears. Anyway we have started off with thirteen months worth, as in the first year most of your money goes in charges and isn't actually working for you. The appealing thing is that it gets money to Switzerland no matter where you are in the world. You can borrow back your money if you want or not pay in for as long as you like. They run a 'Dover' scheme in UK which may be worth your while looking into.

John's £L10 a month rise has just come through. No more for two years though.

We are wondering about getting a tape-recorder. Do you think you could find out the UK prices on four (or two) track stereo models. (Two speakers included in the total price.) Also can you get cassettes (40 minutes in length) in stereo yet and that allow you to make your own recordings? A cartridge is no use as that is 24 hours pre-recorded stereo and is used in *Joe Lyons and such like. We can buy Phillips here but I think that an English model would be cheaper due to devaluation. Anyway if you could get me the prices on a Phillips model and, say, two English models we would be very pleased and would know whether or not to wait for our leave to buy it.

Thanking you in advance,

Love from us both,

Jean and John xxxxx

PS Have just received your parcel of invitation cards. Many thanks. Perhaps you will let us know how much we owe you.

NOTES:

*Valerie was my cousin - my Uncle Terry's eldest daughter. Her daughter was illegitimate but Valerie kept her and named her Sharron. Valerie later married and went on to have two more daughters and a son – half siblings to Sharron.

*OIS went spectacularly down the drain owing money all over the place. It was a pyramid scheme. We were led like greedy lambs to the slaughter.

*Joe Lyons refers to a chain of cafes that had piped music.

*Susan's late arrival to my keep-fit was due to the fact that her Libyan house-maid had put a near lethal mixture of chemical cleaners down the toilet and had nearly passed out with the fumes.

Letter No. 93 (Typed on airmail paper)

Monday 16th September 1968

Dear Dad,

I hope this reaches you in time for your birthday. I am sorry that I could not find you a birthday card, but when I went into town on Sunday all the Italian card shops seemed to be closed.

I hope the torrential rains have not affected you too much, though I expect your garden is in a mess.

The Pughs had a baby girl on Friday 13th, 6lbs 5ozs. She is going to be called

Katie but christened Catherine. John and Jeanette Wilde took me to see Susan on Sunday and we were allowed to look at Katie.

My thumbnail is growing again but there seems to be a split between the old half and new half. I hope it joins together eventually.

Must close now,

Happy Birthday,

Jean and John XXXXX

Letter No. 94 (Handwritten on airmail paper)

Wednesday 25th September 1968

Dear Mr, Mrs, and Miss Noah,

I do hope things are better now and that you, Dad, managed to wade to a pub for a birthday drink.

I am relieved to hear that the parcel reached you safely; I too am longing to see the films. I might be making a film of the Pugh's baby, Catherine Jane (Katie) later on.

On Saturday we had some friends round for a meal. After eating we sat in the lounge nattering and I had Zena on my lap. Suddenly I noticed that she was ferreting around rather a lot and discovered, to my horror, that she had been calmly chewing away on the streamers that hang down the back of my very brightly coloured dress that I bought in M & S. Fortunately I have been able to turn the chewed parts in so it still looks okay.

The poodle, poor thing, had to go back to the Blue Crescent, but apparently an Italian lady is interested in him, so we hope he is okay.

My keep-fit idea hasn't got going yet. Yesterday only Cindy came. Next week Susan Pugh might be coming and Sheila will be able to come alternate weeks.

We, mostly me, are in trouble with Mr Green as it has been brought to his notice that I have been telling people that his wife has never visited me. He told John that his wife doesn't visit – people visit her by invitation. I think it will go in the report against John. Still he is on my side about it as we feel she should have visited at least once.

Mrs Hughes, John's middle-aged assistant at Giorgimpopoli, has a son employed by *National and Grindlays Bank and he is being made redundant at the end of his tour owing to the nationalization of their African branches. That only leaves the bank with a few branches in India and Aden.

Think I will go and feed Sheila's cat now. Sheila and Owen have nipped off to Tunis, lucky devils.

Have just fed the cat, Pussy Willum. She is really wild and chased Zena all over the house. She scratched me as well. I think I will send John in future.

Tonight Dave Pincombe is coming for a meal. His wife, Thelma, has just had a baby boy, Alistair, I think. She had to have a caesarean though. There is only one more baby left to come now in this Tripoli batch, until December time anyway.

Love to you all,
    Jean XXXXXX

P.S. Two favours to ask:

When you send back the films via D.J. Pugh. B.F.P.O. 57 could you also enclose a gilt chain-link waist belt for me? They are all the rage here at the moment but cost between 15/- and 25/-, each which seems rather expensive.

The second favour is for Luigi. He would like, for a relation of his, two 6in to 9in dolls dressed as: a) a guard (must be with busby) and b) a Scottish doll (must have a kilt.) I will square up with you when you tell me how much they cost.

Many thanks.

By the way did the suit and lipsticks arrive okay with the films?
    Love Jean XXXXXX

NOTES:

*National and Grindalys Bank. The bank where I used to work in its St James' Square office in London before going to Tripoli with John.

Letter No. 95 (Handwritten on lined paper)

October 1968? (Undated)

Dear Mum, Dad and Diane,

Sorry not to have written before but I have been so busy. Thanks for your letters.

*Cindy made me a lovely long beige evening dress for the Poppy Ball. It had cut-away sleeves; a low back and a high collar edged with gold sequins.

The ball was a farce. The weather was appalling and to get to the hall one had to splosh through mud and attempt to keep one's hair dry. The hall had one paraffin heater in it and the tables were placed under draughty windows. It was impossible to dance because of the crowd, so one either sat and shivered or shuffled and elbowed a way round the dancing area.

We did two performances of 'Under Milk Wood'; one on Saturday to an audience of twelve and one on Sunday to an invited audience of about thirty at the American Residency. It was only a play-reading but the producer made us all move about so it was more like a proper play only we held our books. Luckily I only had four small parts but nevertheless it was still quite a nerve-wracking experience.

My half thumbnail is now only a fraction behind the half that was left on and then I have about a quarter inch of splits and ridges to grow out before it is back to normal.

We have now got seven-and-a-half hours of recorded music on our cassettes. I can't wait to begin on your selection when we get home. John likes Strauss and Chopin and military marches. (I know you can supply the first two in abundance.) I want to tape your music from shows as they will remind me of the actual performances. The plug that we have is pronged and circular, but you will see it soon enough.

Zena hasn't come on heat yet so I presume she only has it every nine months instead of every six months. A friend of mine is hoping to mate her dog in a couple of month's time so I won't bother mating Zena now as the 'market' will be flooded. John doesn't want me to send her home to U.K. as he feels that I will want to do it every time I have a pet abroad. Still if I start looking well in advance I should be able to find her a good home here.

We have been keeping quiet socially this month but now that John has just about finished his balance work we expect be gadding around again.

Dr Zhivargo has arrived at long last so we will be going to see it soon. Also we owe meals to quite few people so I will have to get that over with in the near future.

By the way, Cindy has left the Embassy so don't worry about sending the extra rollers - I'll manage with the eight I've got. My hair is in a terribly dry condition at the moment so I've only used them once so far.

Sorry this letter isn't very interesting,

> Love from us both
>> Jean and John XXXXXX

NOTES:

*Cindy. We two formed a perfect counterbalance to our dreary work stations, always chatting and chortling and making unrespectful comments about other embassy staff members. It was a light-hearted relationship, with no rivalry although she'd once, laughingly, called me a swot because my three GCSE 'O' levels had contained one in biology whereas her identical English Literature and English Language had only been accompanied by a certificate in needlework. However her sewing skills had proved far more useful than my knowledge of a rabbit's innards or the construction of a bull's eye. She could make me a dress in an afternoon and whilst she was stitching I would iron her husband's shirts.

Ref: *Under Milk Wood. One of my small parts involved drawing circles of lipstick around my nipples. Fortunately I was allowed to turn my back to the audience and keep my clothes on.

Letter No. 96 (Hand written on airmail paper)

Monday 28th October 1968

Dear Mum, Dad and Diane,

As you can imagine we are both very pleased about your forthcoming engagement, Diane. We are looking forward to meeting our brother-in-law and to seeing the photos of him. The only thing you haven't told us about is his job. Does he always have to work night shifts?

I am sorry not to have written for so long, but believe me, we have been up to our eyes in social engagements (or else recovering from them.) Firstly we had *Goronwy Roberts, Minister of State, out from UK, then H.M.S. Torquay paid an official visit – cocktails on board; party at David Pugh's and then our own effort on Monday. The idea was for us to have two cadets for a meal but when John went to the jetty to collect them nobody appeared to know anything about it so Polly, Garry, Dick and us ate an awful lot.

At David's party, Jackie (the Pugh's nanny) was wearing a low cut dress and asked John to protect her from our lecherous ambassador. I told John afterwards that Jackie was quite capable of looking after herself but judging from John's reply he was being as lecherous as H.E.

I have been going to keep-fit with Sheila once a week. Last week we had a curry at her place afterwards, cooked by Owen, her husband. We also took her to see 'The Dirty Dozen' which we enjoyed. Owen does three weeks in the desert and one week at home.

Anyway this week promises to be quieter. I have made out a long list of things that I would like sent out with the films:

- One white collar attached shirt (14½ neck)
- Twenty wax-filled hair rollers. (You boil them for ten minutes and put them in your hair for about five minutes).
- One P.V.C. raincoat. (I think Marks and Sparks have them for about £3. I don't mind if it is a plain colour or flowery but if possible I'd like a matching rain hat.)
- Three pairs of stocking tights – just ordinary stocking colour – size 10.
- Butterick pattern No. 4814 size 12.

The above list, plus Luigi's dolls, will be quite expensive so let me know the cost of it all and we'll send a cheque. By the way, sea-mail will be the best way of sending it all as airmail will probably cost £2 or more. (D.J.Pugh. B.F.P.O. 57.)

We had a bad storm last week and I really felt the need for a raincoat. At lunchtime I went out to get some bread and found that two of the shops were inaccessible owing to flooding. The only one I could reach was by jumping across up-turned fruit boxes that the owner had put down.

Do let me know how Grandad's chest X-ray turns out. Why did he have to go in the first place? How is Eileen's cancer now? I hope she is responding well to treatment.

All the Tripoli 'September' babies are thriving and I know of two more due around Christmas time. (Anika, from the bank, and a Canadian girl down the road.)

Libya has issued yet more stamps, so keep them all for me as I'll need the duplicates for swops and for Barbara from Grindlays (who I still write to.)

John has just joined the National Geographical Society and we have also sent off for a weekly airmail copy of the Sunday Telegraph.

Regarding the tape-recorder – we will find out the makes available here and send you the prices for comparison.

Thank you for looking, Dad.

    Love to you all,
        Jean and John XXXXXX

NOTE: *Goronwy Roberts was the Minister of state for Foreign and Commonwealth Affairs 1967-69

Letter No. 97 (Typed on airmail paper)

Monday 11th November 1968

Dear Mum, Dad and Diane,

Many thanks for your letters. Your letter with the sad news of Aunty Dolly's death and Eileen's cancer coincided with Kay's letter telling us of the death of Jean Lunnon's husband. (Aunty Molly's daughter). Jean married a Mauritanian and is left with a half-caste baby boy. I hope Grandad wasn't too upset by the news of Aunty Dolly. By the way I do remember Reg vaguely, wasn't he Helen's brother?

It seems a shame that Valerie doesn't put Sharron up for adoption, but perhaps she will find someone to marry her and take on the baby later. I hope so. Is she still fairly slim?

We went to a Halloween party and I made John a long black robe and myself a short black dress with a tatty hem. John got re-christened the 'Mad Monk' because of his antics. (He remembers falling on the floor with Cindy but I had to remind him that he fell on the floor with Polly as well.) He has a bad cold and cough at the moment and is nursing it with brandy and whisky.

We still have our canasta evenings with Pat and Bob but on Friday Gary taught us bridge – well the basic idea and the rules - but not the cunning involved when you get expert. You won't forget to keep your eyes peeled for Waddington's Risk? If you can buy it for us and keep it at home we will be very pleased. John tried to get it again, now that the Christmas stock is in the shops, but he was told that it isn't being made anymore.

You talk about us not being bombarded with the American election news – what do you think Wheelus churns out? Our only relief is between 6 – 8pm every evening when the Libyan Broadcasting Service is on the air.

Our hoped for Christmas trip to Tunisia is off, as the banks will be open on Boxing Day which means our having to fly back on Christmas Day. We may go to an Italian Hotel in the country instead (on the Benghazi road), with Cindy, Geoff and Nigel. Failing that Cindy and I will share the work and we'll have Christmas together.

The bank has at long last given a cost of living increase. Also we have bought, on the bank, a vacuum cleaner, two carpets and new curtains. And we have several more things to come.

Garry tells us that the Phillips shop here has some cassette stereo tape recorders and you can tape from your own records or buy ready made tapes. The price is sixty Libyan pounds (about seventy sterling.) Sounds quite good don't you think? Perhaps you would comment, Dad.

Can't think of much else to write but thanks for the shopping you are doing for us.

Love from us both,
Jean and John XXXXXX

P.S. Kay is getting Diane an engagement gift from us. Have a good time on Saturday and Good Luck, Diane.

Letter No. 98 (Hand written on airmail paper)

Monday 25th November 1968

Dear Mum, Dad and Diane,

Many thanks for your letter.

Have you given up smoking and driving in view of the extra 5d tax? I think it is very bad to put up the duty just before Christmas.

We drove down to Kusabat on Thursday (it can be spelt in many different ways owing to it being an Arabic name: Cussabat; Quasabet etc.) and booked into the hotel for Christmas Eve and Christmas Day. The boys, John and Geoff, will drive back at about 6am on Boxing Day and Cindy and I will follow later. The couple who run the hotel said that Zena can come along as well. So I am very happy. I told Peter Bull how pleased we were with the hotel, as he recommended it to us in the first place, and he said that he and Rosemary may come too.

John and I plan to give a buffet supper for about twelve guests on the Thursday before Christmas and Cindy and Geoff are giving one on Boxing Day.

Thanks for posting off the parcel of 'goodies'. I can't wait to get them.

Zena is due to come on heat in the middle of December and I have been asking around trying to find her a suitable mate. Luckily Mr Goulding, Head of Chancery, has two pedigree male black and tan dachshunds and he said he would mention Zena to his wife and perhaps she will let me take Zena along to be mated. Zena has a dachshund head, barring the ears, and her coat is a lovely shiny black which is characteristic of the breed. Of course her legs are too long and she shouldn't have any white fur but by mating her with a proper dachshund she should produce quite nice pups, all being well.

Did you see Zena on film? What did you think of her? By the way did Kay and John manage to see the films?

Kay wrote and said what a lovely evening you had all spent together. John and I miss out on all these family occasions but next Christmas we will make up for it.

Do let me know how much I owe you for the parcel. I also enclose a cheque for presents for Grandad, Nan, baby Sharron and Uncle Bill. We have ordered gifts by a postal service for you three. Actually I've forgotten if we usually send to Nan and Uncle Bill, if not put the extra money onto Grandad's gift.

Many thanks,

    Love from us both,

        Jean XXXXXX

Letter No. 99 (Typewritten on airmail paper)

Tuesday 10th December 1968

Dear Mum, Dad and Diane,

Many thanks for the letters you have sent. I am sorry to have taken so long in answering them but firstly Sheila's cat bit my right index finger, then I developed a cold and finally life has suddenly got very hectic.

I am sorry to hear about the car proving expensive at the moment. I expect Richard can mend most of the things so you are lucky in that respect. John and I found that the labour costs involved when our car (Bertha) was at the garage often exceeded the cost of the part.

We have bought the Phillips stereo cassette recorder and have filled four cassettes from the records of friends so far. It is jolly good and we would like to record a lot off your set when we get home. It is all quite simple, you just plug the cassette set into whatever you are recording from and away you go, with no need for sitting in silence while the taping takes place.

Polly puts up with me arriving very early at her flat with the recorder some mornings (having been dropped off by John on his way to Giorgimpopoli) and then she helps me choose classical pieces from their collection.

Joanne, the GM's secretary is leaving soon and she is taking us out for lunch today. Fortunately I have just about got my sense of taste back so I should enjoy it.

I have practically completed my Christmas shopping and only have a few bits to get for Mohamed, Ali etc. This year the Christmas cards in the shops have improved a great deal and the wrapping paper is also quite good.

Sheila is off to England today so I have to feed her rotten old Pussy-Willum for a month. She has promised to buy Zena a new lead and collar in the UK which is bribery on her part really. Pussy-Willum had to have a rabies injection and so I went along with Sheila and helped hold the cat down. It was during this fiasco that the wretch decided to bite down to the bone in my finger. Even the vet looked worried but luckily, except for deep bruising, it wasn't too bad and is now nearly back to normal.

I had two days off work with my cold but it has loosened up now and I feel more my old self.

The other day I trotted off to the shop round the corner and what should I see coming towards me on the pavement but a hobbled camel. Its mouth was full of horrible looking green saliva, and the little man trailing along behind on the end of a piece of thin rope looked mental and certainly had no control over the beast.

Mum, I remember buying you a birthday card and even writing it but I can't remember posting it. I have had a search around the flat but can't see it anywhere so please forgive me if it doesn't arrive.

Diane, I am pleased you liked the gift Kay got for you from us. We have arranged for a 'bottom-drawer' Christmas gift to be sent via a catalogue and I was so pleased that it wasn't on your list of engagement presents. It is both decorative (I hope to your taste) and useful (if you like doing that sort of thing.)

The weather is very changeable at the moment. We have had temperatures in the 70's followed by cold winds, sand storms, rain etc. all in one week. Last night the temperature changed drastically three times.

Better close now, please don't worry if you don't hear for some little while. I daresay you are as busy as ourselves.

Lots of love

Jean XXXXXX

Letter No. 100 (Typewritten on airmail paper)

Monday 23rd December 1968

Dear Mum, Dad and Diane,

Many thanks for the parcel, which I collected at work today. Unfortunately the BFPO part of the address should have been written as the last part of the address but because it had been put directly under David's name the English post office had missed it and therefore the parcel went to the ordinary post office here and had to be cleared by our Admin. Section to save paying duty. There is just one other thing regarding the gifts and that is the hair-curlers. I'm afraid eight won't be enough. I am sure when I asked for them I said to send about twenty. Anyway there is no hurry as I won't need them desperately before the summer, but perhaps you could send me another two packets after Christmas. Send by sea and I will square up with you. This time you'd better use Cindy's name (she chatted up the Post Corporal and has her parcels sent BFPO even although she is locally engaged.)

> Mrs G.P. Humphrey
> c/o The British Embassy
> Tripoli,
> Libya.
> BFPO 57

The white jumper looks lovely and I am looking forward to going home and trying it on. Luigi is in Malta at the moment but I feel sure he will like the dolls.

John and I decided to cut down on Christmas cards this year and we only sent 28 but now we keep getting cards from people that we should really have sent to but thought that they would not send to us.

Sorry this letter is in such a muddle and barely comprehensible but it is only a quarter to nine in the morning and I haven't woken up properly yet.

We had our supper party on Thursday and it went very well. Twelve people came and I did a cold turkey with sausage meat stuffing one end and chestnut stuffing the other. I bought a 5 lb. tin of ham as well.

John is pretty jealous about Dad getting in all those kisses with Kathleen Jones and can't wait to catch up on you. Mind you he doesn't come off badly here for kisses and I am sure he will find a substitute in Cindy or Rosemary over Christmas.

Apparently I have won an electric fire in the Military Mission raffle. Even if I had wanted one we couldn't afford to run it.

We are off to Kussabat tomorrow. John was unlucky with the ending of Ramadan. Because it ended on Thursday night he had Friday, Saturday and Sunday off and then had to work today but has Tuesday off for Independence Day and Wednesday off for Christmas Day. If Ramadan had ended on Friday night he would have had the Friday anyway and then straight through to Thursday.

Coffee is ready so I'd better close off now. I hope you have a lovely Christmas and thank you once again for the super parcel.

Love from us both,

Jean and John XXXXXX

Letter No. 101 (Handwritten on airmail paper)

Sunday 29th December 1968

Dear Mum, Dad and Diane,

Thanks for your newsy letter Dad. I enjoyed hearing about the romancing that is going on in Chesham Crescent.

John is still up on you, Dad, re Kathleen Jones as he gave her over twenty kisses before he left. Admittedly they were all at the same time (I was watching) but it goes to show that he foresaw what would happen once he was away.

We drove in convoy to Kussabat on Christmas Eve, in a sandstorm, only to be told at the hotel that they only had one room. Eventually we got the three we'd asked for and spent the evening around a miserable electric fire, which only glowed slightly, even with all the lights off. Hot water was unavailable and the loo, when flushed, brought to the surface all that had gone down before. (We never did discover who had done the one the size and shape of a tennis ball.) The beds were warm and comfortable but out of the three meals we had there two were fried gristly steak.

We drove back in the early afternoon on Christmas Day to Peter and Rosemary's. We leapt one after the other into hot baths and had a lovely meal. All in all it was quite comic but never again.

I haven't been able to see the films yet as our projector won't take the size of reel that Albert put them on. I am hoping to buy two small reels and split the film. Unfortunately I won't have any 'run-ins' but when we get home and sort the films out I expect we will think of something. Did Kay and John ever see them?

By the way, you know we have now got a Phillips cassette outfit? Well the cassettes can be either thirty minutes each side or forty-five minutes each side so we would be grateful if, whenever you play one of your records, you could note exactly how long each side takes. Don't include run in or run out, just the actual playing time.

I'm dreading the 31st. Both previous New Years have been bad times for

John at the bank and we have had to miss out. Lady Sarell has asked us to the residency again this year and John is determined to make it there this time. The Sarells have their Poppy Dance on 4th January at the Piccola Capri and we are going at the great expense of £L2½ each. After the Poppy Dance we are going out of circulation, except for cards, so that John can get his end of year stuff through.

Happy New Year to you all,
    Love Jean and John XXXX

Letter No. 102 (Handwritten on airmail paper)

Undated. Probably January 1969

Dear Mum, Dad and Diane,

Many thanks for your letter. John says 'yes please' to the book. So perhaps you could send it out. P.O. Box 2308 should be okay as it isn't banned or anything here.

Sorry about all your colds. Our weather is changeable but on the whole, during the daytime, you could sun bathe in a swimsuit. If you have £80 to spare why not come out, Mum, and have a good rest.

About Diane and Richard's wedding in 1970, we should be home for the January and February but of course, they must choose the date to fit in with their own arrangements. I'm afraid that John and I will have to get used to missing out on a lot of things.

Good for you, Dad, taking driving lessons. I must learn when we get home then perhaps John will let me have the car sometimes. As far as we can make out it is going to cost us £100 to have the steering changed and pay tax if we sell it in the UK. So we may as well pay freight and ship it to our next posting, as long as we don't have to pay a high import duty.

On the 16th January Martin Pugh turned himself into a 'human torch' to quote David. Fortunately David carried out the correct first aid and got him to Wheelus hospital in twelve minutes. Martin should be out in three more weeks and is making a good recovery. The little devil got hold of some petrol and soaked tissue paper in it and then threw it onto a garden fire whilst David was indoors pouring himself a cup of tea. Susan has been spending most of her time at the hospital and has arranged for friends to look after the baby and Sally.

This last weekend French twins did practically the same thing but they both died. I should think the whole of Tripoli has been hunting out cans of petrol and hiding them away in view of the accidents.

The other sad thing that happened was that Cindy had a miscarriage about two weeks ago. She is much better now after the initial shock and has cheered up.

We are doing another performance of 'Under Milk Wood' tomorrow because so many people missed the first one and have said how much they wanted to see it.

We, the ladies of the embassy, had tea with the Queen of Libya on Thursday. It followed the same pattern as before and was enjoyable.

Now that we have the cassette outfit we have decided to invest in a Phillips turntable so that we can borrow records and tape them at home, rather than lug all our outfit to other people's homes. The Phillips' shop has sold out at the moment but are expecting some more next week. 'Inshalla'.

The Libyan TV is just for the locals. They have pinched the Wheelus wavelength so now the expatriates have had to pay to have their sets altered to the new Wheelus channel. John and I haven't seen TV for months and certainly don't feel the need for one.

I went to close the front gate today only to find a praying mantis sitting on it – Uggh.

The bird is now renamed Louise as it has laid four eggs to date.

Zena nearly died one night as I'd accidentally left a gas tap on in the kitchen. She was very dozy but perked up after some fresh air. I saw the dachshunds that I'd wanted to mate her with and they were half her size in width but about as long in body. As she hasn't come on heat yet I have given up the idea, especially as it might do her out of a new home when we leave.

Polly and Garry have gone now and we are down to seven months – hooray. I am surviving and keeping cheerful but John is exhausted and needs a lot of sleep. I sleep a lot in the afternoons (4pm – 6pm) and only do housework prior to having visitors.

I felt proud of my effort on Saturday. We had four people in for a meal and I managed two vegetables, roast beef, roast potatoes, Yorkshire pudding and gravy using one oven shelf, three saucepans and one coffee pot. My, what an evening. The Hughes' never stopped talking and even had an argument at the table with each other. I got collared by Mrs Hughes and John was nattered to by Gerry's wife, Pat. I had such a feeling of relief when they all left. The meal was a repayment for hospitality so perhaps we can get out of anything else that involves them in the future. But at least two of the guests left happy.

We have had a sizeable pay-rise at the Embassy but now have to work two afternoons a week and pay income tax and INAS contributions (National Health) as well as £L3 a month for transport, so I am just £L4 a month up but have longer hours. What a swizz.

Must close now; hope you are all over your colds etc. Please give my love to Eileen.

Love,

Jean and John XXXXXX

Letter No. 103 (Handwritten on airmail paper)

Sunday 23rd February 1969

Dear Mum, Dad, and Diane,

Thank you for your letter Mum. I will let you know when the book arrives. I daresay John will sneak it home in his briefcase and not let me see it 'till he has finished. We have both just read a Frank Yerby book called 'Benton Row' which was excellent.

Martin Pugh is now out of hospital and recovering well. I expect he will still start at Boarding school in September. I'm sorry to hear about Eileen's decline. She must be the last one left in her family, poor thing.

Guess who walked into the embassy to register last week? Bruce Warner from St. John's days. I must admit that I did not recognise him but he insisted that knew me from somewhere, until it finally clicked. Do you remember him? He has a sister, Pam, and he used to take the collection in church. I asked him home for a drink and ever since he has either rang John or me everyday. Actually he grows on you (which is lucky) although he spins a few yarns.

I don't know if Diane told you that the bank are wondering if John should do four years here straight off as it is a first tour. John has been so depressed about it all that I feel like clouting the bank with a ledger for even thinking up such a mean trick. If they do decide on four years the only way out for us is to break our contract and maybe loose our six months leave pay. Anyway if the worse comes to the worse we will send a copy of the contract to an English solicitor and see how we can get out of it to our best advantage.

I've managed to catch a cold which seems an incredible feat with temperatures in the 90's.

Zena, still on heat, has had so many callers that it isn't funny anymore. Two of them have been sleeping in the road guarding the gate and one of them has been up to the inside door of the flat. I had to carry him back down the stairs because he wouldn't budge. Another sat at the main door of the flats and thumped on it for admittance.

At the moment I have got a plain-clothes policeman watching out for a youth on a blue bicycle who assaulted me once and attempted a second attack another day. (He cycled up behind me and put his hand up my skirt – it was horrible.) The idea is for me to spot the youth and then tell this poor old policeman, who is then to catch him. Still I am pleased about the prompt police action.

My bird has been with Ian and Monika's male in the hopes of a proper fertilised egg but nothing has happened so she should be coming back today.

Monday

John has been ferreting around in Tripoli office and according to snippets of conversation that Nigel and Alan have overheard things look brighter for us. We may even get away in August when John's work permit expires.

I have just bathed Zena as her heat suddenly finished and am soaking her bedding (three old curtains) in disinfectant.

The Haj is beginning on Wednesday. Lots of Libyans have left for Mecca. Those remaining here are leading their sheep around on ropes ready for the slaughter, which is gruesome.

Tomorrow the Pughs and the Foremans are coming up for the evening and as John has Wednesday off I have promised to leave him the washing up as I have to work. I don't expect Mohamed will be around.

It's little wonder that so many others and I have colds as the temperatures have jumped around this last week between 42 degrees to 93 degrees Fahrenheit.

Sunday March 2nd.

Sorry that this letter is in so many instalments, but I'll make this the last page.

We have been out the past few evenings or had people in and next week we have a busy time ahead: two parties; canasta; and a reception at the British Pavilion of the TIF. Next Sunday is also my meat market day so I'll have to be up early. I hate preparing the meat for freezing as it takes ages to sort out and trim but it makes it is easy for the following four weeks as the meat is all prepared and ready to cook. The main problem is allowing for people eating with us. I usually buy a large joint of pork, which I keep to one side.

I bought a tin of chocolate sauce the other day, which should solve any pudding problems. I love pears and ice cream with chocolate sauce over the top.

My two attempts at making the sauce myself were failures. It tasted okay but was so runny.

We hope you are all well and we are also counting the weeks to our leaving Tripoli. We don't know yet how long we will take getting home – see how the money lasts. But two months at the outside I should think.

Love from us both,

Jean XXXXX

Letter No. 104 (Handwritten airmail paper)

Monday 10th March 1969

Dear Mum, Dad and Diane,

Thanks for your letter Dad. My face screwed up in sympathy at the description of Mum's injured fingers.* I do hope they are healing up quickly. It must have been agony.

Guess who did some gardening yesterday – me. I helped Sheila rake and weed and thoroughly enjoyed it. It was bright and warm with just the hint of a nip in the air.

We have a public holiday for the King's birthday on Wednesday so I am hoping that we can go out for a drive and walk, if not I'll do some more gardening.

John isn't very bright at all but can you tell Kay that the pills have arrived safely and that he is taking them according to instructions. Kay thinks he is anaemic which is quite possible as it is a common complaint here. We eat liver and steak a lot already so I don't think it is anything to do with his diet that has made him so run down.

We went to the British Day reception at the TIF on Saturday evening and had a lovely time as we knew so many people there. I got a free sample of ten Liptons pure coffee bags which are quite nice. As you went into the pavilion the ambassador and other embassy staff were standing in a reception line and last year John was annoyed because the ambassador greeted him as 'Tungate'. This year the old idiot was telling me how nice my hair looked whilst shaking John's hand and ended up by saying nothing at all to John.

After the TIF reception we went to a party down our road and got tiddly on champagne punch. John, of course, mixed his with whisky. We hadn't planned staying late but John suddenly looked at his watch and exclaimed in surprise, 'Goodnesh itsh ten pasht one'. So we downed our drinks and rushed – or rather wobbled – home. We took Zena out for a meander and just as we were getting into bed I noticed that the bedroom clock said a quarter to twelve. I checked with John's watch and found that in his drunken state ten past eleven had looked like ten past one.

We really have been gadding about this month and have a lot more things to go to before March is through.

Pat took me to the meat market yesterday and I bought four weeks supply – including some tuna fish, all for £L.9 which I thought quite reasonable. I will have to buy a couple of frozen chickens and sausages and perhaps more fish next week to help last out but all in all the meat wasn't too expensive. Groceries are a fantastic price though; 3/- for a medium sized can of tomatoes and yet for 12/- I can buy a 1lb tin of lovely ham. Soups cost over 2/- for a tin of the condensed type.

I have had to go to the police station three times so far in an effort to identify the youth who grabbed at me – no luck yet though. I keep telling the police that he rode a blue bicycle and was plump and young but they don't get the message – I have been shown some really scrawny fellows and all with different coloured bikes.

The pets are fine but the bird hasn't laid an egg for six days which is a shame as I am sure it would be a fertilized one as I have Monika's male in with it and they have definitely been trying. (Caught them at it one tea-time.)

Zena is as daft as ever and getting so fat but she only has raw meat each day, unless Ali has been sneaking food to her in the morning.

Better close. By the way John's GM's wife is expecting a baby. I'll be interested to see if she has it here or goes home.

Love from us both,
    Jean and John XXXXXX

NOTES:
  ref. My mother's fingers. She got them caught in the hinges of a car door that was being closed.

Letter No. 105 (Typewritten airmail paper)

Wednesday 26th March 1969

Dear Mum, Dad and Diane,

Thank you for your letters. I will try to get all your bits and pieces Di.

Kay wrote and said how much she had enjoyed the Ladies Festival, it sounded very well organised on your part.

John is much better since he has been taking the pills and he has given up his sleeping tablets. Another five months to go and we will be on our way. I don't know how long it will take driving home, maybe two months – it depends on how the traveller's cheques last.

My gardening days are over as Sheila and Owen are leaving for Canada just as soon as they can sell up. I can't say I mind too much as I have just bought a second-hand Jones electric sewing machine and am endeavouring to make some dresses. I have little enough time to do anything so I am pleased in a way that I needn't garden anymore.

I am well pleased with the machine, although John teases hell out of me as I struggle trying to discover the difference between an interfacing and a facing (I know now) etc. I have nearly finished the plain dress on the pattern you sent me although I haven't dared try it on in case it doesn't fit. The machine is rather old and plods on nice and slowly which is just how I like the speed to be.

Cindy and Geoff took us horse riding last Saturday afternoon and after a wait of over one-and-a-half hours, due to a lack of horses, we got a ride. I was meant to have a chestnut horse but when the man in charge heard that I hadn't ridden before and that Geoff intended having me on a leading rein he made poor John dismount from his grey and let him have the chestnut instead. Evidently the chestnut was more lively as John was last seen disappearing down a leafy lane whilst the rest of us were still mounting. Cindy went after John and Geoff took me around on the rein. I managed trotting but naturally couldn't stay down in the saddle and I got very sore. When the hour was up we went back to the stables and I managed to get off the horse okay but couldn't get my legs unbent and back together. I must have looked ridiculous. I remained stiff until today (Wednesday). John was okay on Saturday but he stiffened up later. He was pleased with his effort as he hadn't ridden since he was six or seven years old but found he remembered it all. He will only be able to play golf for a few more weeks before David goes on leave for a month so I expect he will ride whilst David is away. I may go again with Cindy in the afternoons as I feel confident enough. It is just a case of getting the horses, who are mainly lazy or old, to go where you want them to, as they only seem interested in finding their way home.

The weather is, on the whole, warm, in the eighties but I haven't attempted swimming yet. I hope the water skiing starts soon as I'd like to get good at it. The feeling is marvellous when you skim over the sea and look down into the depths below.

Sheila has asked us for a curry tonight so John is well pleased as he loves curry.

Brian and Deidre are off on the 6th but they have invited us to stay with them at Walton-on-Thames when we get back, which we will probably do. Most of our friends seem to be leaving at the moment and we are just left with Cindy and Geoff and Pat and Bob. I expect we will find some more but at the moment we don't particularly care as there seems so little time left anyway. We still have enough acquaintances to keep us going.

Better close now, give my love to Eileen when you next see her and tell her I am thinking of her.

Love from us both,
    Jean XXXXXX

Letter No. 106 (Handwritten on airmail paper)

Sunday 13th April 1969

Dear Mum, Dad and Diane,

Thank you for your letter. I can't think of anything to say about poor Eileen except how sorry I am for her. Does Terry visit her at all?

We have had a couple of weeks of blustery weather and I heard about one English person who arrived here a couple of days ago saying she would have done better, weather wise, staying at home.

I am very keen on horse riding now. Although I can only afford to ride once a week I have been up to the stables several times with friends just to watch. I took Zena yesterday (on her lead of course) and she sat by my side above the school arena as good as gold. She was absolutely fascinated by the horses and her head moved round and round as she followed their positions.

The school arena is a rectangle shape with thick shrubbery on three sides and a grassy bank on the fourth side. The surroundings range from orange groves, scrubby grass fields and clusters of Arab huts. When I go on Monday with three others I expect we will go to the fields for a ride. I only hope my horse is old and tired.

My poor little bird escaped on Tuesday. I left her cage on the balcony wall and when I got home from work at lunchtime I found the cage on its side on the balcony floor with the door open. The poor thing could hardly fly and the weather was very rough so I doubt if she survived for long. I looked around the garden and nearby roads for ages but couldn't find any trace of her.

Sheila and Owen left for Canada on Friday but unfortunately their cat, Pussy-Willum, developed enteritis and had to be left with the vet. All being well I should be able to collect her this afternoon and deliver her to her new owners.

We had Zena's prospective new owners over last Sunday. They liked her very much and she jumped around from lap to lap very happily. (This jumping around must sound bad to you but she only does it if you let her.) Anyway a lot depends on whether this couple still want her in June when they come back from leave and whether or not John and I stay on in Tripoli with another company. John has been putting out feelers and we hope something good will turn up. He absolutely hates the bank and the way they treat you and feels he can do just as well leaving it. Naturally he will have to be able to save between £800 and £1,000 a year to make it worth while but the great advantage of being out of banking is that his money will be to hand and can be spent if we want, whereas in banking you don't see it until you retire.

Four and a half months to go. I don't really want to come back here but it may be the only way for John to get an accountant's position without qualifications as the people with jobs to offer know him and realise that he is efficient and capable.

Better close now,
Love from us both,
Jean XXXXXX

Letter No. 107 (Handwritten on airmail paper)

Sunday 27th April 1969

Dear Mum, Dad and Diane,

Sorry not to have written before - usual rush with trying to fit everything in.

You seem to be having a rough time at home with so many people you know getting cancer. I don't suppose Eileen is any better even though she is at home now. Give her my love when you see her next. Do you think I ought to write? Perhaps just a chatty letter to them all? If so could you let me have their address.

My dressmaking almost came to a stop because every time I saw a decent pattern that I wanted to buy in the pattern book the shop was out of it. There are only two shops in Tripoli selling patterns so I was really discouraged. Anyway I bought some more material and decided to use the same pattern as before. Cindy put a stand-up collar on it for me and I ironed Geoff's shirts in return. Anyway

I now know how to put a stand-up collar on a dress, a style I like very much.

For our birthdays could you please send out a 'mixed-bag'? John would like the usual M & S collar attached white shirt, size 14½ and I would like three patterns – one for a plain sleeveless dress (possibly a front zip for a change) size 12 (or 12½ if from the Simplicity new sizes); one for a summer housecoat, again with a zip, as I don't feel up to making button-holes; and lastly, one for summer shortie pyjamas. Next on the list, some thin elastic (the stuff that is on a reel and nearly like cotton); some sewing machine needles and a spool or two. The machine is a Jones and the spools are round with five little holes around the edge.

I hope all the above doesn't take up too much of your time as it can be a problem choosing patterns. Do you think you could send them out as soon as possible as I need to make up the things for the summer and our trip home. I know I won't have a surprise for my birthday but time is short between mid-June and the end of August.

Cindy and Geoff will be driving around Europe about the same time as us and we have jokingly arranged to meet at the top of the Eiffel Tower on 30th October at midday. Wonder if we will?

We did some recording at Bob's the other evening and have added forty-five minutes of Barbra Streisland and forty-five minutes of Dionne Warwick to our collection. Unfortunately we didn't have time to fit Herb Alpert onto our Chris Barber and Bert Kaemphert cassette. We played Scrabble in between recording and Bob got F-A-R-T- but I teased him that it was actually spelt P-H-A-R-T.

Riding is still going strong. The last time I went I let Bob have the very old and quiet horse as I had ridden a couple of times more than him. I had Armenia lll and felt petrified as he seemed to want to gallop. Cindy kindly swapped horses with me and I had Sedida instead. Even so he was quite fresh and I ended up in the sand, plonked firmly on my bottom - the horse had decided to trot before I did. The only problem was re-mounting, as by then I was stiff – bruises to prove it. Bob kindly got off his smaller horse, Armenia 1, and I changed again.

Bob and Suzie went up another afternoon and Bob got Sedida. This time the animal ran away with him for several yards. Still he said he would have it again if I wanted the quiet one – which I do. I hope I have time to take some lessons at home.

Better close now – hope you are all well. I expect your flat is looking smart now. Does Dad know when he will be tested?

Love from us both,
    Jean and John.

Letter No. 108 (Handwritten on airmail paper)

Saturday 3rd May 1969

Dear Mum, Dad and Diane,

I do hope you are feeling better now Mum, and are resting as much as possible. Thanks for the letter Dad, and all the news.

Glad to hear that your driving lessons are going well and we shall certainly be thinking of you on 28th. Do you take the test in Bromley or Beckenham? I think I will take mine in Swyre, Dorset. The Mini isn't too bad at the moment, although it often lets John down when he is overtaking and trying to get into third gear. We would have bought a Renault 4 instead if we had known at the time how cheap they were. We went to Tunisia in Dick's Renault 4 and found it very comfortable and roomy.

I don't think John and I will be around for Diane's wedding on 4th April, which is a shame. If John changes jobs and we have to come back here maybe I will be able to fly home for it. I don't relish the idea of another tour here but John doesn't think he will stand much chance of applying for an accountant's position with a firm that hasn't seem him in action at Giorgimpopoli. Two companies definitely want him at the moment, if they have suitable vacancies. They are Robert Ray (or Mandrell as they are known at home) and Baroid. Baroid is John's first choice as they have worldwide coverage.

Mum, referring back to my last letter. I was telling Pat of my pattern plight and she lent me a Simplicity pattern book that is a shortened version of the usual one. I saw a sleeveless dress pattern that I really liked. It is simplicity No. 7976 size 12 (6/-), so if you can get it for me I will be very pleased. They also had patterns for a housecoat and nightdress. Just one for each. I quite liked them both but you may see something better in the larger book. Anyway, the numbers are 7138 and 7141, both size 12. So if you are in doubt you can always get the above two and know that I like them and feel capable of making them up.

Our weather is hotting up – 92 degrees today, but it is a ghibli and instead of brilliant sunshine we have thick swirls of grey sand and hot gusts of wind. The sea is grey and choppy, the sky overcast and the air is thick with dust.

I don't know what Zena has rolled in, although I could hazard a guess, but she stinks. She was bathed only a few days ago, so rather than go through that performance again I have powdered her with 'Flea-tic' which is said to 'get rid of doggy odour'.

I had a letter from John Keeling, the previous vice-consul, who is in Aden, and who came to your flat when on leave from here. I had hoped to meet him when back in UK but he will be going back to Aden on 12th September.

The horrible Lebanese chap, Isaam, that I work with is now a father. His wife had a boy. *Lady Sarell sent a small gift for the baby, which I thought very kind of her.

Talking of 'ladies' Lady Wheeler, wife of Sir Mortimer, came into the embassy the other day enquiring about antiquities, so I sent her off to Leptis Magna and the Castle Museum. She is quite plain and wore a scruffy divided denim skirt.

Surprise, surprise, we have been asked to dinner by Roy Young the number three in the bank and the following week we have been asked to the GM's for cocktails. I don't know if they have heard that John is thinking of leaving the bank, and are feeling worried about their lack of interest in us socially, or if it is just coincidence.

Last Wednesday the head of Commercial Section at the embassy, Jimmy Reeve, asked me if I could step in at a luncheon party as he had been let down by one of the female guests. He was entertaining a trade delegation from UK. I hurriedly telephoned John, to let him know what was happening, and off I went in the best embassy car, along with the Queen's Messenger, to Jimmy's villa. The Trade Delegation arrived – two unprepossessing chaps from Leicester. I dropped my best accent immediately, tucked into the sherry, ate a superb meal and enjoyed it all no end. After lunch we all drove back to Tripoli; the 'delegation' to the Waddan and the Queen's Messenger and myself to the embassy. It was only on the drive back that I discovered what the 'delegation' was trying to sell in Libya – cheap knitwear. I chuckled so much when I got home and thought it all over.

I hope you are all well now and that Grandad enjoys his birthday.

Love from us both,

Jean and John XXXXXX

NOTE: *Lady Sarell was generally regarded with respect by the embassy wives for her approachable and ladylike demeanour. However is was said that she could (and did) swear like a trooper when behind the wheel of a car.

Letter No. 109 (Handwritten on airmail paper)

Monday 12th May 1969

Dear Mum, Dad and Diane,

Thank you for your letter Mum and for being so quick sending off the parcel. Don't worry about the dress pattern mentioned in my last letter. I hardly expected you to have got everything so quickly especially as I thought you might not have been feeling up to shopping. You certainly had a bad bout of 'flu and I hope you are 100% fit now.

Diane's wedding arrangements sound very good. Where is the Hotel Philomena? Is it similar to *The Crest?

We have planned a rough route home: a week on Djerba; a week in Tunis; boat to Marseilles; a quick look around the South of France; up to Switzerland; Black Forrest; down to Toulouse; up to Paris and home by hover craft. We don't know how long we will take but we will drop you cards and give you forwarding consulates to write to.

So many people are leaving Tripoli at the moment. John and I are going to another spate of farewell parties – it seems never ending. I also owe a few people meals so I'd better decide what to give them and start inviting. Once I have made up my mind about the food I am okay but I spend days worrying about it beforehand. We had a funny meal at the Young's last week - corn and crab soup followed by roast potatoes, ham, peas, sprouts and corn in one dish, and asparagus in an egg and cheese sauce in another dish. There was only a little of everything – Oh, I forgot, we had gravy as well. The evening itself was enjoyable though. They have a huge Airedale that is only six months old. He eats a pound of meat a day as well as eggs, biscuits and vitamin tablets. In fact he costs them as much to feed in a day as it costs me to feed Zena in a week.

Zena has dandruff so I consulted Vic, the chap at work who used to train police dogs. He said to massage against the fur, brush with a soft brush, again against the fur, then buff with a chamois. On top of all this I have to completely change her diet for a few days and give her cod-liver oil. I have followed his instructions and there is a marked improvement, except she stinks of fish.

I have just got back from riding which is why my writing is so bad – I still feel shaky. In fact I am not riding anymore until I have had some lessons at home. This time the horse decided to roll in the sand with me still on it. I got away, bar a foot. Luckily it was only a little bit under the horse and protected by the upside down saddle (where I was meant to be sitting.) Suzy leapt off her horse and hauled mine up and said 'Get on then'. So I got on again but didn't feel happy until we were back at the stables dismounting.

I am glad Grandad is well. I hope he has received my letter and money by now. Thanks for reminding me about Rosalind's birthday. Can you also let me have Duncan's date of birth as I don't seem to have it written down.

John and I went into town to order my birthday present and the shop still had the *bracelet that I had fallen for in January. It is really the most beautiful thing imaginable. It is composed of filigree gold links, each with a dark blue enamelled centre, hand painted with pink roses. Anyway I will be able to show it to you soon. I have promised John some gold cuff links for his birthday.

Better close now and thanks again for getting the parcel off so quickly and for the housecoat. I had a feeling that you would take pity on me – thank goodness.

Love from us both,

Jean and John XXXXXX

NOTES:

*John and I had held our wedding reception at The Crest Hotel in Beckenham. The Philomena was situated in the same road.

*I gave the bracelet to my eldest daughter, Adele, in December 2014 as it no longer fitted me.

Letter No. 110 (Handwritten on airmail paper)

Sunday 25th May 1969

Dear Mum, Dad and Diane,

Thank you very much for your letter. Also thank you for the parcel which arrived safely yesterday.

I'm afraid that my dress-making has fallen by the wayside as John keeps bringing home cassettes from a shop in Giorgimpopoli, which have to be taped over-night and then given back to the shop-keeper by the next morning. (Illegal but cheap.) We have a lovely lot of music now – a particular favourite being a Shadows recording that is very noisy. In fact the Shadows have taken over from the 1812 as a Sunday morning blare-out. (I like the neighbours to know all about it.)

The insect-biting season is here once again and I am covered in bites. Last night I draped the bed-sheet right over me but I must have left my left index finger unprotected as it is swollen and itchy today - most annoying. John never gets bitten as apparently insects don't like the taste of alcohol in the blood, so tonight I am gulping apricot brandy as a preventative.

Please let me know Duncan's date of birth as I must send him a card. Talking of cards Diane and Richard's one to John arrived today. It really is funny.

John is very pleased with his shirt, and so am I with my gifts – thank you very much.

John will need his shirt for our wedding anniversary and the Queen's Birthday celebration at the residency. I shall probably get some materials on Thursday for the patterns you sent, which are super. I have had to wear the housecoat already as my old one is falling to pieces.

I threw out a lot (most of) my winter clothes until John saw what was happening and said, 'I'm not bloody made of money'. So reluctantly I salvaged my mauve suit and big grey coat. He has thrown nothing away yet.

Oh, to be away from here. I am getting jumpy and, I'm afraid, short-tempered. We are all in odd moods at work – John Wilde's wife's baby is due any day; Luigi is getting married on 14th June and Isaam's wife is ill so he is up half the night looking after their new baby. We all take it out on each other. One day, I was arguing as usual with Isaam - he couldn't understand that I had no belief in a god. I told him that I considered myself a self-styled humanist. David Pugh walked into the section at this point and chuckled when he heard me explain to Isaam that a humanist was a sort of good-hearted atheist.

Luigi had stood slacked mouthed and silent during the altercation but when things had quietened down he gave me a worried look, shook his head and showed his genuine concern that, in his opinion, I would have no afterlife.

I can't think of much else except Good Luck, Dad with your driving test.

Love from us both,
Jean and John XXXXXX

Letter No. 111 (Handwritten on airmail paper)

Sunday 15th June 1969

Dear Mum, Dad and Diane,

Today is my birthday! Ugg – twenty-five years old. Thank you for your cards – could you thank Grandad for me please for the one he sent.

Yesterday was the Queen's Birthday celebration and I had to prepare 400 canapés for it. It took me over four hours to make them. We get our money back from the embassy but nothing for labour. What a penny pinching idea though. There are at least two hotels and numerous little pastry shops in Tripoli that could have made a far better job of it than us 'ladies' of the embassy. I cheated on one hundred by making a dip and buying Ritz crackers etc. Then I made about twenty-five asparagus shoots rolled in slices of bread; thirty five sausage rolls and lots of pieces of toast with assorted bits on them. I reckon my four trays looked pretty good compared with some of the soggy messes that were handed round at the 'do' in the evening. Have you ever made dips, Mum? We can either buy tinned sour cream or dried sour cream that you mix with milk. The sour cream is the base and you can add blue cheese; garlic and onion; shrimps etc.

Tonight we are going to a Lebanese restaurant in Giorgimpopoli with Pat and Bob for my birthday. Originally we had intended seeing Twelfth Night on June 5th and then going for a meal with them but Bob suddenly had to go to the desert so we just took Pat to see the play.

I've just realised that this letter will be waiting on the carpet for your return from holiday but I'll plod on in case someone is forwarding them for you.

John isn't very bright at all – he is eating and sleeping reasonably well but he is on tenterhooks about changing jobs. He should be hearing from all three prospective companies this week.

Zena's new home is all fixed. I shall let her go in six weeks time so that I can visit her once or twice before we leave. Also if Judy and Brian have any questions or difficulties with her I should be able to help sort them out. We will really miss having her.

Cindy has returned from the UK after having her tonsils out and now the poor girl is down with flu. She seems to have one thing after another go wrong. They gave a supper party last Friday and they ordered a stuffed cooked lamb for it. It was absolutely delicious and fed the sixteen of us.

I am hoping to get a cheap Kodak Instamatic next week ready for our trip home. The cheapest is £5 but films cost £2 here. Could you check on the price of films at home for me please as I think they may be a lot less. For £2 you get twenty shots. If they are cheaper I'll get you to send some out BFPO. Thanks.

I have had the trots for a week now and feel pretty grotty. I eat a lot as I feel so hungry but I just feel weak all the time. Tomorrow a girl at work has promised to bring me some tablets that are better than Entroviaform, so I hope they do the trick.

Saturday 21st.

Feeling okay now, the tablets did the trick. John got the camera for me from a shop next to the bank. He was talked out of the £L5 one and got a £L7½ one with a flash instead. The bulbs last for four pictures. When he brought it home we took it into the bedroom to examine it. John was holding it and wondering what a certain button on it was for and now we have a lovely snap of the bedroom ceiling.

Have you Jeanette's address in Switzerland? We will certainly visit her as we are going that way to Germany.

Two embassy families are giving a joint farewell beach party on Sunday for the Sarells. They are catering for over one hundred guests. The beach is difficult to get down to so goodness knows how they are going to get the nosh and booze in place.

The weather is most unsettled. Yesterday it dropped twenty degrees in a very few minutes. Some days it is dry and hot and others it is clammy with a damp warm wind. Then we have ghiblis every four or five days and sand blows in under doors and through closed windows.

I hope you are enjoying good weather on holiday and come home brown and rested.

As I am writing we are listening to Johnny Mathis who always puts me in a lovely mood.

Better close now,
    Love from us both,
        Jean XXXXXX

Letter No. 112 (Handwritten on airmail paper)

Undated possibly towards the end of June 1969

Dear Mum, Dad and Diane,

Not very much news for you but I was pleased to receive your letter and hope my one to you has arrived now.

Give my love to Aunty Eileen when you see her. It is such a shame for the rest of the family as well as for her. I only hope that Valerie and Janis settle down soon.

Have you been to see your cousin *Sheila yet? I can still remember parts of a visit we made to Aunty Lou shortly after Sheila's first husband had been killed and Christine and Judith were just young children. Ask Diane if she remembers. I think a lady with thick glasses took us to a sweet shop.

My stomach bug seems to have gone although there are still lots of food and drink stuffs that I just can't face, although I liked them enough before. Pat had more-or-less the same bug as myself some months back and she is still 'off' certain things. Anyway I have cut down on my smoking a bit, which is good.

Did I tell you in my last letter that John's next bank posting is to be Aden? They want him there in January, which is a month off his leave, so they can stick it. We are still waiting to hear from Haliburton but even if nothing turns up we will still leave the bank. John thinks that he will be able to get a job with either a Canadian or Australian bank. Apparently the Australian banks fix you up with a job in Australia and you travel out as an emigrant. So even if we don't fancy settling there we need only stay three years before paying our passage back home. There are quite a few Australians in Libya so it seems as if there are opportunities for travelling from Australia.

Neither of us feel like settling in England just yet so we may as well see as much of the world as we can, as long as the pay is good.

I dropped *Rosa a line wishing her all the best. What will her name be now?

Zena and I were asked to tea yesterday by her new owners to be. She behaved very well and made a fuss of Brian when he came in from work. They didn't seem bothered when I told them that she chewed things occasionally or when she leapt up on their settee. Their flat is set back off the road so they will be able to let her take herself off for a walk if they want.

I sometimes used to let her out by herself but worried so much that it really wasn't worth my bothering. She has no idea about cars and some of them really speed along our road.

This afternoon we are going over to Dick's and then to the beach. So I will take my new camera and get some final shots of Zena and Rupert together. Dick is endeavouring to find Rupert a new home too, as he has been naughty lately – cat killing and Arab chasing. Dick feels that he would settle down more if he had a family around him.

I will have to start thinking about a farewell party soon. I don't know whether to make it drinks and snacks or buffet supper (30 to 40 people). Probably the former, then we can ask more people. On second thoughts, perhaps we won't have one at all, as it will cost a fair bit as well as the problem of getting rid of all the unused drink.

Better close now,

    Excuse writing,

        Love Jean XXXXXX

NOTES:

*Sheila was Aunty Lou's daughter and therefore my grandmother's niece. Sheila's husband had been a test pilot and had been killed in an aeroplane crash.

*Rosa Cook was a middle aged widow who I used to work with as a 'Saturday girl' in a local cake shop. My family had taken her to their hearts and were thrilled when she found love with Reg in later life.

Letter No. 113 (Handwritten on airmail paper)

Friday 18th July 1969

Dear Mum, Dad and Diane,

Thanks for your letter Dad. We were sorry to hear about your driving test and hope 'third time lucky' proves true for you.

I had to laugh at your excursions to the swimming baths with Alexandria. I trust you got Diane out of bed this week. I can't really see myself accompanying you when we get home, I have softened up a lot here and like to be baked by the sun before swimming in a warm sea.

Guess what rotten news John received? His last hope, Halliburton, have said that he is not sufficiently qualified for an accountant's position with them. The two American bosses here can't understand it and one is going to write again to London. The thing is that John's banking exams look pretty good listed as individual subjects and although the Americans swallowed them, the London office must have realised that John is nowhere near being a qualified accountant.

Aden, here we come.

Rather than hand in his notice on 1st September John is going to wait until he gets home and see what the prospects are like for gaining a job abroad outside of banking. At the moment we are persuading ourselves that Aden is the place to be. (Not very successfully I'm afraid.)

Our weather is first-rate at the moment, 80 to 82 degrees in the day and dropping at night allowing everyone to sleep comfortably. The night sky is fantastically clear and the stars shine brilliantly. I still hate looking at them much though; it fills me with dread at the vastness of it all.

David Pugh is due back at the end of this month and the idiot wrote and asked me to look out for a large friendly dog for him. Naturally I remembered Dick and his dilemma about Rupert but I don't think David will accept my glowing description of Rupert as 100% true.

Zena will be going at the end of the month to Judy and Brian, so John and I are spoiling her like mad at the moment.

Last night (about mid-night) John and I drove back from our card evening and were followed, from the carport to right inside the flat stairway, by a meowing scraggy cat. We relented and I took down some milk and cubed cheese and put it in the garden for it. The cat pounced on the food uttering delighted meows and attracting at least six other cats, which popped out from behind every plant in the garden. Two of the cats were kittens and most attractive. John had to carry Zena past the feeding felines for her last little walk of the day and she got most jealous and wouldn't concentrate on the job in hand. She kept jumping up at us for affection. I only hope the cats don't catch us again tonight.

We've been out a bit more this week and have a few things lined up for next week as well. (Two barbeques – lovely.)

Rather than give any sort of farewell party I am going to give a few small dinner parties for closer friends. I shall start next Friday with the Mowforths, and Dick and Deidre. Then we will have another two or three.

With a bit of luck the bank will be paying our shipping costs, which will be a great help as the car is going to cost us about £L30 for an export licence, which we hadn't anticipated.

Better close now,
    Hoping you are all well,
        Love from us both, Jean XXXXX

Letter No. 114 (Handwritten on airmail paper)

Friday 25th July 1969

Dear Mum, Dad and Diane

Thanks for your last letter. I was sorry to hear about Eileen and all the trouble afterwards. I hope the funeral went off peacefully.

I hope Janis settles in Australia, it seems a good idea for her to go, especially in the circumstances.

I feel tired today, missed my afternoon nap yesterday and this evening we have four people coming for a meal. To complicate matters I couldn't get a large enough leg of lamb for them all and will have to cook two this afternoon, as well as a fruit pie. I am hoping that the meat will only take two hours apiece otherwise the meal will be really late. The oven will be in use from 2pm to 9pm, as I have roast potatoes to do as well.

We are being 'evicted' from our flat on August 31st when the lease runs out. It is a yearly lease and has always been renewed previously without trouble. Anyway the bank has said that under the circumstances we will be away on September 1st. (They sure get their pound of flesh.) Nigel and a chap in the Benghazi office have been given permission for local leave with fares paid to Malta. I am so annoyed at the unfairness of it. John is going to try to get the fare to Malta out of the bank in lieu of leave. I hope he can as it will be about £40.

It is going to cost us about £30 – £35 for an export licence for our car so the Malta money would be jolly useful.

We played cards last night and only have one more card evening left before Pat and Bob go on leave, so I don't expect we will be seeing them again.

Poor Zena has a nasty two inch cut behind her ear and another deep graze on her cheek. I thought at first that she had been bitten by another dog when she escaped from the garden over a week ago, but now I am wondering if she got knocked down by a car. I duly took her to the vet because they looked rather septic. The vet was in a foul mood before we even started and because Zena wouldn't sit still he just wrote out a prescription for 'gents in violet' and told me to cut her fur away around the cuts and dab it on. At least he didn't charge me. Anyway, after several attempts of seeing to her and pinning her down before dabbing, there is a marked improvement. My only problem now is how to remove the gentian-violet staining from my body. I am covered in it.

Saturday 26th

HAPPY BIRTHDAY DIANE!

Our meal went off very well yesterday, they didn't leave until gone 2am. I am tired again now but will be able to have a sleep this afternoon.

I've no work to do at the moment except write out some sort of job guide for my replacement. I think the embassy will have difficulty getting a replacement as the salary is quite low compared to the oil company salaries.

Will close now,

    Love from us both

       Jean xxxxxx

NOTES: There is a longer than usual gap here between letters that I shall explain. I had recently had a pregnancy confirmed, with the baby due at the beginning of February 1970. It was unplanned due to the uncertainty of our next posting and also the costs that might be involved in a private delivery abroad. John hated the idea of any financial strain and I had therefore had a contraceptive device called a 'coil' fitted a few months ago. The device had obviously failed and I had it removed once it was certain that I was pregnant. I was so happy to be having this baby and planned to stay in England for the birth and follow John to Aden after my sister's April wedding. I was very excited about surprising my parents with the news that they were to become grandparents but I wanted to keep it a secret until we were back in England and I could tell them myself. Then one morning I began to have severe pains and noticed blood in the toilet. As I never wrote anything down about the miscarriage I am now relying on a confused memory of something that happened forty-five years ago.

Pat Rumph drove over to the flat and stayed with me whilst I lost the baby. I can remember feeling very cold and being wrapped in a coat for the drive to the Moasat Hospital. Then I remember being lifted onto an operating table whilst struggling and fighting the anaesthetic mask before I finally lost consciousness.

I awoke in a private room feeling groggy and saw John standing anxiously by the side of the bed. The doctor who had performed the D & C came in beaming; for him the procedure had been a success and he proudly pointed to a plastic container on the bedside table that held a grey ridged lump of matter about the size of a child's fist. This he happily explained was the tiny placenta that he had removed.

Thereafter, every night before dropping off to sleep I would experience an uncontrollable mental replay of the events of that day. I didn't stop crying inwardly for a long time.

Letter No. 115 (Handwritten on airmail paper)

Tuesday 12th August 1969

Dear Mum, Dad and Diane,

John and I have been sorting out our trunks and getting things arranged for shipment. As we were given a large crate by the Foremans we have no need for Diane's very old cream case or Dad's old brown case so we were wondering if you want them back. We don't have room for them in the car so they will have to be freighted home empty, which we will do if you really want them, if not we will pass them onto someone else.

The packers are coming next Wednesday, 20th and you would be amazed at the number of forms needed for this 'simple' procedure. It's going to cost us approximately £100 just to get out of this place. Certificates for this and certificates for that; car export; injections; translations.

I hope my teeth last out until October. The back ones twinge a bit. It costs about £10 here for a filling or two.

As we will be moving about quite a bit John thinks that Jeanette's address will be the only useful one for you to write to. It is: - Mrs J. Bider-Swan, Haltenstrasse 146, 8706 Meilen, Switzerland. Perhaps you could pass it on to Kay and John.

We are moving into David Pugh's villa for our last few days, which will mean Mohamed can give the flat a good scrub out before Ross Holden moves in.

The only set dates we have are: September 1st leave here, hooray, and September 9th take the Tunis-Marseilles ferry. Anyway, I will send you post cards as we troll along. At the moment all we want to do is GET OUT, so our trip round Europe is rather unplanned. John bought some maps of France and Germany and judging by the way his index finger was skimming up, down, and across France I think we will be spending a lot of time there. Devaluation should help a bit to stretch our holiday money.

Life may be rather hectic in the remaining three weeks so don't worry if you don't hear much from me.

Please let me know about the cases soon.

 Love from us both
  Jean XXXXXX

P.S. Dad, I hope the 8th was your lucky day.

Letter No. 116 (Handwritten on airmail paper)

Tuesday 19th August

Dear Mum, Dad and Diane,

Thanks for your letter, Mum. I haven't forgotten Diane's shopping. I have just sold the sewing machine for £L20 so will be able to finance her ring (probably about £5 sterling tell her.) I also want a ring for Jean Andrews, as we will stay with them for a few days. I will get the Barbara Gould lipsticks in France as the ones in the shops here have probably melted by now. I've decided against buying sheepskins, as they have to be thoroughly cleaned with insecticide and then brushed. We will probably buy pouffes and camel saddles in Gabes, Tunisia, as they are better quality than the ones in the Tripoli suk.

Jean Andrews wrote to say that she is expecting a second baby next March. Apparently young John is looking forward to having a brother and has already divided his toys out, keeping all the good ones for himself and saving all the broken ones for the baby.

Pat and Bob have left for home leave, so our card playing has come to an end. John and Jeanette Wilde are off on the 9th and most of our other friends have already gone so we aren't having a farewell party now. On Thursday we are having the Robinsons, Ute and Maurice, and David Pugh in for drinks and snacks. On the following Thursday I am giving a buffet for Alan and Anika, Nigel, and Philip and Ava, then, except an occasional meal for David, we are finished with entertaining. We must do our packing then and get the shipment off. David has said that we can stay with him for our last few days, which is marvellous. (I expect he wants me to cook for him as Susan doesn't get back until mid-September.)

I tried to persuade John to sell the cine-projector to some interested friends but he wants to keep it, so he is now in sole charge of movies. I am just sticking to my Instamatic camera. I have taken nearly twenty pictures but won't get them developed until we get home.

Zena went last Tuesday and Brian and Judy popped in on Wednesday to say that she was fine. Apparently she hadn't whimpered at all and had gobbled up her food with no trouble. At one point she escaped and started haring down the road, looking over her shoulder but when she saw that Brian wasn't chasing her she came back. I hope they pop in again. I don't want to go there in case she remembers me and it upsets her. (Doubt if it will though.) I took some final pictures of her and hope they turn out well.

John's mother sent us an advert for banking positions in South Africa with the Netherlands Bank of South Africa. It looks promising. Anywhere is better than Aden and South Africa sounds a fab. place. Fresh pineapples and big black grapes for me, brandy and wine for John.

Did I tell you that Jeanette wrote back asking us to stay with her and Heini in Switzerland?

We are waiting for a reply from the A.A. before deciding definitely on our route.

Love from us both,
Jean and John XXXXXX

Letter No. 117 (Hand written on airmail paper)

Monday 25th August 1969

Dear Mum, Dad and Diane,

This should be my last letter to you from here unless something drastic happens.

Please make appointments for us at the dentist from 22nd October onwards (but not November, unless in the first week.) Can you ask him to do the check-ups and part of the treatment in one go i.e. allocate 1 hour to 1½ hours for us both. A morning appointment would be best I think, as we can recover at your flat before driving to Cobham. We both definitely need treatment. Mr Press should still have our charts from three years ago.

We originally intended taking a flat for our leave but we plan a trip around UK for six weeks, seeing and staying with people, in November. By the time we get back Christmas will be upon us and then January will be taken up with packing etc. so we will probably stay at Cobham with Kay and John.

We seem to have needed the brown case Mum, for part of our shipment, so it will not be abandoned. We also think that Diane's will come with us, somewhere in the car, to put our en route purchases in.

For some unknown reason both John and I are very much on edge at the moment. The actual trip doesn't bother us – we are very excited about it but I don't think we will relax until we are through the border customs and on Djerba.

I've bought Diane's ring. She has a choice of two, a plain gold one or one with imitation diamonds in it. (Respectively £4 and £4½ approx.) I also bought baby Sharron a sterling silver bangle. Other than a few bits and pieces we don't expect to be bringing much back; too much customs duty at UK (33⅓%).

I was told today that M & S, Oxford Street, keep a large summer stock in store and let overseas visitors buy it and then they send it to the departure port and deduct purchase tax. This sounds a good idea especially as Aden is a free port. I hope Coronells in Beckenham will let me browse as well.

John Keeling wrote to say how pleased he was that we were going to Aden. He likes it there very much - much better than here. Poor old Geoff Bishop is in UK now, suffering from an unidentified disease.

We will probably pay Zena another visit this week and on Friday we will see Rupert for the last time when we go to Dick's to clean the car.

Better close,

Lots of love, and longing to see you all,

Jean and John XXXXXXXXX

Monday 1st September 1969

Something Drastic Happens:
Gaddafi takes power

Our mini-traveller was packed ready for our journey home and waiting in the carport. We were excited and in the process of eating an early breakfast before setting off when there was a loud banging on our front door. Audrey and Jack from downstairs were standing there with shocked looks on their faces as they told us that they had just heard that a coup had taken place and all movement was forbidden. We stood frozen. Three years to the day since John had arrived in Tripoli and except for a short visit to Tunisia he had not left the country in all that time. To be foiled at the last moment was unbelievable and filled us with indescribable dismay. Audrey kindly offered us lunch later as she knew our cupboard was bare. I can remember the meal to this day; a peculiar mix of cubed tinned luncheon meat, smothered in a thick tomato sauce and served on a bed of spaghetti.

David Pugh had fortunately realised our predicament and in the afternoon he called at the flat to escort us to his villa, relying on his CD plates to get us through. For the next week we stayed with him (Susan and the children were in England) and I was able to make myself useful keeping house and answering the phone. David worked long hours ensuring his 'flock' of British expatriates were kept informed whilst handing out good advice. He spent his time either at the embassy or checking up on British people in their homes.

Then, after seven days of uncertainty; all the while sharing David's home, he drove back from the embassy with the news 'They're giving out exit passes at the harbour castle'. John immediately jumped into the mini and headed towards the castle. After a long wait he finally managed to obtain two exit visas. It was six o'clock in the evening when he got back to the villa and the passes were due to expire at midnight. Our farewells were hasty and we promised David that we would call on the consul in Tunis to report on things and to let him know that we were safely away. Later David told us that he had used us as 'guinea pigs' to test the effectiveness of the passes at the borders. He said he knew that we would be 'sensible'. A compliment or what?

The road to Tunisia was long and straight and we drove tensely into the fading evening light, taking a last look at silhouetted palm trees with a darkening sea behind them. The Libyan border post was eventually reached and the passes and our passports accepted and stamped by armed guards. We were out of Libya.

Relief overwhelmed us as we drove a few hundred metres on hard packed sand to the Tunisian border post. This would be easy we thought. But for some reason the Tunisian soldiers did not seem pleased to have us there. They escorted us, without facial expression, from the car, one on either side of us. Moonlight reflected on the metal of their rifles as they guided us towards a collection of huts. Once inside the main hut we were told to sit. We took the two hard chairs offered us in front of the desk, facing a stern looking well-braided soldier. He took the passes and passports and held them in that special way that people who can not read very well hold pieces of official looking paper. He stared at them, almost unseeingly whilst all the while John kept uttering the Arabic greeting 'kerfalik' in an effort to get him to acknowledge us and break down the barrier of suspicion. Eventually he sighed and nodded to the two khaki clad militia that we could go. Silently we left the hut. We walked stiff legged with nerves to the car, the soldiers staying behind us. Our shoulders were tense and our arms firmly by our sides not daring to offend Arab propriety by touching each other, although we felt like holding hands for reassurance.

We drove off into the black night shortly before midnight. Our relief at getting away left us muted, we had no energy left for vocal celebration. Tiredness swept over us, persuading us to pull off the Tunisian road and drive into a small collection of trees lit only by our headlights. We fell asleep in our seats.

We awoke as the sun's warmth was stealing the early morning chill from the air. Our ears were filled with bird song; they too were waking up to a new day and relishing its freshness. It was an orchard that had given us rest and shelter for the night and after a few biscuits and some bottled pop we drove back onto the road and reached Tunis on the 8th of September just in time to catch our evening boat to Marseilles.

The End

Postscript

RUPERT
Rupert stayed in Libya with Dick until about 1972 and then accompanied him to Belgium where he lived a long and happy life.

ZENA
Zena returned to England with Judith and Brian and lived with them for several years until run over by a car.

JIM AND FLORENCE
We lost touch but understand that they had another son.

NANCY AND ALAN
We lost touch.

GWEN AND ERIC
Corresponded for a few years but then lost touch.

POLLY AND GARRY
Lost touch but understand that they had two daughters.

ANNA AND JOHN
Lost touch.

JENNY AND IVAN
Lost touch.

SHEILA AND OWEN
Lost touch.

BARBARA AND PETER
Lost touch although we did visit them once at their Manchester home during our leave.

JENNY AND TERRY
Met up in Bahrain. Kept in touch.

DAVID AND SUSAN
They lived in their house in Bromley for a while before being posted to Paris.

CINDY AND GEOFF
Met up in 1972 at the Gower Penisular. Lost touch later.

PAT AND BOB
We visited them and their baby son at their Farnborough home in Kent but lost touch afterwards.

JEAN AND DEREK
We visited them and toddler John during our leave. Still in touch.

CAROL AND ALAN
Stayed in Canada. Still in touch.

THE SARELLS
After her husband was made a KCMG in 1968 Mrs Pamela Sarell became Lady Sarell.